IMAGES
of America

MADISONVILLE

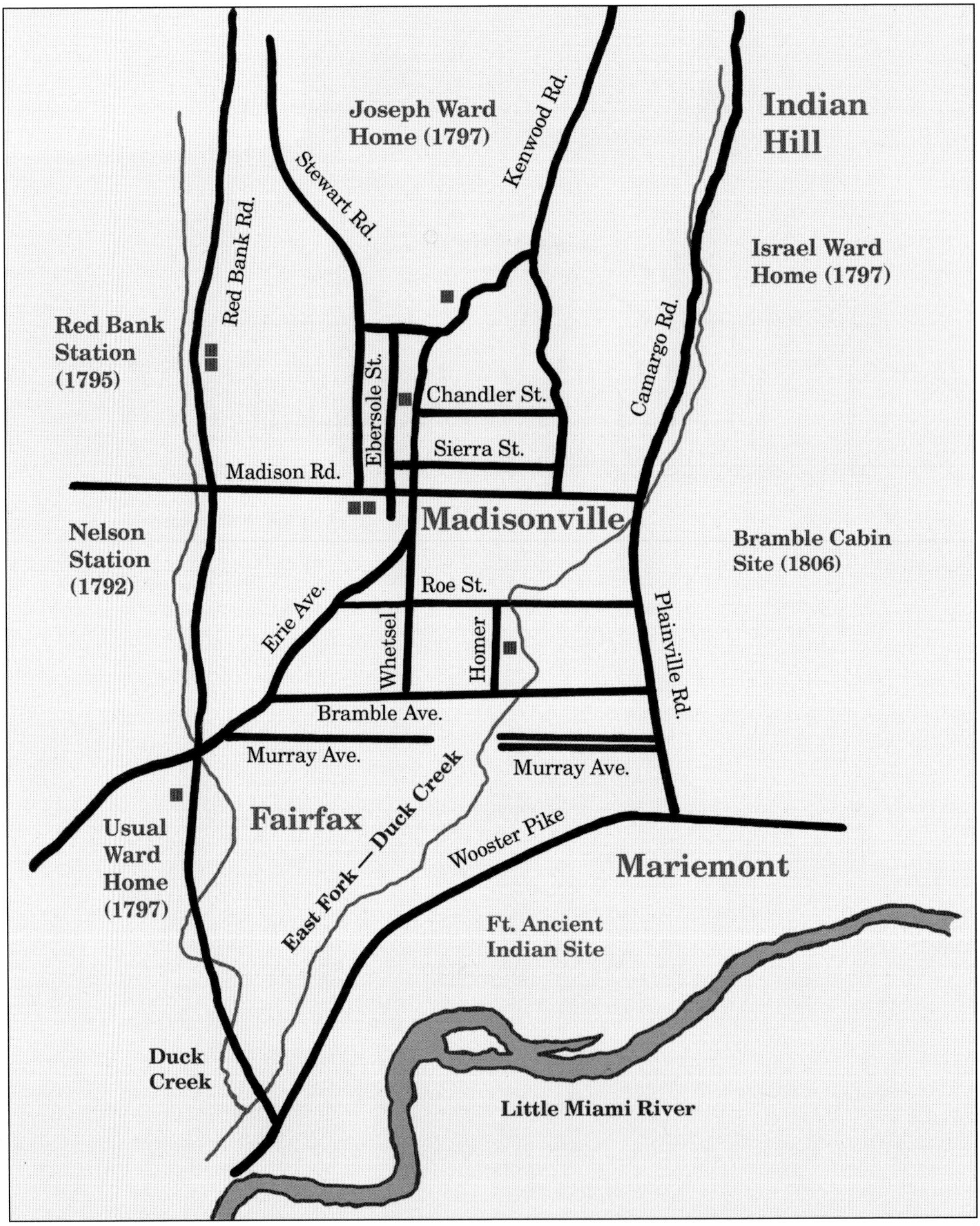

This map shows Madisonville in 1880. Madisonville was incorporated as a village in 1876, and the first officers were Louis W. Clason, mayor; Calvin Fay, clerk; George J. Settle, marshal; and Timothy Maphet, W.W. Peabody, Michael Buckel, William Settle, James Julien, and Louis Cornwelle, councilmen. Madisonville had 1,247 inhabitants by the census of 1880. (Courtesy of the Madisonville Historical Society.)

On The Cover: This building, 4906 Whetsel Avenue, was constructed in 1886 with a third story added in 1896. It was owned by F&AM 419 Masonic Lodge, which held its events on the second and third floors using the side lodge entrance. The first floor housed the Madison Building & Loan No. 2 and First National Bank. (Courtesy of the Madisonville Historical Society.)

IMAGES *of America*

MADISONVILLE

Ruth Ann Busald, Nancy Hanseman,
and Janet Meckstroth-Blank

ARCADIA
PUBLISHING

ISBN 978-0-7385-9366-1

Published by Arcadia Publishing
Charleston, South Carolina

Printed in the United States of America

Library of Congress Control Number: 2012937703

For all general information, please contact Arcadia Publishing:
Telephone 843-853-2070
Fax 843-853-0044
E-mail sales@arcadiapublishing.com
For customer service and orders:
Toll-Free 1-888-313-2665

Visit us on the Internet at www.arcadiapublishing.com

This book is dedicated to the past, present, and future residents of Madisonville.

Contents

ACKNOWLEDGMENTS

This book was made possible by the dedication of the Madisonville Historical Society in gathering photographs, postcards, newspapers, and familial accounts and compiling this information for others to share and enjoy. Special recognition is due to Nelson Hoffman and Emmanuel Hack, who were early guardsmen of Madisonville's history and treasures, and to Ruth Ann Busald, who has been Madisonville's historian for over 30 years and founded the Madisonville Historical Archives. We would also like to thank Theresa Blank Galan, a fifth-generation Madisonville resident, for assisting her mother in writing the captions for this book.

Introduction

Madisonville celebrated its 200th birthday on April 24, 2009. This monumental occasion prompted residents to recall Madisonville's humble birth in 1809, its vibrant childhood through the beginning of the 20th century, and its sometimes trying adolescence since the 1960s. Since Madisonville's conception, many have chronicled important events in its history, whether by notations on a photograph or postcard or the writings from a local resident. One such prominent Cincinnatian, Judge Joseph Cox, wrote a dedication for the souvenir booklet of the opening of the village waterworks in October 1892, recounting the first 100 years of Madisonville history. The following is an excerpt from his historical account:

> The State Legislature enacted a law, January 27th, 1809, providing for the distribution of school sections, under which the town of Madison, named in honor of James Madison, then President of the United States, was laid out upon the site of what is now Madisonville. The survey was completed in March, 1809, and John Jones, William Armstrong and Felix Christman chosen trustees, and the first sale of lots was made by auction April 24th of the same year, the prices realized ranging from $3.50 to $31.00 per lot. The post-office was established in 1826, and named Madisonville. The first house was built of logs, and located where Rief's saddler shop now stands, near the corner of Main street and Central Avenue [now Madison Road and Whetsel Avenue]; the second, of logs, was built on the southeast corner of Central Avenue and Centre Street, and the third, also of logs, stood on the southeast corner of Main and Mathis Streets. In the year 1811, the first house of any pretensions built by Patrick McCollum, the frame of logs, the outside covered with weatherboards and painted, was located on the present site of Klein's drug store, and a part of the old building still stands. Here the first church was organized through the efforts of Mr. McCollum, an ardent Methodist.
>
> The early history of the village boasted of several manufacturing enterprises of considerable magnitude for the times. Among them a manufactory of wooden bowls, the machinery operated by horsepower; a pottery where was manufactured the crude crockery and earthenware used by the early settlers. There were also in operation a fulling mill and three tanneries; a gristmill was erected in 1823, the power being furnished by an over-shot wheel and the supply of water brought from the springs on the hillsides. A distillery was also operated in connection with the gristmill. The manufacture of whiskey was an important industry in the early days, and the village boasted of three distilleries.
>
> On the ground, Madisonville seems to be a plain, but seen from the surrounding hills it is situated on a hillside that slopes gently to the Southwest. The village has already begun extensive improvements, and it does not need great foresight to see that the time is not distant when Madisonville will be an attractive field for the industrious and ever-present speculator. With the unequaled advantages nature thus affords, with the conveniences the railroad company extends, with the easy access to and from the city, with its fine views,

> fine air, the wholesome character of village like, it is not surprising that the movement of population is setting steadily and strongly in this direction.

By 1900, Madisonville was a bustling community with a strong local economy and school district. In 1911, Madisonville was incorporated into the city of Cincinnati, and in the following years, the business district was revitalized with an influx of residents, money, and building projects. Madisonville, like many communities, was hit hard by the Depression but was able to rally itself and survive, still opening new businesses. Judge Joseph Cox wrote that Madisonville was always noted for the loyalty and patriotism of its citizens in reference to the Mexican-American War and the Civil War, but the same is true for World Wars I and II. Many of Madisonville's churches housed memorials to the local sons who served. As the soldiers returned, the community flourished through the end of 1950s.

Madisonville began to decline in the 1960s as newer communities were developed and businesses shifted out of the city into the suburbs. The timing of Madisonville's bicentennial in 2009 was fortunate in that it highlighted efforts in creating a renaissance for our community, which has struggled in recent decades. New businesses are coming into the community again, bringing building projects, employment, local revenue, and beautification to the area. However, with the new building projects, there is also an effort to preserve our historic structures. As our bicentennial slogan declared, "We are celebrating our past and creating our future in Madisonville."

One

Village "Country" Life Before Incorporation

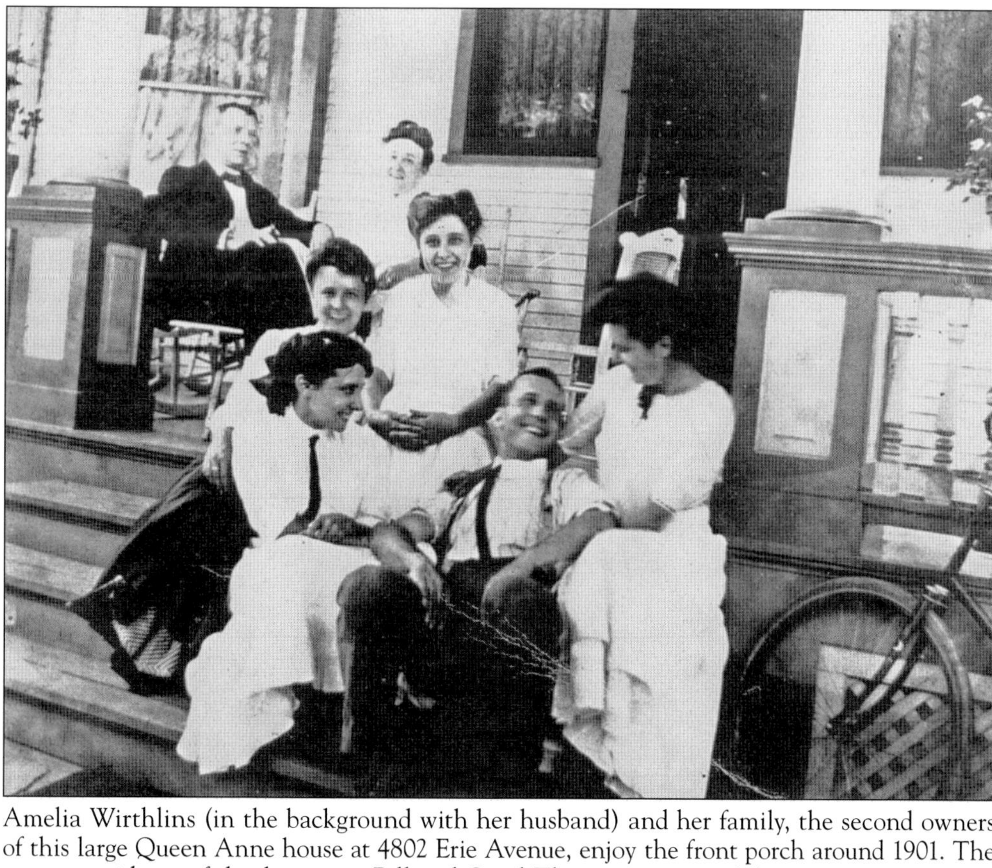

Amelia Wirthlins (in the background with her husband) and her family, the second owners of this large Queen Anne house at 4802 Erie Avenue, enjoy the front porch around 1901. The current residents of this house are Bill and Carol Thomas, owners of the BBQ Revue at 4725 Madison Road.

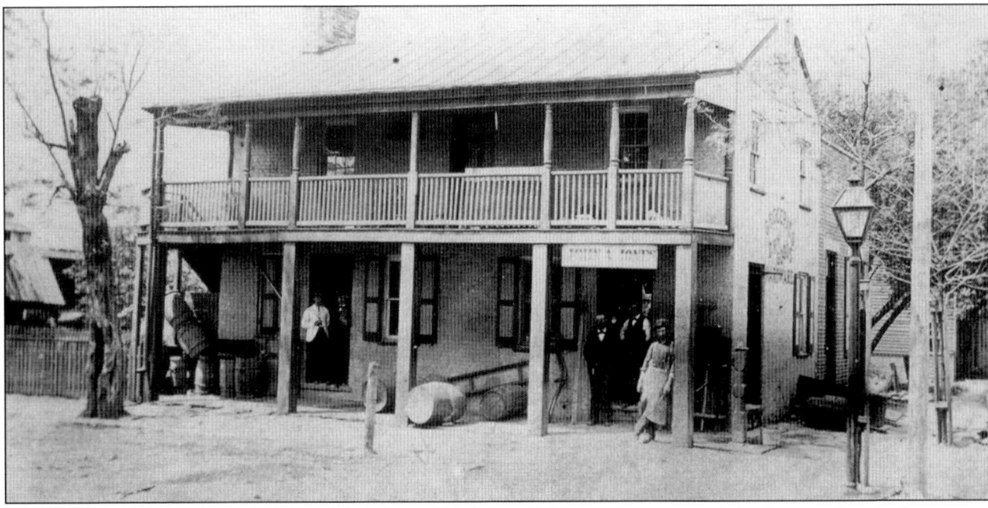

According to the Hamilton County Atlas, published in 1869, John A. Jones Grocery Store was located at the southwest corner of what are now Madison Road and Whetsel Avenue. One of the first grocery stores in the area, it served the residents of Madisonville for many years. The building was demolished about 1896 to make way for a new structure that housed John Stirnkorb's Tavern and later Stein's and Statman's department stores. The building was rehabilitated but again fell into disuse and was demolished in 1996. The land is now vacant.

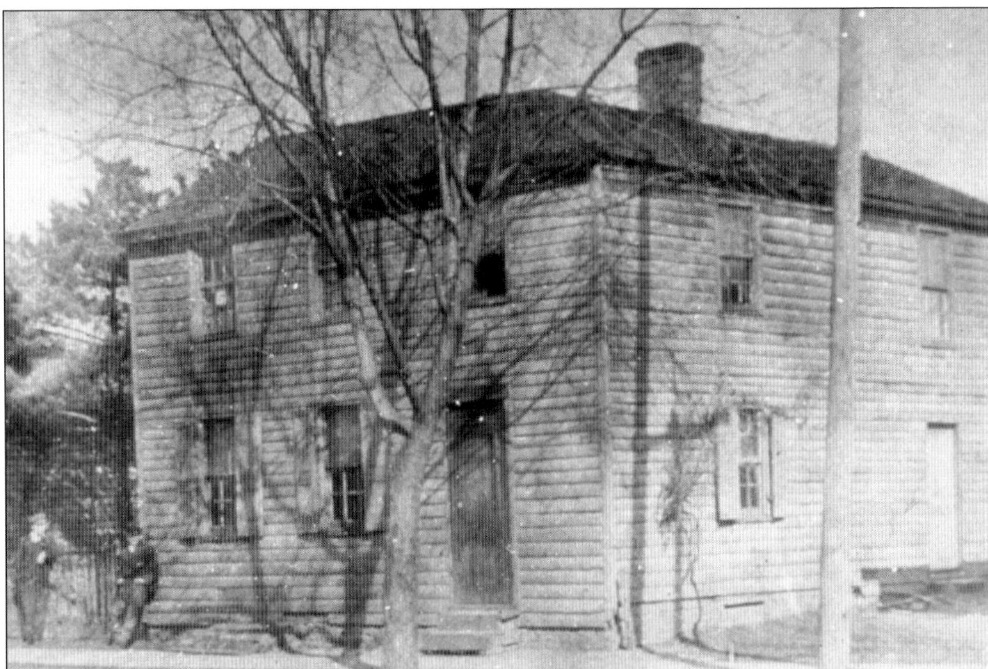

The Goggin House, built around 1830 on the northeast corner of Main Street and Central Avenue (now Madison Road and Whetsel Avenue) was probably the first Madisonville hotel. It was built at the site of an 1809 tavern, possibly incorporating the log building into the structure. For many years, it served locals and travelers passing through Madisonville. Around 1854, a modern brick hotel, the Madison House, was built on the northwest corner of the intersection, and it gradually replaced the Goggin House.

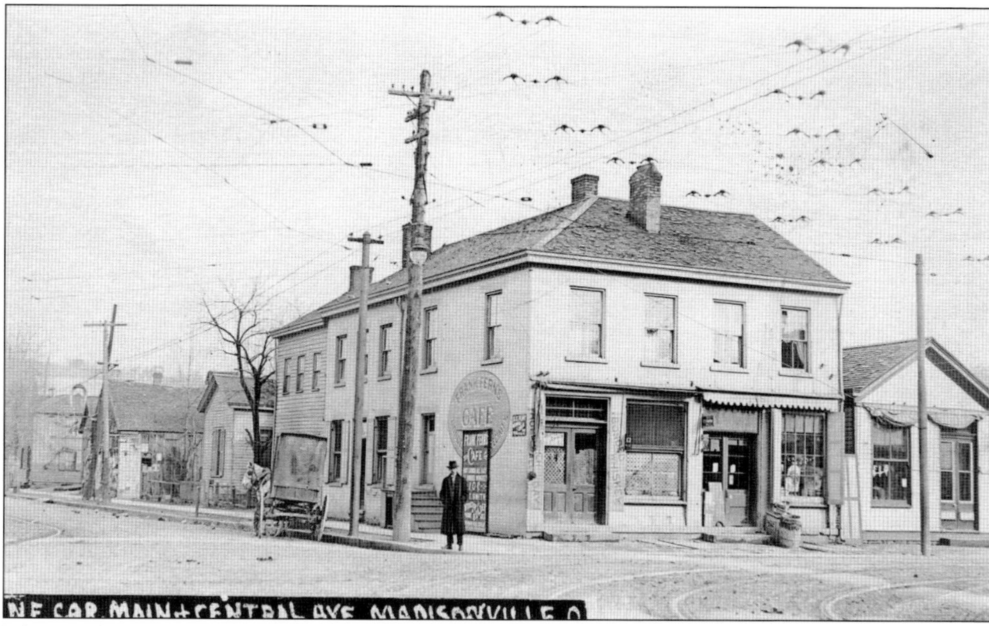

The northeast corner of Main Street and Central Avenue (now Madison Road and Whetsel Avenue) changed hands many times over the years. Shown here is the Frank Ferris Café with a sign reading "Bonded Whiskey" in the 1860s. Later, Timothy and Lon K. Maphet bought the building and operated the Maphet Brothers Grocery for about 30 years. Timothy also served as a councilman in the corporate village of Madisonville in 1876. Bainum's Drugs operated the site for several years until the Fifth-Third Bank was constructed on the same lot in 1927.

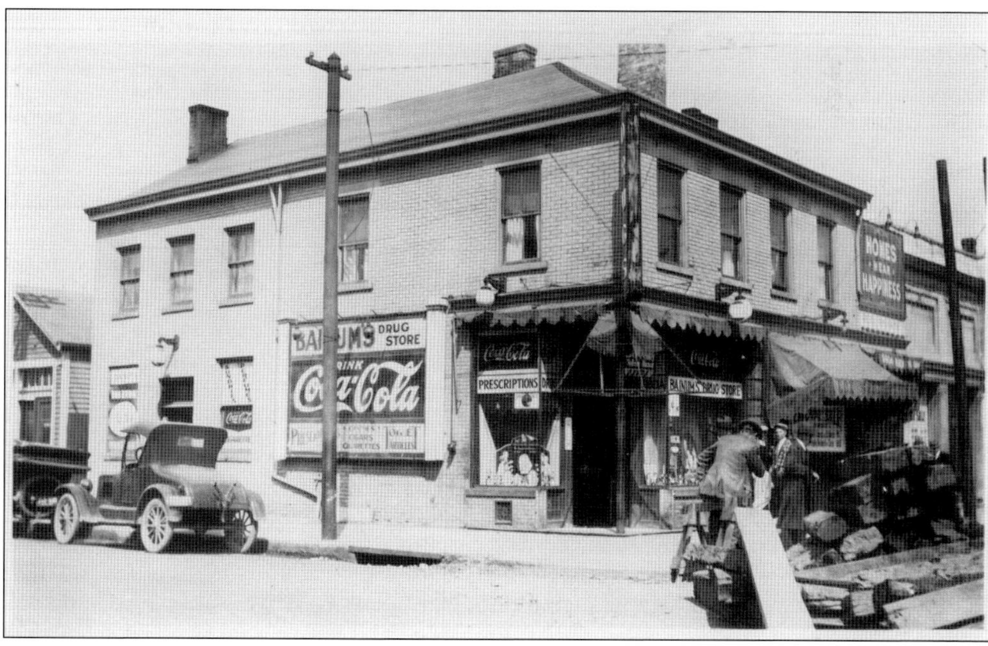

Bainum's Drugs is seen here shortly before its demolition in 1926.

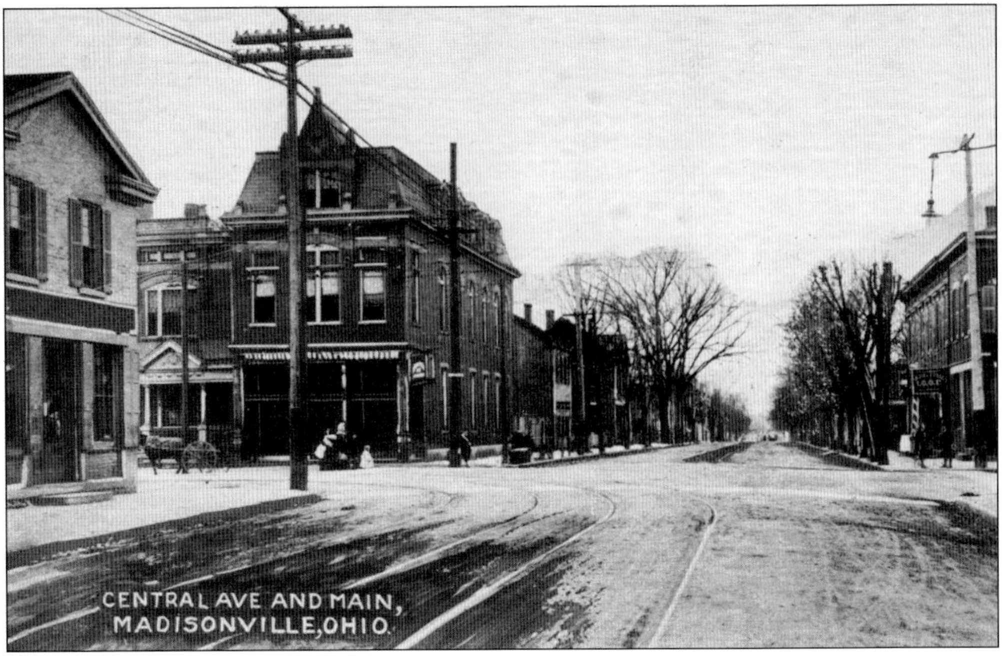

The intersection of Main Street and Central Avenue (now Madison Road and Whetsel Avenue), seen here looking west along Madison Road about 1907, has long been considered the focal point of Madisonville. The southeast corner at the time housed Sprague and Aiken's Grocery Store, which was built in 1860 and later become Aufderhar's Grocery. The second floor of this building housed the first home of the Madisonville Masonic Lodge 419, F&AM, from 1868 until 1876, when the lodge moved to its newly constructed building on Whetsel Avenue.

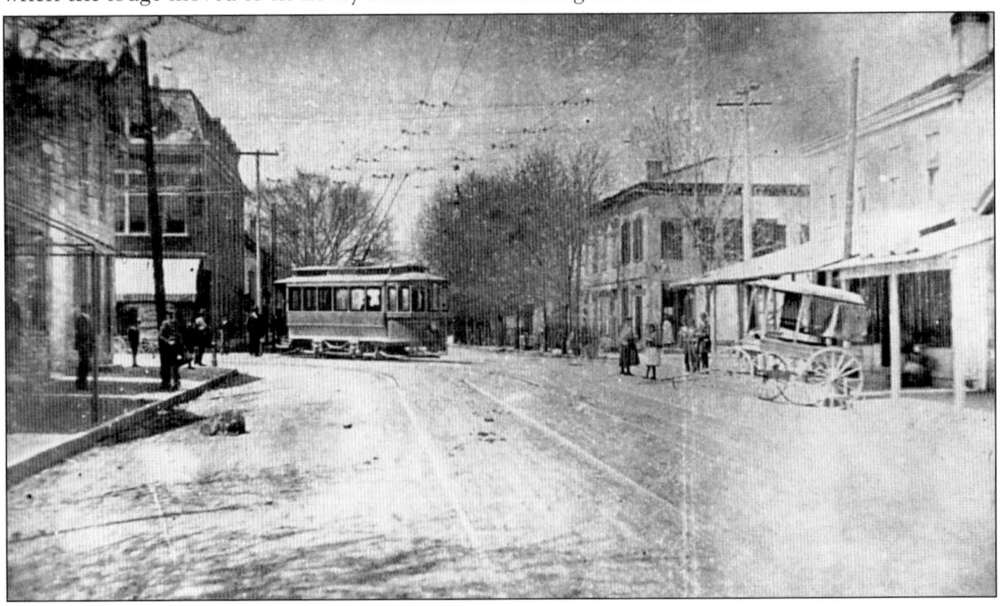

The streetcar turns left onto Central Avenue on its way back to the city. This streetcar was one of the first cars to serve the business area of Madisonville. Until the B&O overpass was built over Central Avenue around 1905, it was considered too dangerous for streetcars to cross the double tracks, so they would stop at the tracks, reverse trolley wires, and return to the city.

A hotel was constructed at the northwest corner of Main Street and Central Avenue in 1854. By 1872, it housed a tavern, but the tavern was sold to John Beiswenger, and he turned it back into a hotel, the Madison House. About 1885, the Madison House changed its name to the Madison Hotel, as this photograph depicts.

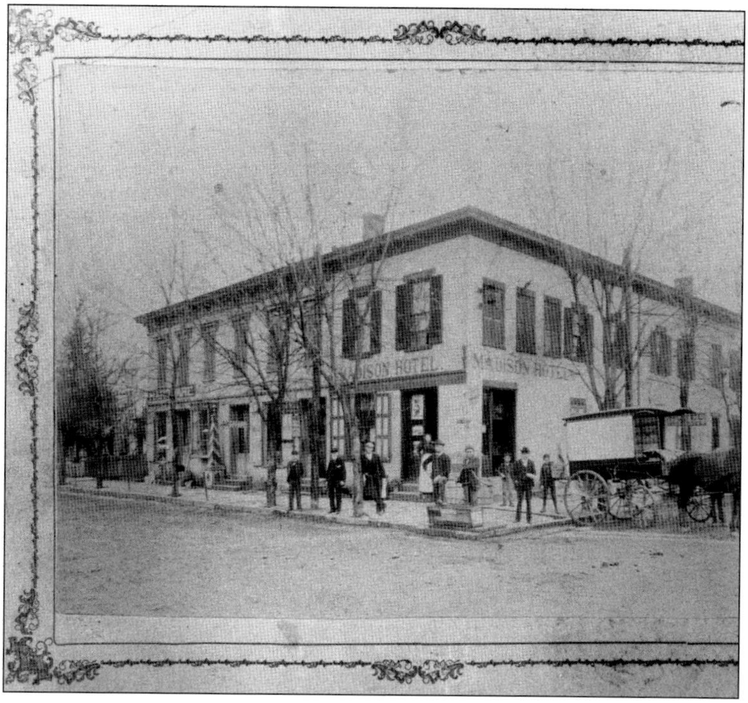

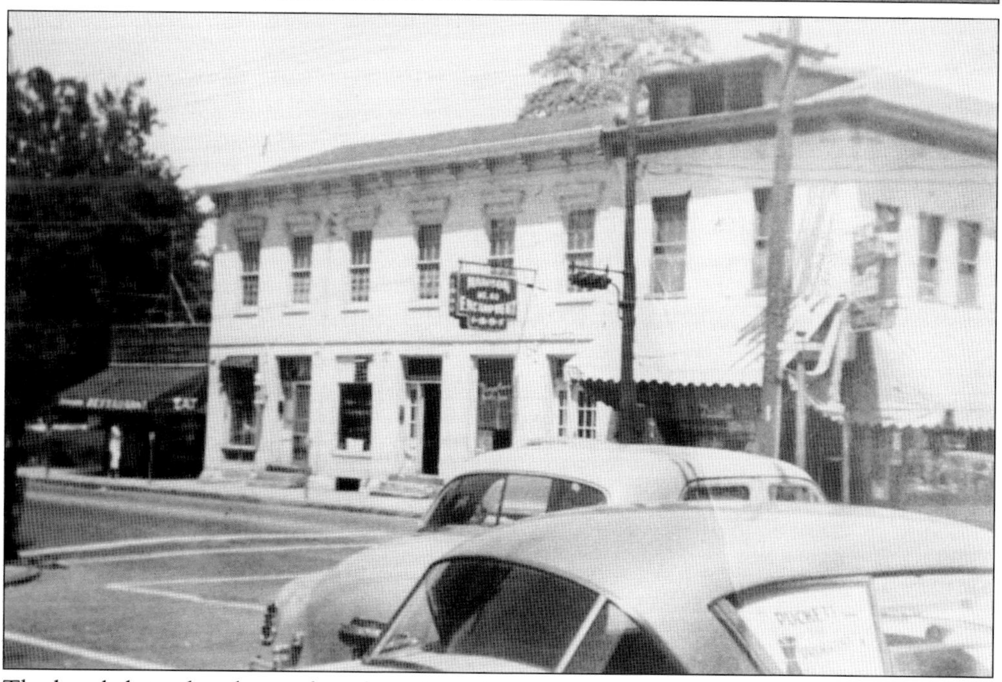

The hotel thrived and served as the informal headquarters for local statesmen and township politicians of the early period, but by 1912, it had ceased to be a hotel. Dr. C.W. Kramer, a local druggist, purchased the building and extensively remodeled it. From that time on, the structure was occupied by a succession of drugstores until the 1960s. After years of neglect had taken their toll, the building was demolished by 1982. Today, the corner is the site of the Madison Center, built in 1991.

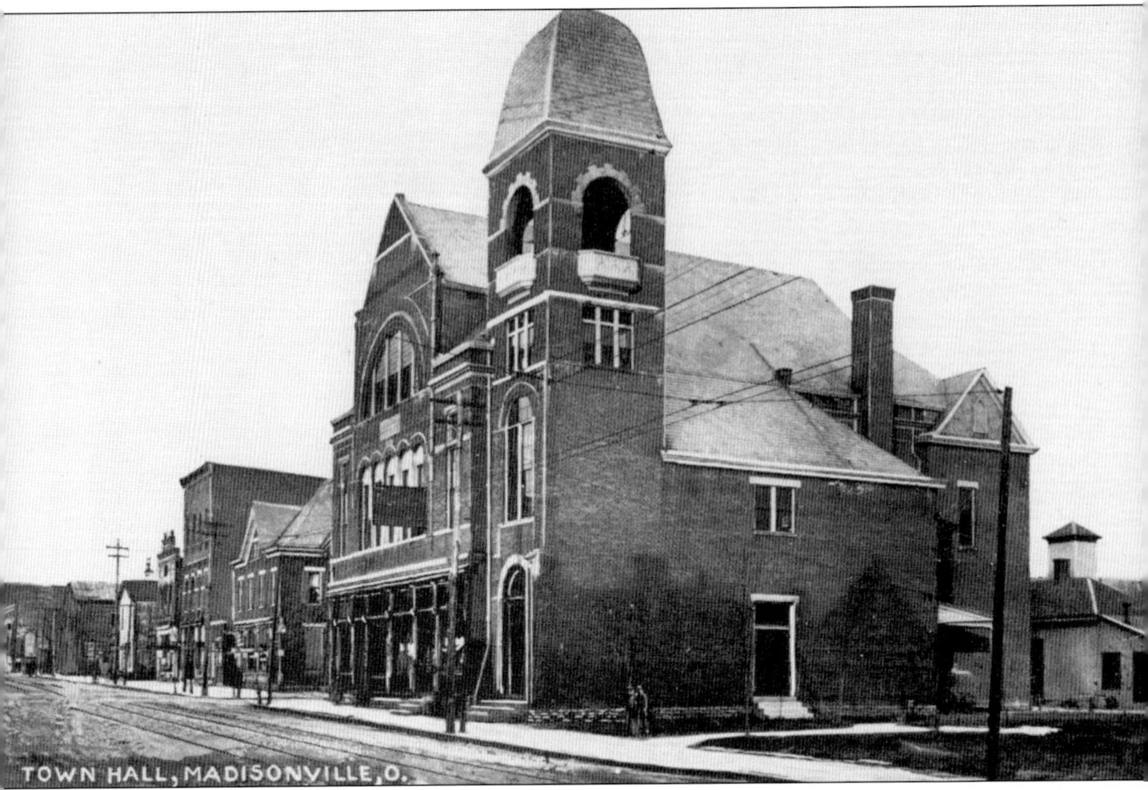

The town hall, seen here in 1896, was an imposing structure towering over other buildings in the village. It was completed and dedicated in 1888 at a cost of $12,000. Marvin Ralston, a historian and member of the Madisonville Round Table Literary Club, gave the only known eyewitness description of the inside of the building: "On the first floor was a large reading room, two stores [one being Kroger's] and an imposing entrance and stairway which led to the second floor village offices and a huge meeting room." A jail and the town marshal's office were also located in the building. In 1900, the large reading room became a branch of the Cincinnati Public Library. When Madisonville was annexed to Cincinnati in 1911, the town hall was no longer needed as a seat of government but was used for other purposes. The Monday Club, a women's literary group determined to keep the branch library in Madisonville, gained ownership of the building, had it razed in 1923, and constructed a new library building on the site. That building, still in use today as the Madisonville branch of the Public Library of Cincinnati and Hamilton County, opened its doors in 1925 at Prentice Street and Whetsel Avenue.

This lovely boardinghouse at 5813 Madison Road, seen here around 1900, was home to, from left to right, Madaline Fena, Kathryn Fena, Grandma Grimm, and Anna Fena. The boardinghouse was on the right side of the house, and their sleeping quarters were on the left.

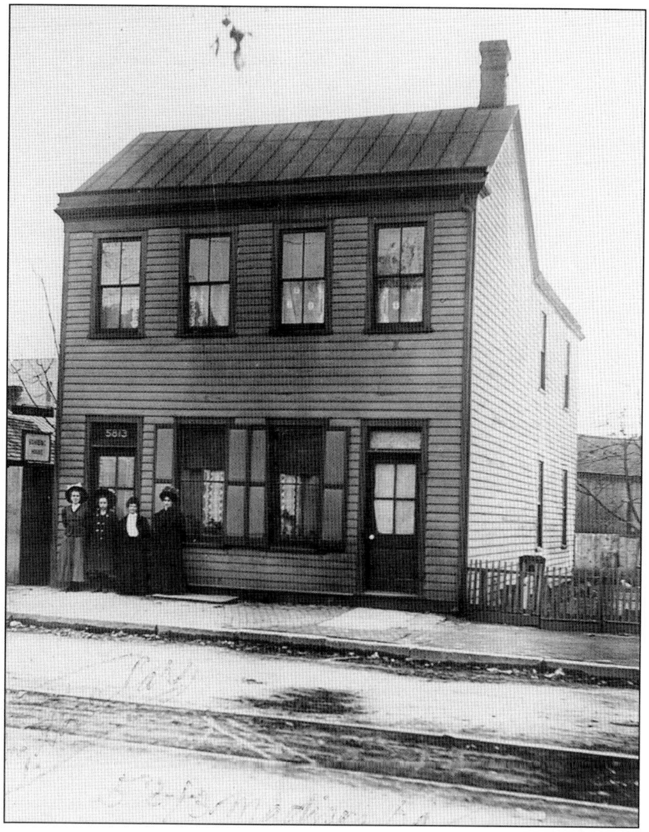

The ladies of the Battenburg Sewing Club pose in this photograph. Young girls of the day went to finishing school to learn to sew, embroider, and tat—all the necessary skills to make beautiful clothes, lace, and household embellishments. These fine works of art, known as school samplers, are highly prized today, with costs that can range in the thousands of dollars.

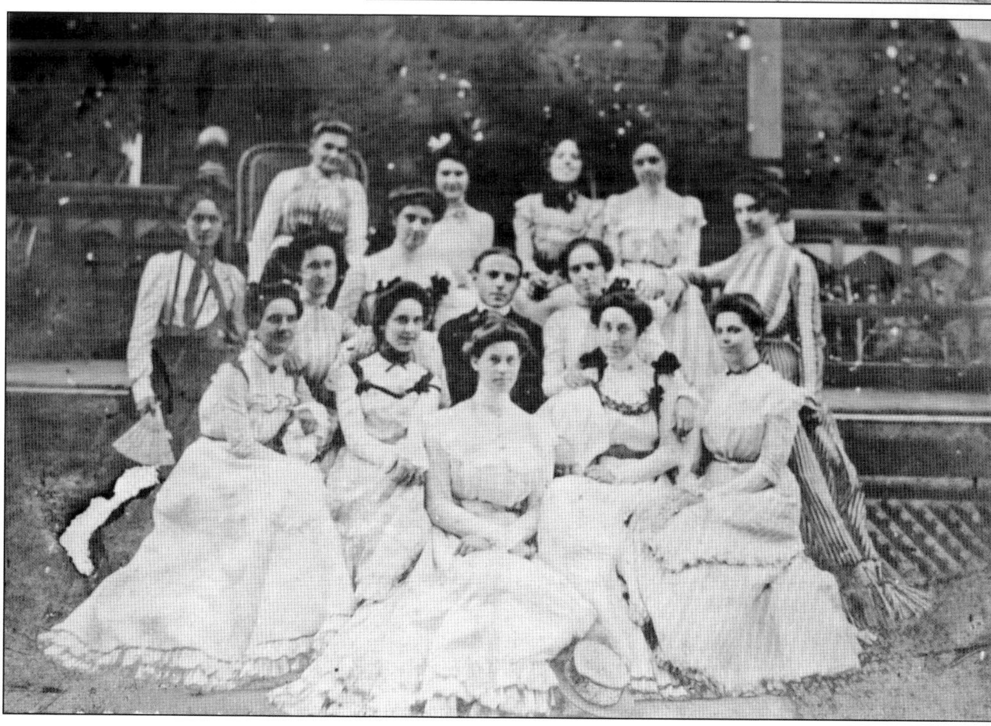

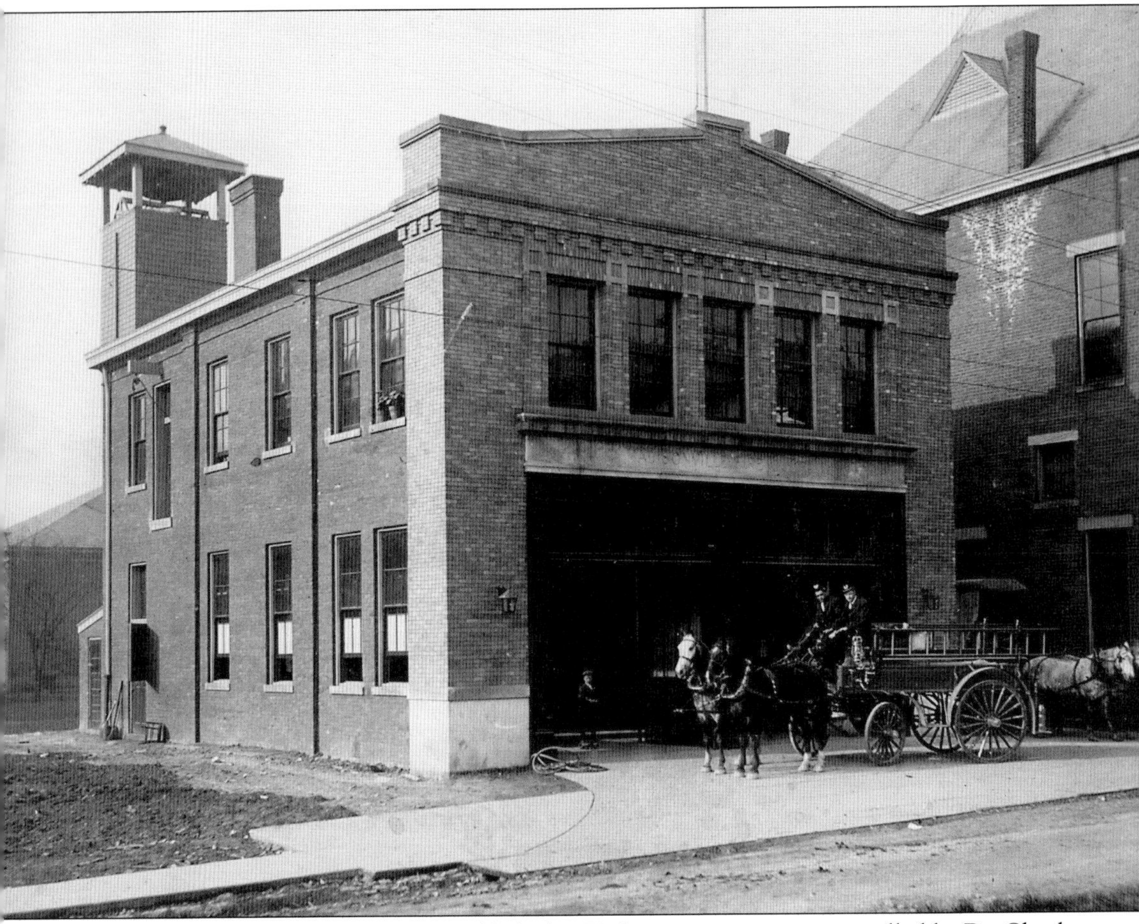

A volunteer fire department was established 1872 during a town meeting called by Dr. Charles Metz, and 50 men signed up. Community events funded the buckets and ladders, which were initially kept on the porch of the Jones Grocery Store on Madison Road and Whetsel Avenue. When an alarm sounded, grocers would lay out the ladders and buckets to be available to the firemen. After four years, a firehouse was built on Prentice Street. In 1888, after the purchase of a hook and ladder truck, the fire department was reorganized under the new name Madisonville Hook & Ladder Company No. 1. In 1903, the Madisonville Village Council agreed to pay $25 per alarm to the firemen, and the name was changed to Madisonville Fire Company. This fire station was built 1909 on the same lot as the old station, which was moved to Ward Street.

This postcard marked the dedication of the Madisonville Fire Company station on January 1, 1910. In 1911, Madisonville was annexed to Cincinnati, which continued to use the new building. Today, Cincinnati Fire Department Station 49 is still in operation serving the residents of Madisonville. Station 49 shares the honor of being the oldest fire station in Cincinnati with Station 39.

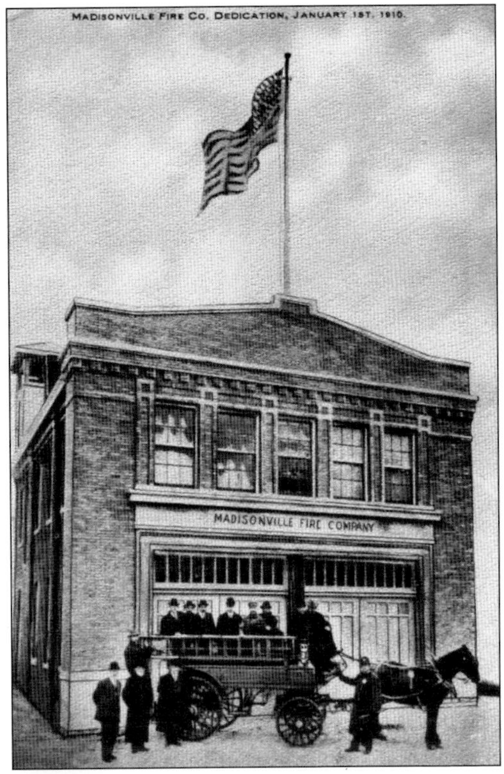

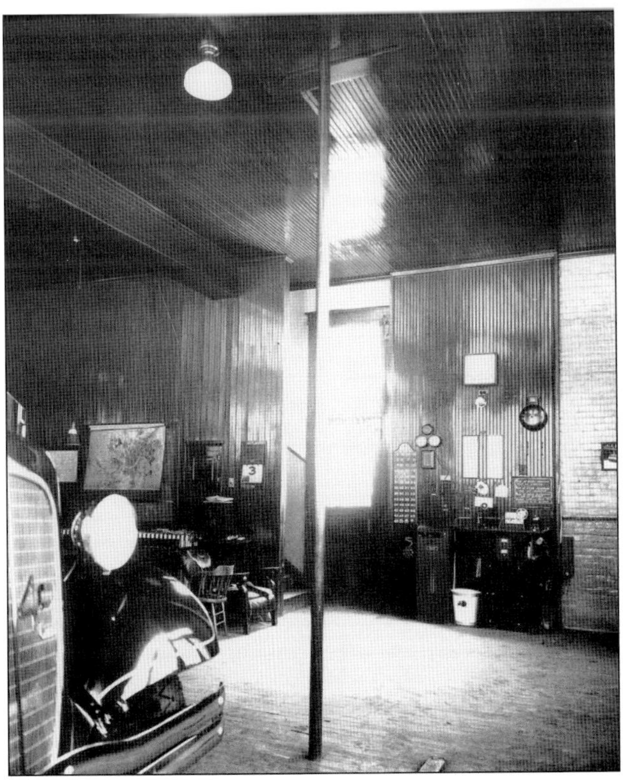

According to locals, when the new firehouse was dedicated in 1910, Dr. Charles Metz was the first to slide down the pole. He was given this honor because of his ongoing support to the Madisonville Fire Department since its founding. This image shows the interior of the fire station. The city removed the second-story hayloft to build sleeping quarters for the firemen, and the floors were renovated to stand the weight of modern fire trucks.

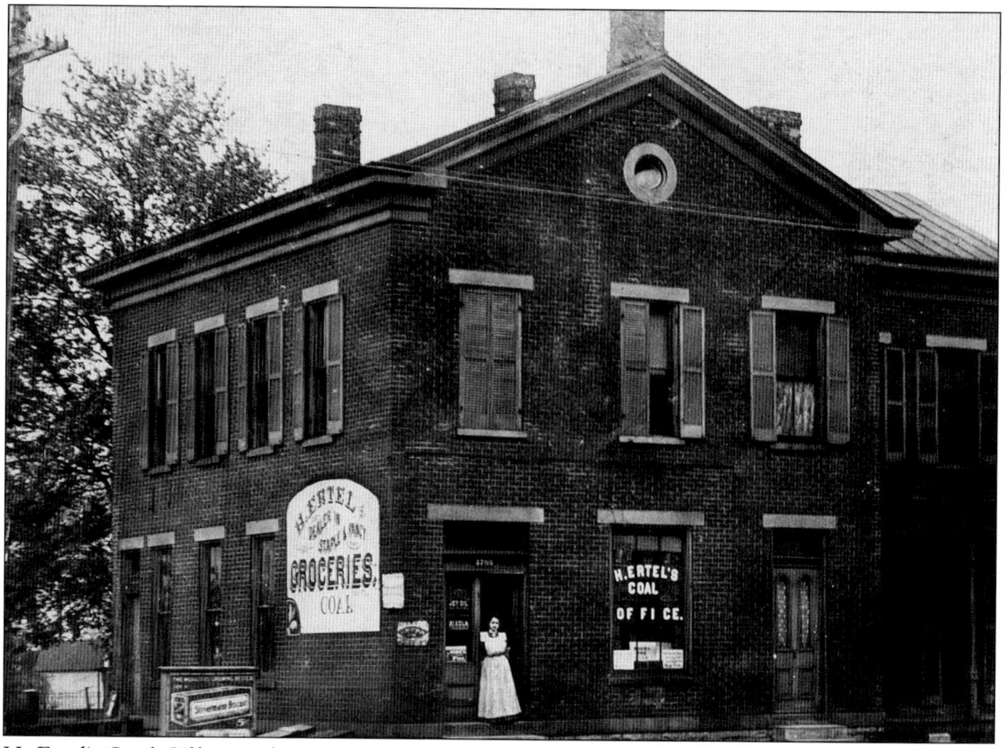

H. Ertel's Coal Office and Groceries at 4700 Peabody Street is across the street from the west railroad station. This building is still standing but is no longer an active grocery store.

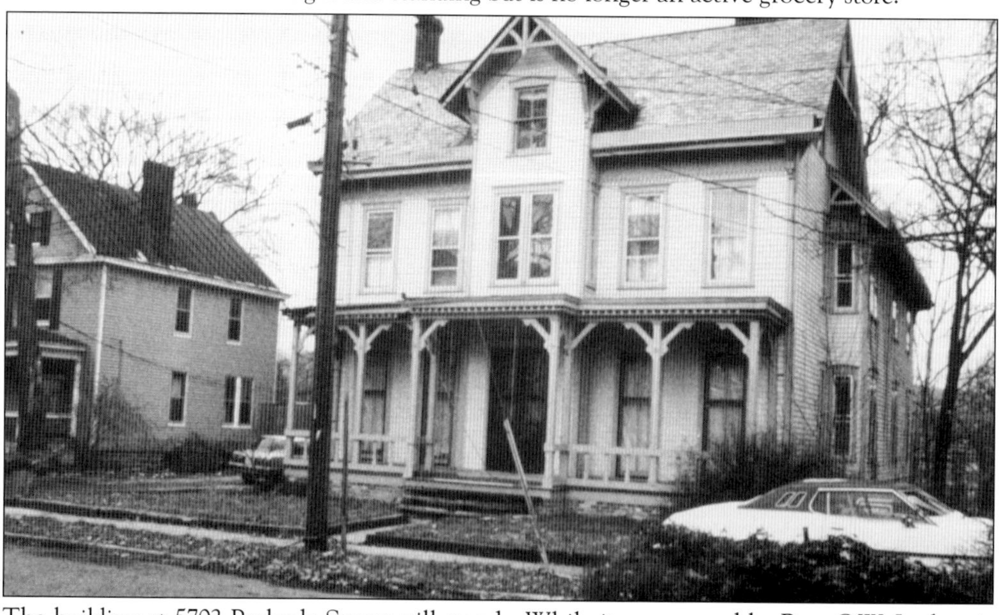

The building at 5702 Peabody Street still stands. While it was owned by Rev. G.W. Lasher, it was the meeting place for the Round Table Literary Club, founded in 1892. Dr. Arthur Knight was a cofounder of the club. George F. Sands and several of his colleagues were members of the Madisonville Round Table when it was dubbed "the University of Madisonville." It was still meeting up until 1997.

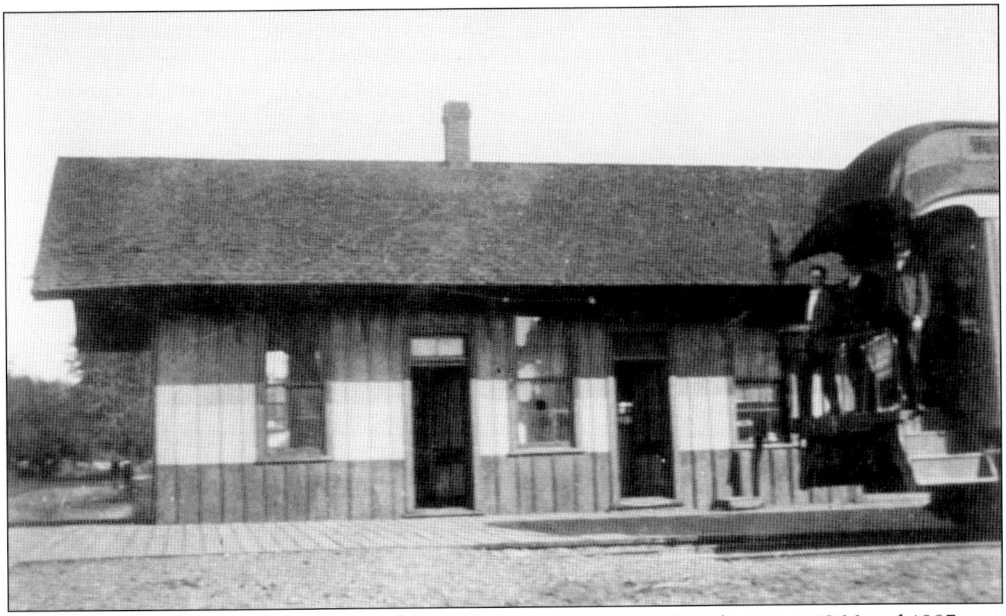

This first Baltimore and Ohio Railroad (B&O) west station, seen here between 1866 and 1887, was located on Orlando Place and Peabody Avenue and was torn down to make way for a new station on the same site. In the booklet "Suburban Homes," published in 1866, the railroad was selling the idea of railroad travel over other means of getting to the city. This made it highly desirable for workers who wanted the "country" life. The B&O offered to "furnish free transportation from Madisonville to Cincinnati, the first year, to the head of the family, if a new resident and building a permanent residence, costing not less than $1,000." Madison's housing boom was on!

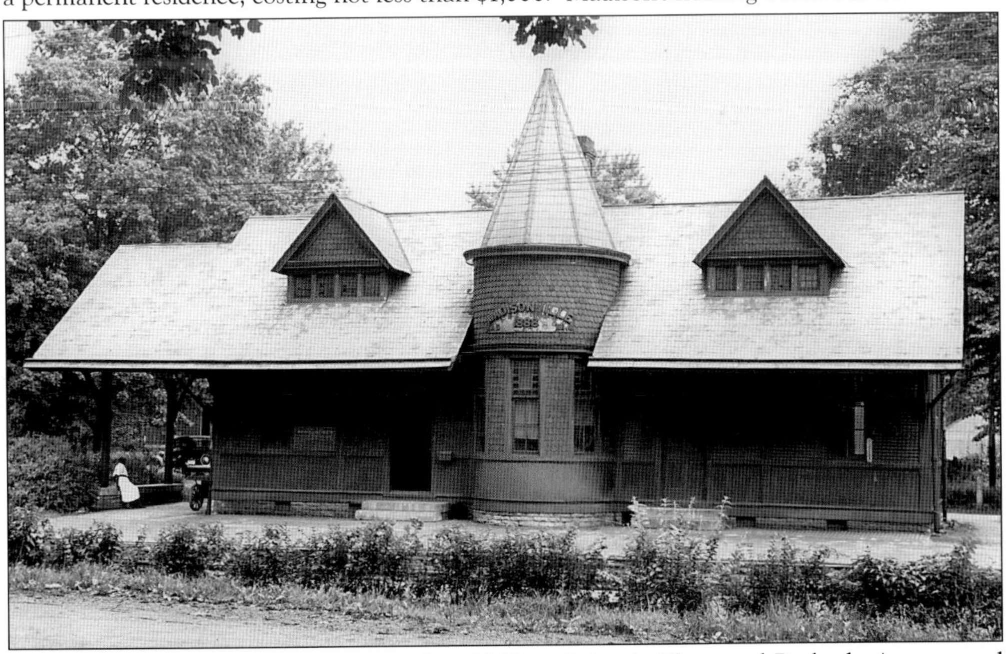

The new west station was constructed in 1888 at Orlando Place and Peabody Avenue and continued in operation until the mid-1940s. By then, the commuter system was a thing of the past. The building was demolished in the late 1940s.

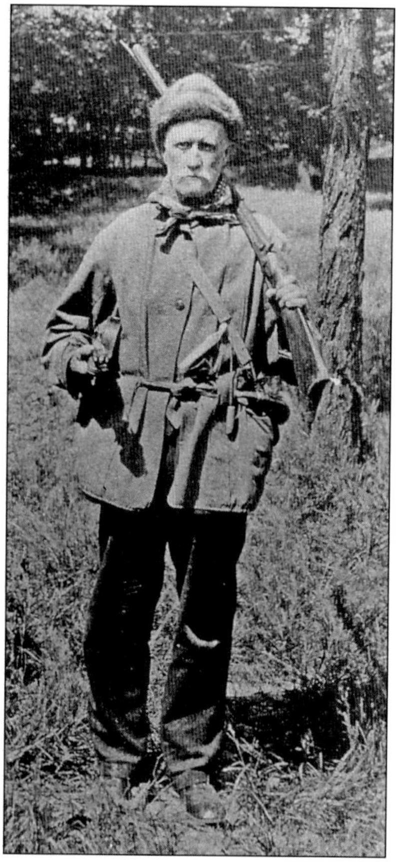

Frank Miller was the paymaster for the railroad beginning in 1866. He was also secretary of the Cottage Building and Loan until shortly before his death in 1958 at the age of 105. His father, Levi P. Miller, was a pastor for many years in the mid-1800s. Frank Miller was also a great-grandson of a founder of the Madisonville Methodist Church, Smith Clason.

This was Frank Miller's home on Erie Avenue, ironically now owned by an unrelated Miller. Lynn Miller is a longtime singer and piano teacher of the kids of Madisonville and the surrounding area and performs in downtown Cincinnati.

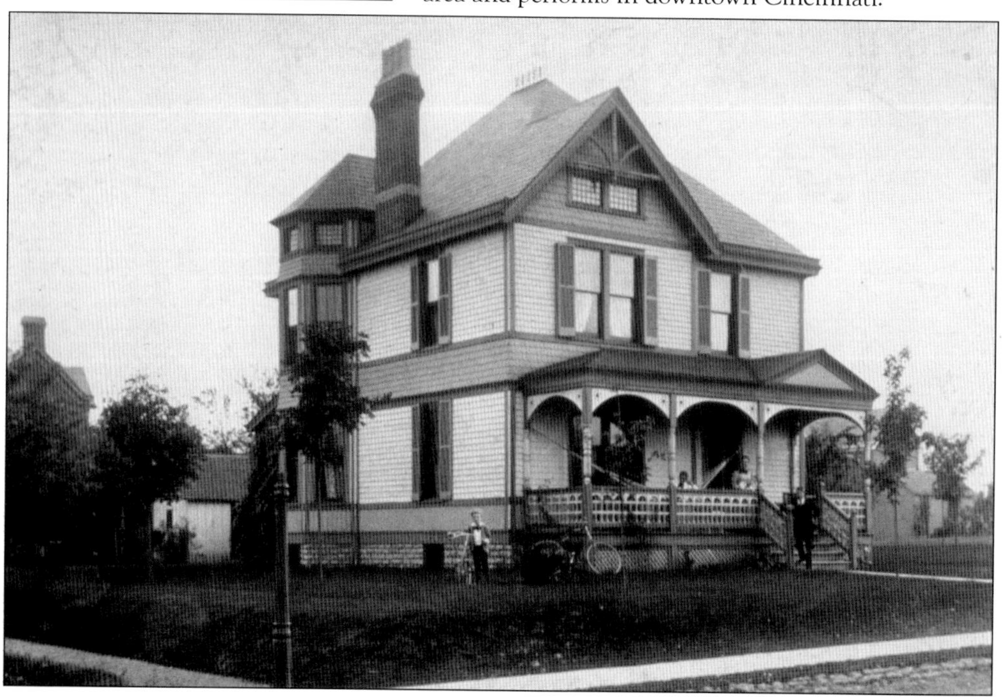

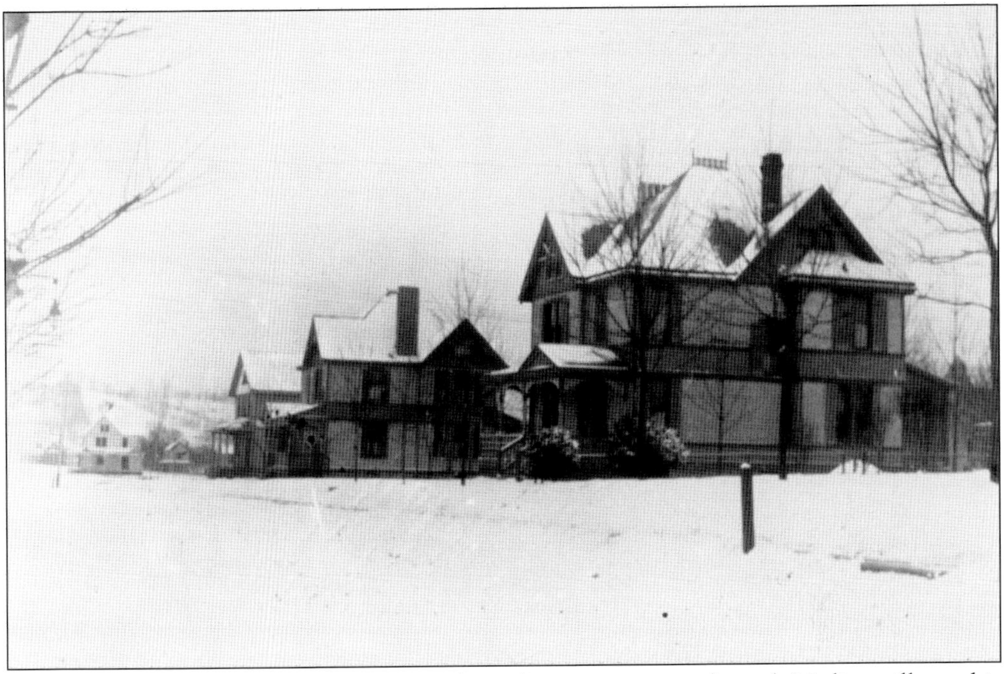

As paymaster, Frank Miller could keep watch on the trains coming through Madisonville out his bedroom window. This view was taken around 1900.

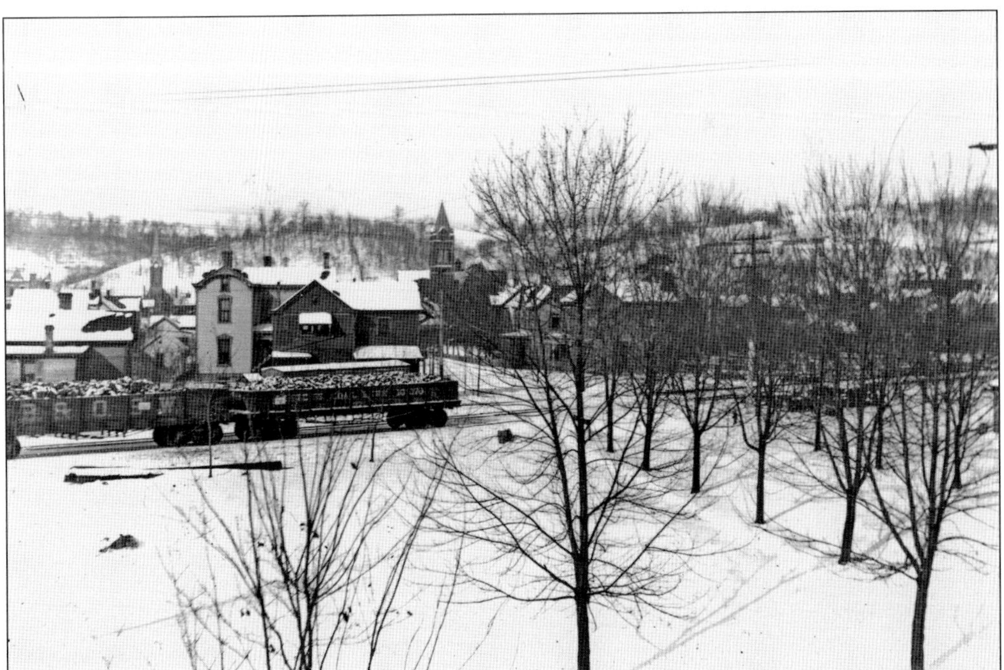

This picturesque snowy view of the Erie Avenue railroad tracks was taken from Frank Miller's front bedroom window.

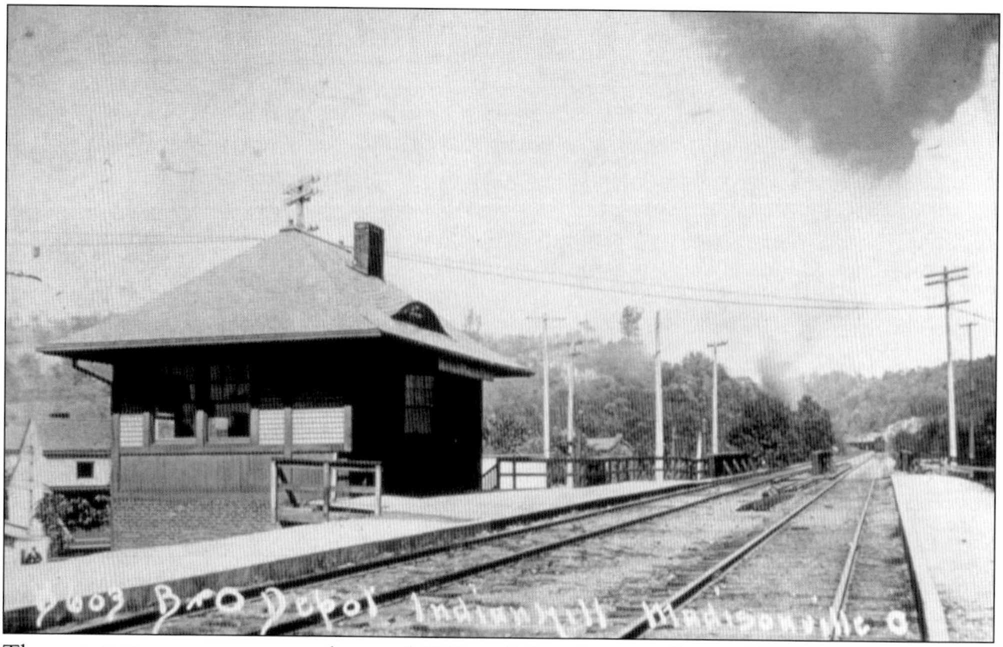

The east station was constructed around 1892, and this photograph was taken in 1910 from above the Mrs. Rogers Candy Store, located on Madison Road adjacent to the railroad tracks near the overpass at Madison and Kenwood Roads. The stairs along the side go to the second-level railroad station, where tickets were sold for boarding. Between 1900 and 1930, one could board a train from either station for trips to the city or any other location along the route of the B&O Railroad. The east station was demolished in the early 1940s.

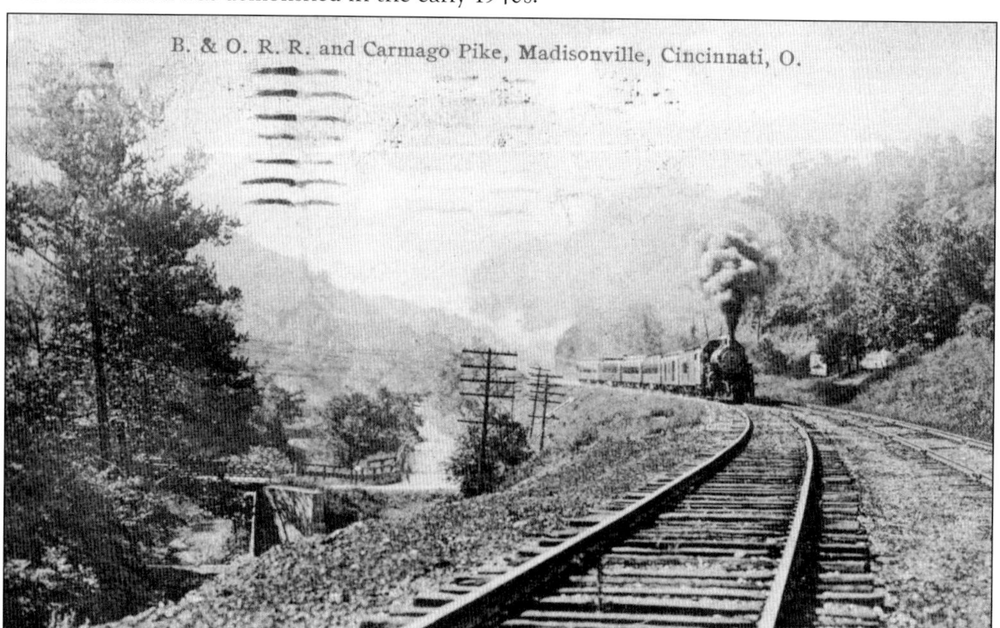

This photograph shows the B&O train coming from Maderia down Carmago Pike into Madisonville in 1910. Its first stop in Madisonville would have been the east station to pick up passengers for their commute to Downtown Cincinnati or any stop along the way.

William Wirt Peabody, born in 1837, migrated to Ohio from the northeast at the age of 17. He took work with the Marietta-Cincinnati Railroad as a stake-driver on a surveyor team and, after many promotions, became superintendant. In the Civil War, Peabody rose to the rank of captain in the 149th Ohio. From that time forward, he was generally referred to as "Captain Peabody." As superintendent, he introduced public relations to the railroad industry and took the radical approach of investigating train wrecks and giving accurate information to the press, earning the respect of his employees and the public. During the Great Railroad Strike of 1877, Captain Peabody's Marietta-Cincinnati Railroad was the only line with uninterrupted train service. Eventually, Captain Peabody became the vice president of the B&O Railroad Southwestern Division, headquartered in Cincinnati, and took up residence in Madisonville.

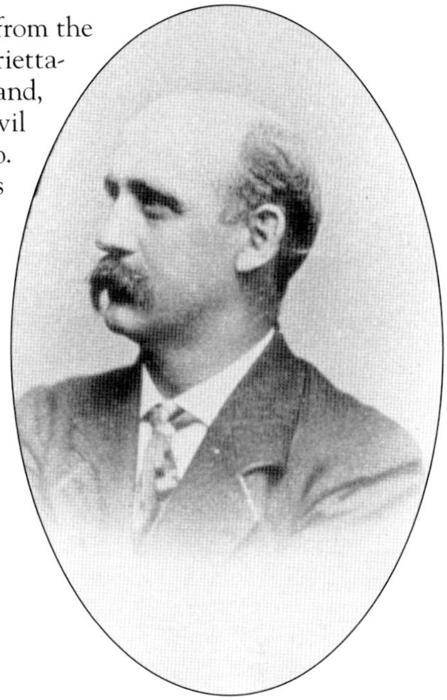

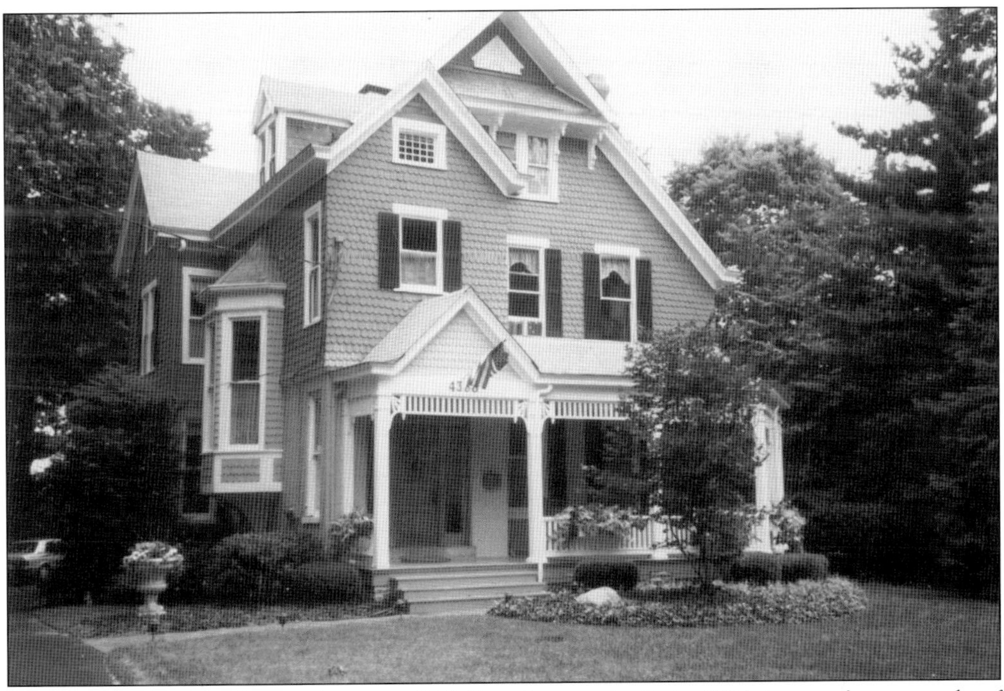

Capt. William Peabody's residence at 4338 Erie Avenue, built in 1884, is a perfect example of Victorian architecture and has been lovingly restored to its former glory by its current custodian, Robert Brown. He has not only restored it to period but has also added a unique feature—a Lionel train traveling along the ceiling through the living room and tunneling through the walls of the dining room, kitchen, and entryway, making the complete circle of the first floor. The captain would be proud to see such an engineering project done in his very own house—how appropriate for the past president of the railroad!

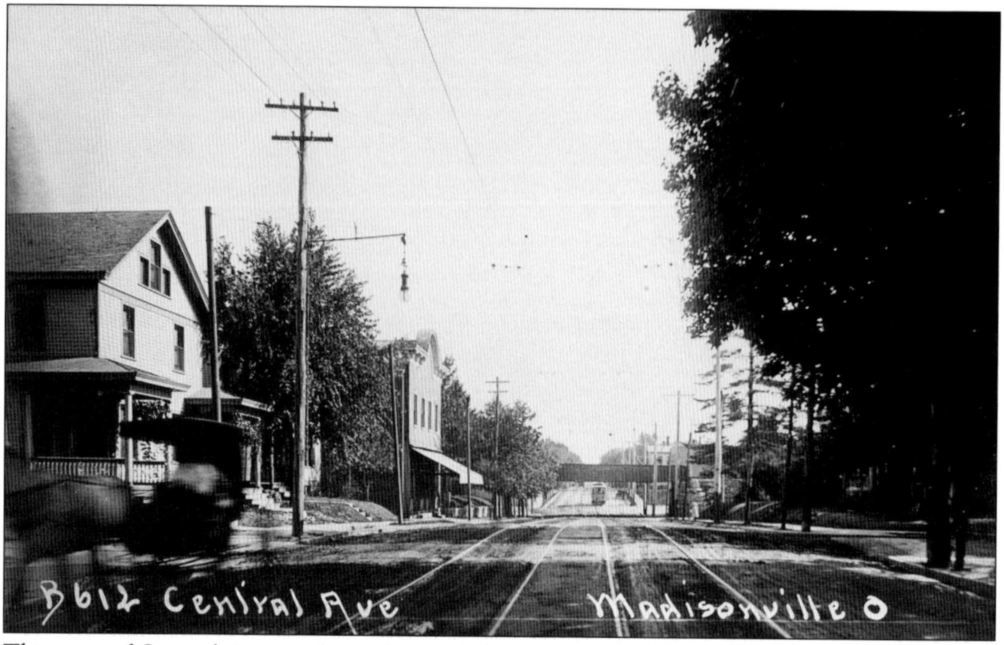

This view of Central Avenue shows the B&O Railroad overpass, visible in the distance.

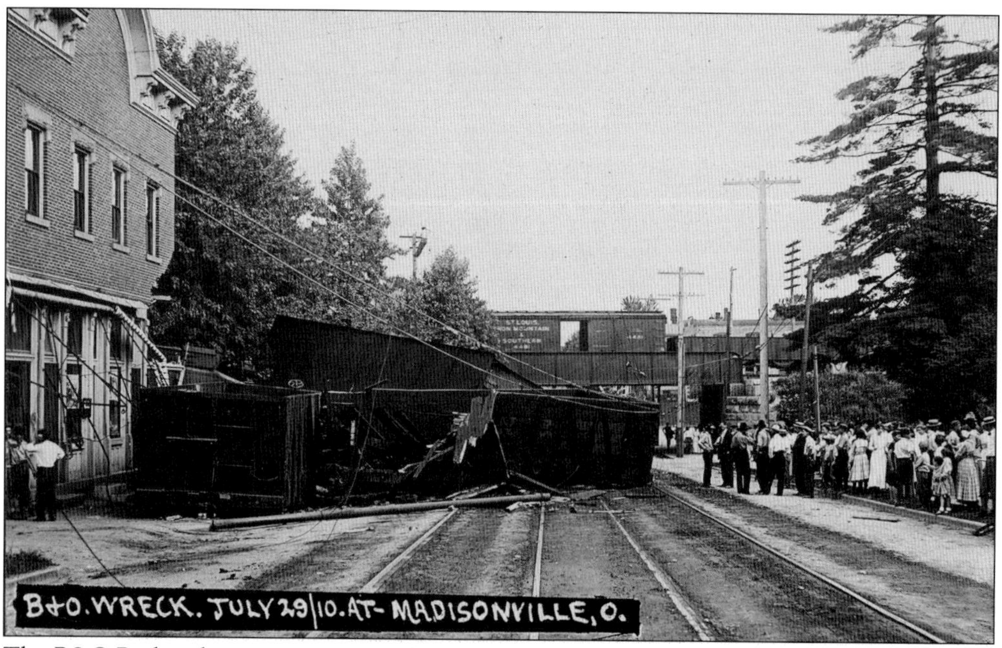

The B&O Railroad overpass at Central Avenue was built around 1905 and was the site of the first train wreck in Madisonville on July 12, 1910. According to a local newspaper report, a freight engine clipped the corner of the W.H. Settle & Co. building on Central Avenue and struck a switch engine that was pushing a freight car into the street and had come to rest in front of the building.

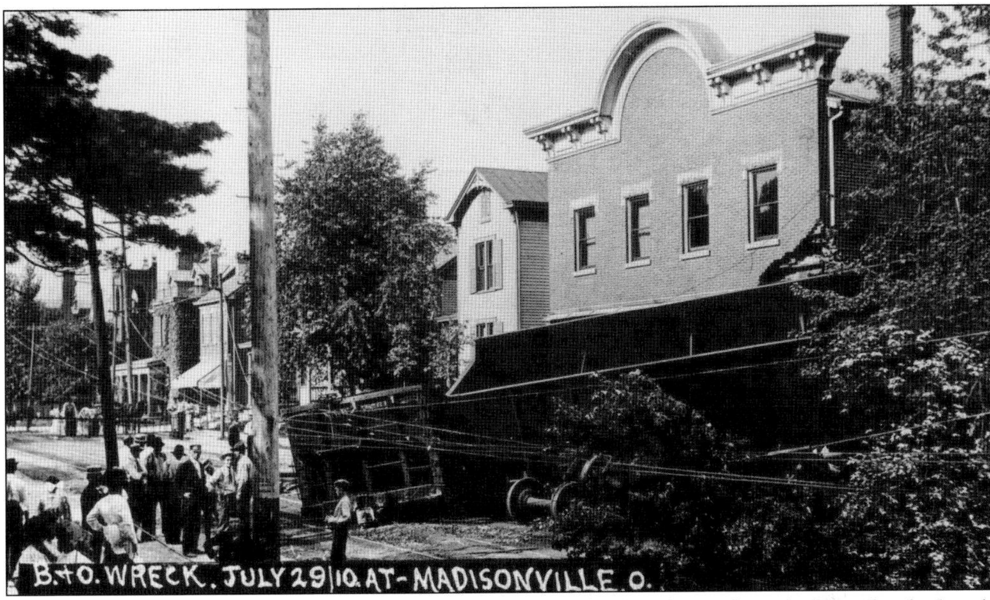

Marks of the train disaster can still be seen today in the brick patchwork. The Settle family home, adjacent to the railroad track and their family business, was miraculously not affected in the accident. Both structures are still in use today, with the business remaining the Settle Supply Company, which stayed in the family until 2006, and the home has been occupied by the Fraternal Order of Eagles since 1939.

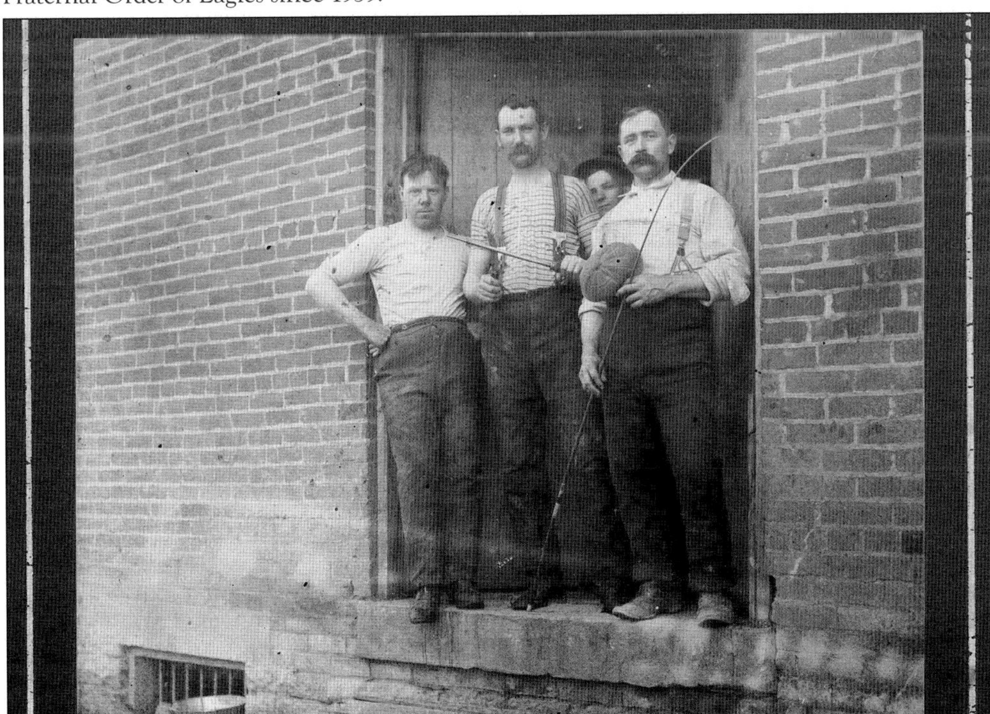

Frank Kneipp (center) and other unidentified employees of W.H. Settle & Co. Real Estate, Coal, and Feed pose in the side loading doorway at 4735 Whetsel Avenue.

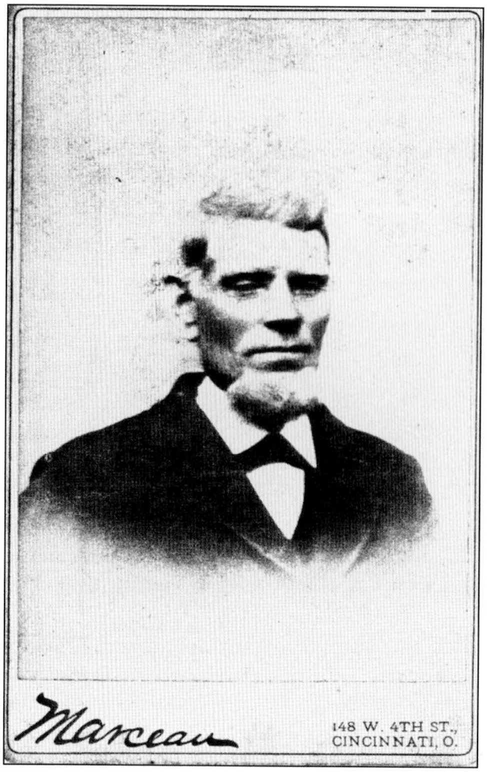

William Henry Settle (1827–1887) was born in Cincinnati to Joseph and Hanna, who migrated to Cincinnati from Yorkshire, England, about 1810 and moved to a farm in Madisonville in 1832. William became a whitesmith, hammering white metal. His place of business was at the corner of Eighth and Main Streets in Cincinnati. William married Esther Kitchell, and they established their residence on Cross Street (Clephane Street), owning a considerable amount of property. William was killed in a railroad accident.

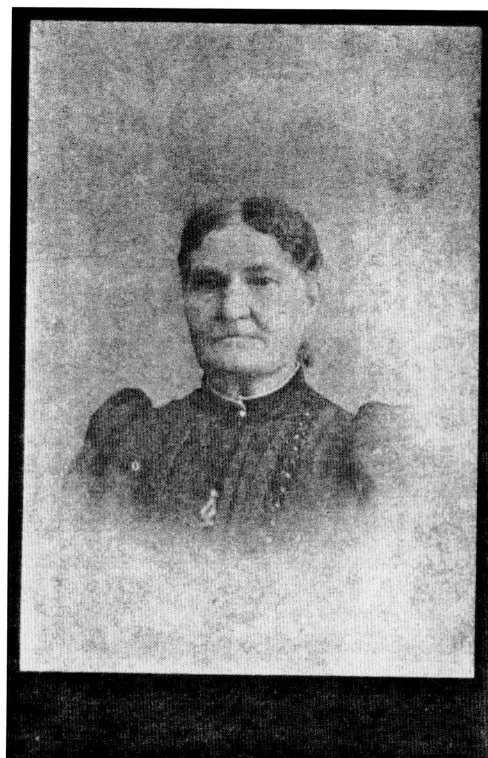

Esther Marriah Kitchell Settle (1830–1911) was also a native of Ohio and of English descent. She and William were the parents of seven children: George I.; Charles M.; William H. II; Carrie J.; Anna; Florence, wife of Edward Gomien; and Leota. When Esther died at the age of 90, she was still living in her home.

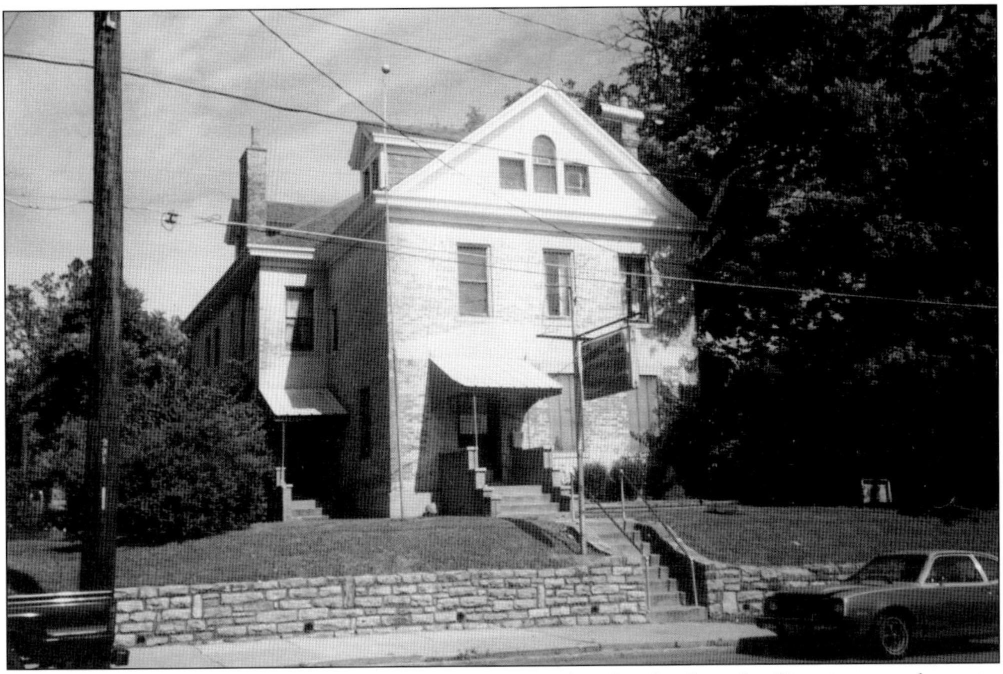

The Settle home on Whetsel Avenue, next to the Settle Supply Co., is seen here in more recent times.

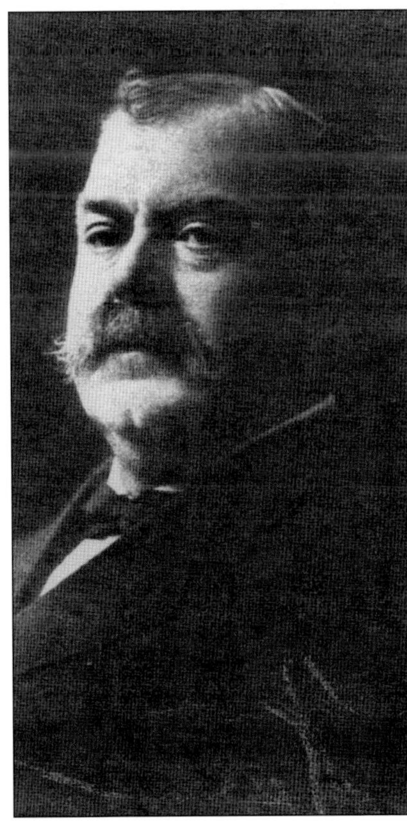

W.H. Settle II was a dealer in hard and soft coal, lumber, and feed and a real estate agent. Born in Madisonville in 1859, he received a public school education completed at Madisonville High School. He founded Settle Coal and Feed in 1890 across from his family home. The business quickly grew, and he opened a lumberyard on Settle Street and Stafford Avenue, one block off Madison Road. William H. Settle II was a very active and well-respected figure in the Madisonville community. He and his partners reportedly built the railroad overpass at Whetsel Avenue, which enabled the extension of the trolley line to the center of town at Madison Road and Whetsel Avenue. He also constructed many of the original sidewalks in the town, operated a water wagon for the dusty streets, and served as an officer of a local bank. In 1888, he was elected township trustee, and he was re-elected in 1892. He was also treasurer of the corporate village of Madisonville. On April 29, 1886, he married Mary B. "Mamie" Clephane, the daughter of William B. and Mary A. Clephane, and they had two daughters, Mable and Myrtle. They were members of the Baptist Church and he was a member of the Knights of Pythias and the Masonic Lodge. Over the years, he was in business with his wife's brother, G.W. Clephane, and his sister Florence's husband, J. Edward Gomien.

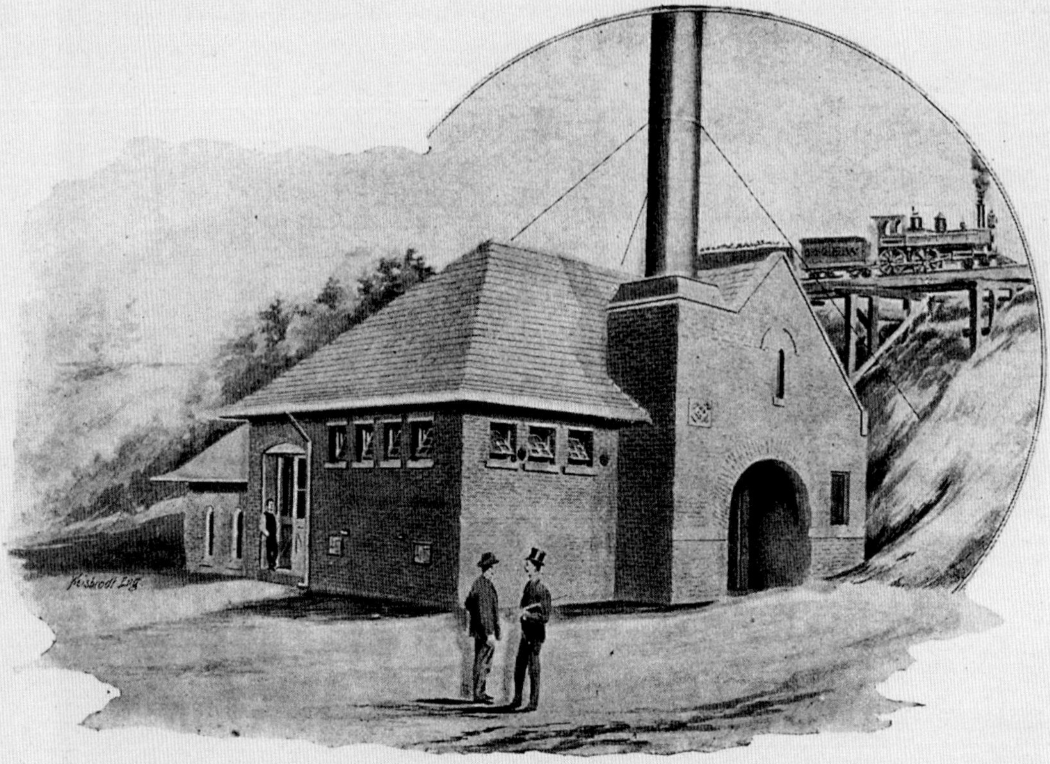

Pumping Station. Madisonville Water Works.

In the dedication to the souvenir booklet of the opening of the village waterworks, Judge Joseph Cox wrote: "The village water-works was completed 1892, located to the east of what is now Red Bank Rd., near the railroad overpass. It provided abundant supply of pure water drawn from wells sunk to the lower levels, rendering contamination from surface drainage impossible. At the time ten miles of mains had been laid with sufficient number of plugs for ample fire protection. The pumping station was a neat brick structure, with engine of sufficient capacity to supply water for domestic purposes, and of sufficient force to throw water over the highest building in the village at the time. The plant was constructed on what is known as the Holly or direct pressure system." After Madisonville was annexed to Cincinnati in 1911, the plant continued operation until about 1917. By that time, Cincinnati was able to provide utility services at a cheaper rate than the old station. The plant was eventually demolished.

· . · MADISONVILLE IMPROVEMENT · . · ASSOCIATION.

I. G. RAWN, ... President.

W. J. BEHYMER, ... Vice President.

F. J. ZINGERLE, ... Secretary.

D. KLEIN, ... Financial Secretary.

F. R. MILLER, ... Treasurer.

WATER-WORKS CELEBRATION COMMITTEES.

INVITATIONS AND ADVERTISING.

O. P. McCarty, W. W. Peabody, Jr., W. S. Rulison
Wm. Driehaus, Dr. Krieger.

PROGRAM.

Dr. W. G. Hier, I. N. Miller, John Crugar, Dr. C. L. Metz.

FINANCE.

J. Anderson Ward, B. T. Clemons, D. D. Carothers, Dr. C. P. Gray.
C. M. Settle, W. B. Shattuc, G. F. Potter.

DECORATION.

David Kline, Paul Megrue, W. J. Behymer.
Rev. Charles Hahne, Samuel Hill.

RECEPTION.

J. G. Luhn, F. J. Zingerle, William Blair, W. J. Behymer, Dr. W. Hier, Charles B. Crugar, W. C. Rogers, Dr. A. L. Knight, I. N. Miller, Dr. C. L. Metz, William Settle, Paul Megue, Capt. W. W. Peabody, I. G. Rawn, D. D. Carothers, S. W. Stone, Oliver Jones, E. A. Conkling, Rev. J. F. Pollock, Rev. D. Lee Aultman, Rev. G. M. Shott, Rev. D. C. Cox, Rev. Charles Hahne, Prof. F. B. Dyer.

The souvenir booklet made for the opening of the village waterworks was an important piece of early literature for the town.

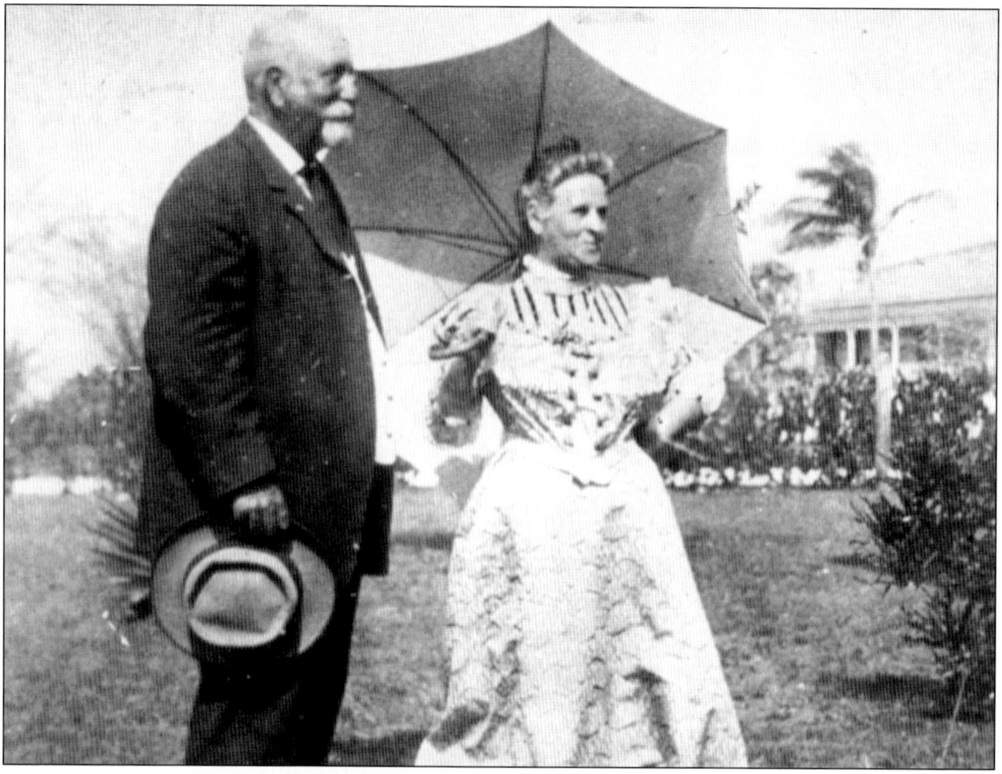

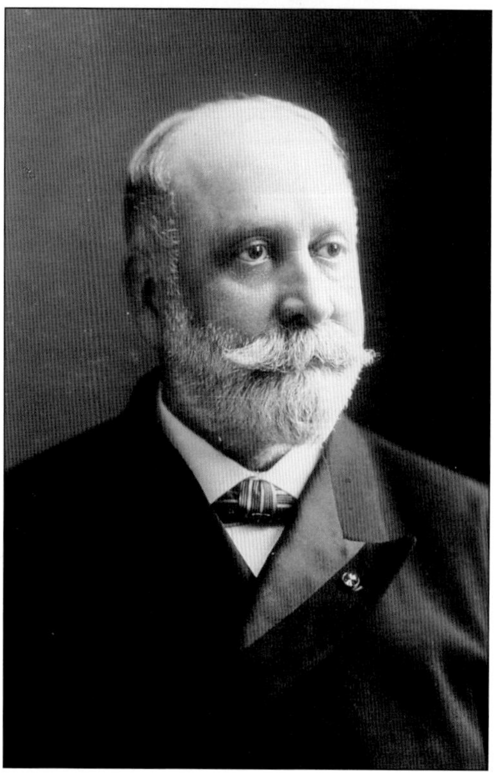

I. Newton Miller, a prominent citizen of Madisonville, is shown here with his wife while on vacation in Florida. He was the general manager of Western Union Telegraph Company and lived in a large Victorian house at Thompkins and Roe Streets. During the Great Railroad Strike of 1877, his employees were the only ones who operated trains in and out of Cincinnati, largely due to the actions of Captain Peabody, who was so well-respected by his employees. He was mentioned in the dedication booklet of the town's waterworks.

William Bunn Shattuc was born in 1841 and moved from New York to Ohio as a boy with his parents. He enlisted in the 2nd Ohio Cavalry during the Civil War with a commission as a second lieutenant, serving two years. Following his military service, he worked for the Mississippi Railroad as a passenger agent for nearly 30 years. Afterwards, he was elected to the Ohio state senate and then to three terms in Congress, where he served on the Committee for Immigration and Naturalization. He died in 1911 at his Madisonville home.

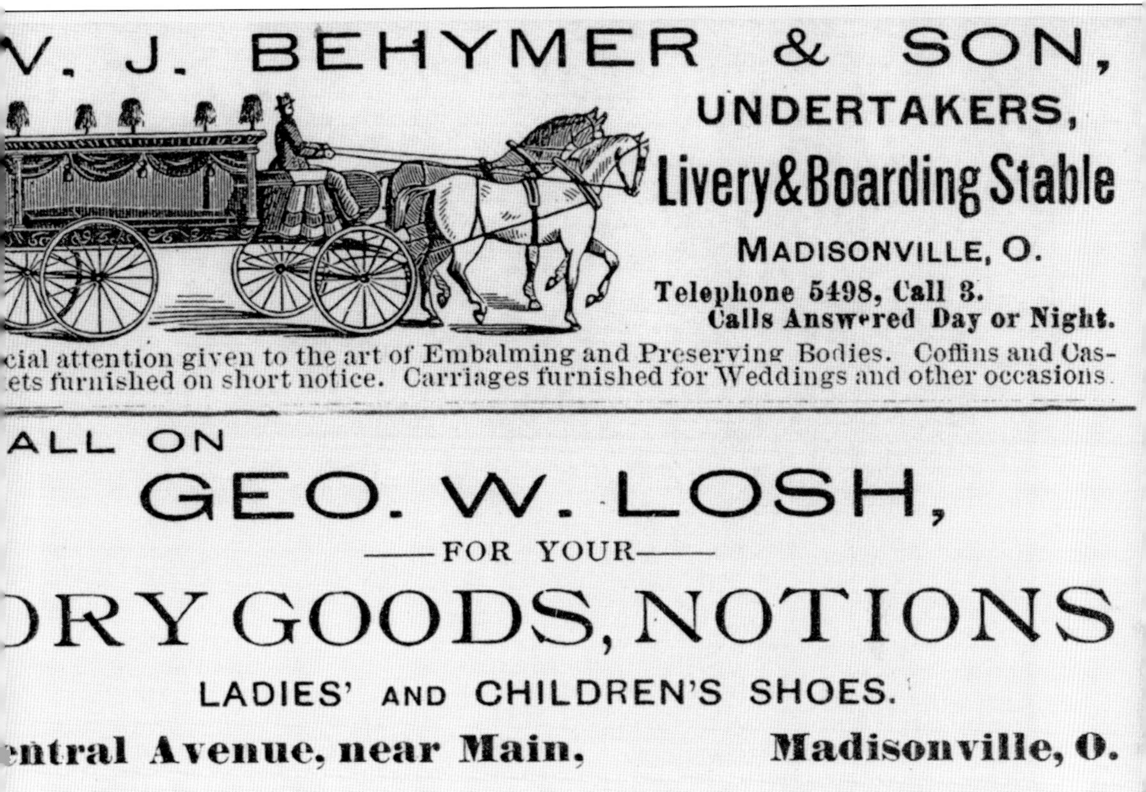

W.J. Behymer, born in 1842 in Clermont County, was an undertaker and proprietor of livery stables in Madisonville and Norwood. He enlisted in the 89th Ohio Volunteer Infantry at the start of the Civil War and was taken prisoner at the Battle of Chickamauga. Behymer was held at various POW camps, including in Andersonville, Georgia, until his release near the end of the war. He held offices in several state organizations and served on the Hamilton County agricultural board, the Madisonville council, and as an officer for Madisonville Building and Loan Corporation No. 2, among others. George W. Losh was born on his family's farm in Indian Hill in 1843. As a young man, he moved to Madisonville and took a clerkship at the general store, which he purchased a year later. This marked the beginning of a diverse business career spanning over 40 years. Losh was a clerk at the county treasurer's office and a salesman before working in the coal and feed business and the dry goods business—for which the above advertisement was made. He also served as treasurer of the Madisonville Building and Loan.

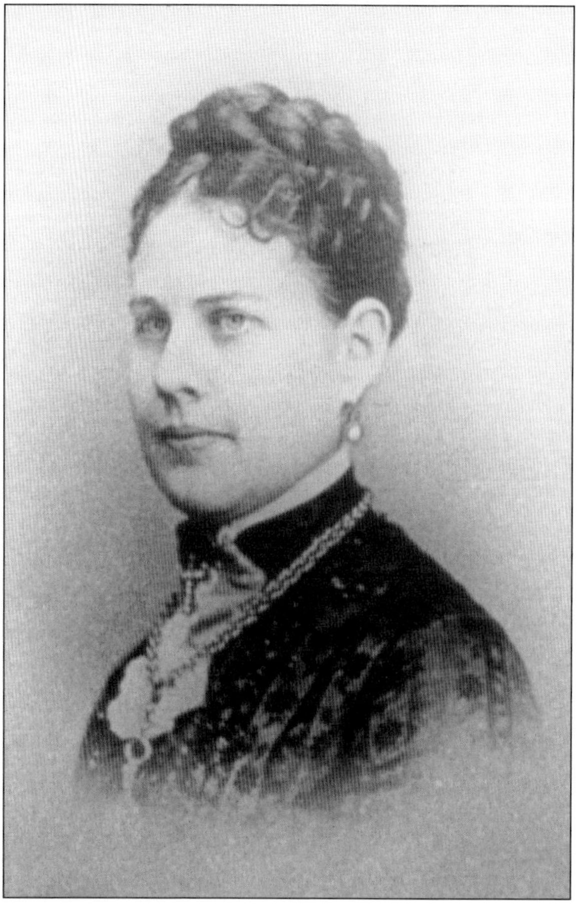

The Madisonville Monday Club began as an idea in 1892, when E.S. "Fanny" Emerson and Mrs. D.P. McCarty felt Madisonville was ready for a ladies' cultural organization. The club, with 37 charter members, was a literary and intellectual group whose aim was to "stimulate intellectual growth and moral development; to promote general philanthropic work along practical lines; and to aid by its influence such interests as may enlist its sympathies."

The Emerson residence, seen here about 1900, was located on a knoll above today's Erie Avenue. A circular driveway approached the house, and several cedar trees were planted on the property, which Mrs. Emerson lovingly referred to as Cedar Heights.

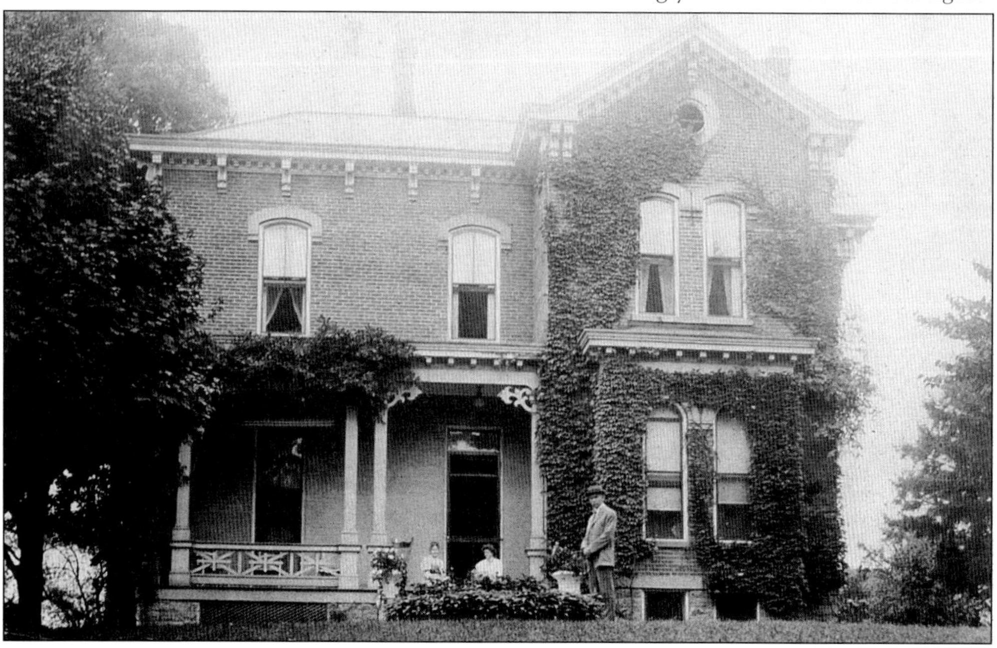

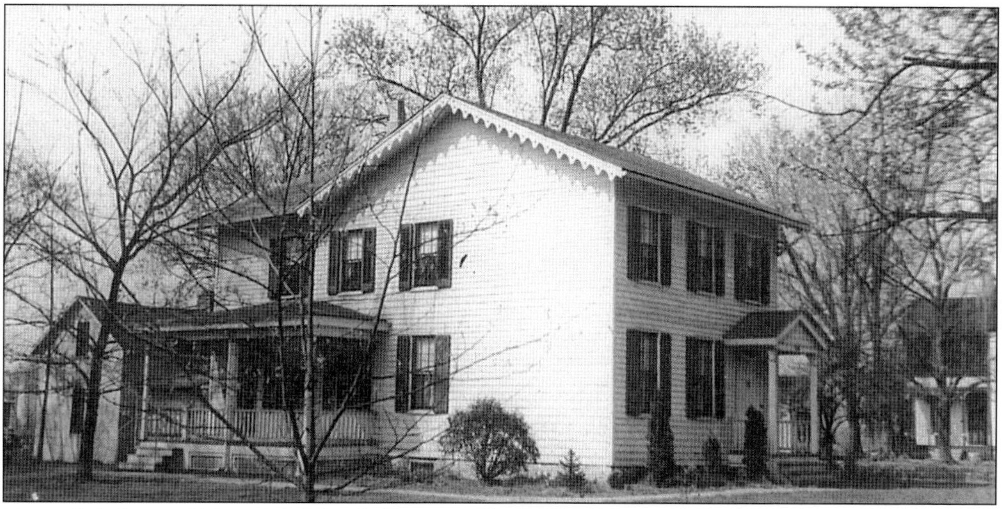

One of Madisonville's earliest family homesteads, Hidden House, was a white two-story Colonial frame house built in 1851 by William and Jack Stewart with a portico to one side and a green shingled roof. The house was near the northeast corner of a 15-acre parcel. This house was demolished in 1976 to make way for the new St. Paul Lutheran Village. (Courtesy of Jane Zultowski.)

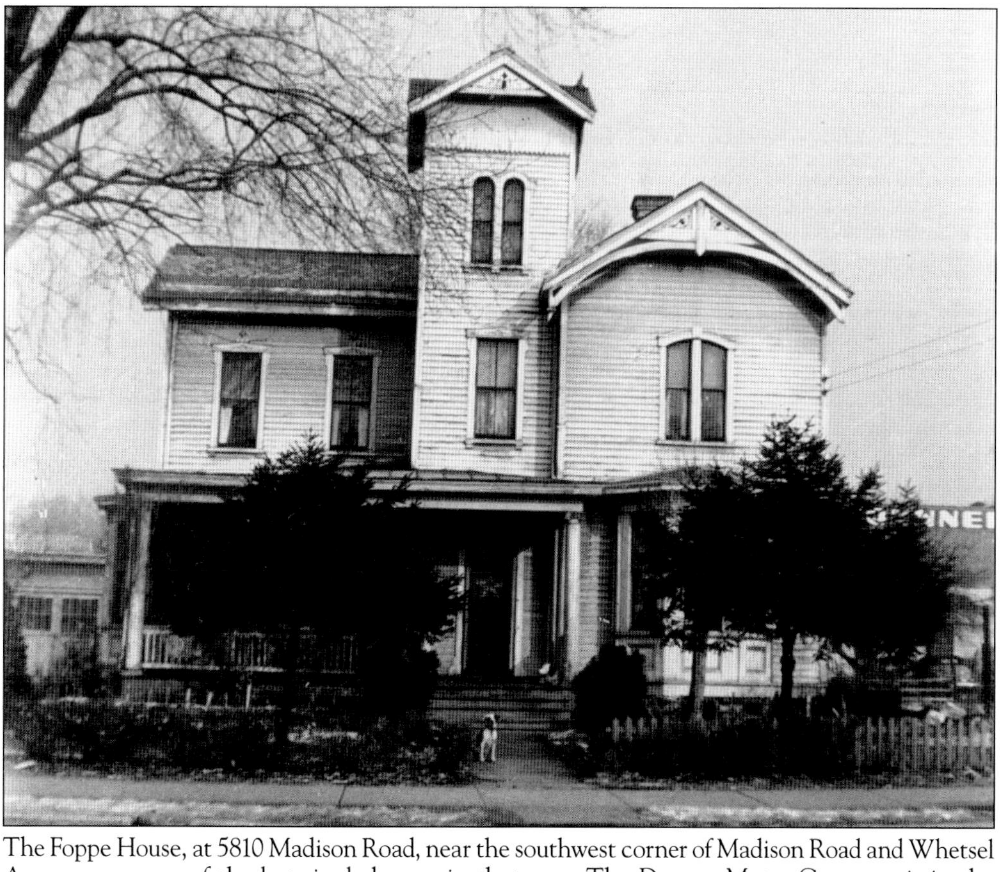

The Foppe House, at 5810 Madison Road, near the southwest corner of Madison Road and Whetsel Avenue, was one of the last single homes in that area. The Danner Motor Company is in the background, indicating that the house was probably demolished around the 1940s.

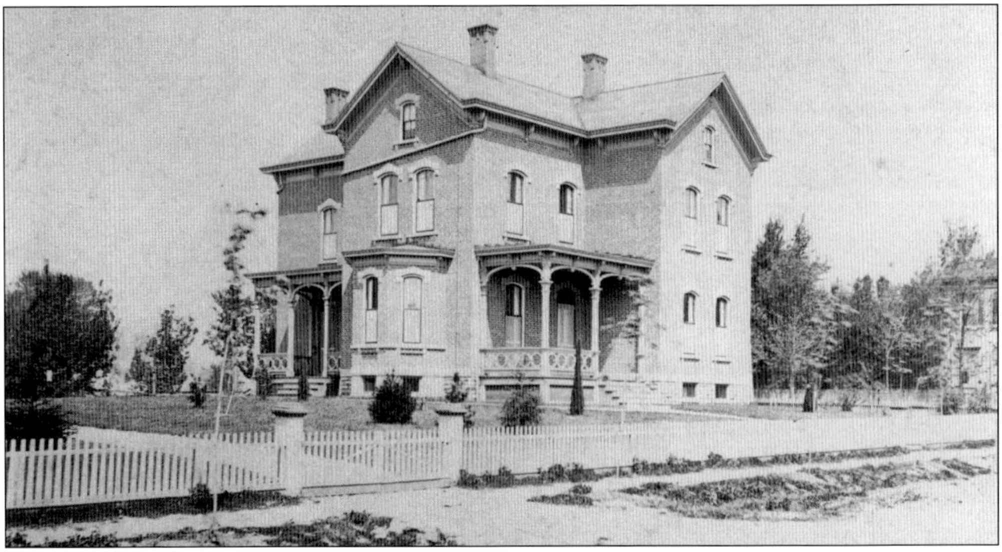

The house at the southwest corner of Madison Road and Stewart Avenue is another landmark of the community and part of the Madison-Stewart Historic District in the National Historic Register. It was built by Scottish immigrant L.C. Weir, who sold it to Dr. and Mrs. George Dart. Dr. Dart was a Methodist circuit rider. They had three daughters who lived in the home until their deaths, at which time the house and property were turned over to the Methodist Church, as stipulated in their wills.

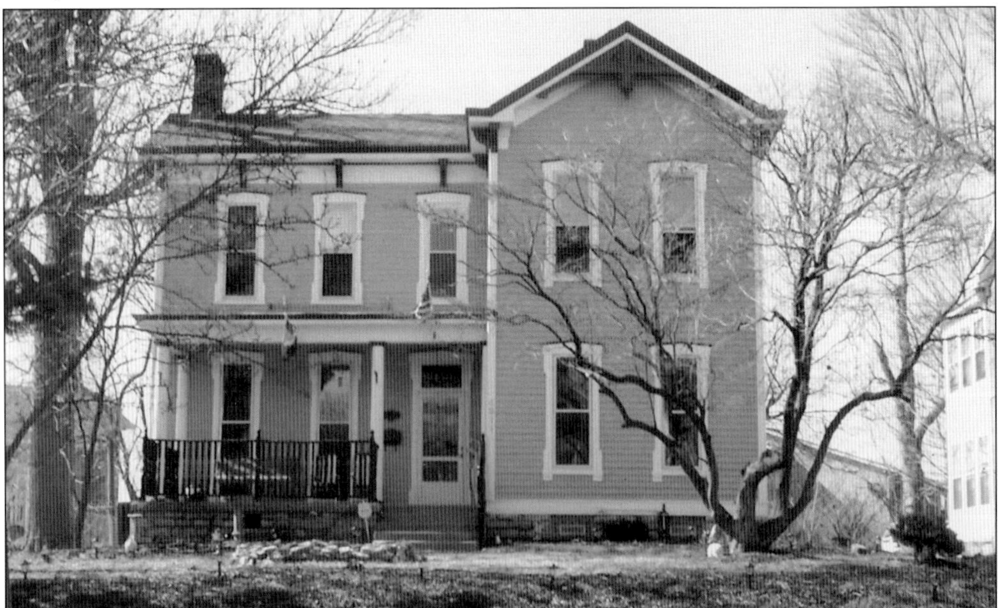

The houses at 4911 and 4915 Stewart Avenue were built by two brothers, Charles B. Cruger (1847–1908) and Jonathon H. Cruger (1842–1922), who purchased the land from Benjamin M. Stewart for $500 in 1870. These homes on Stewart Avenue were inducted into the National Register of Historic Places in 1969 as part of the Madison-Stewart Historic District. Charles Cruger worked for the St. Louis–Cincinnati Railroad, and Jonathon Cruger was as a teller at the Fourth National Bank in Cincinnati.

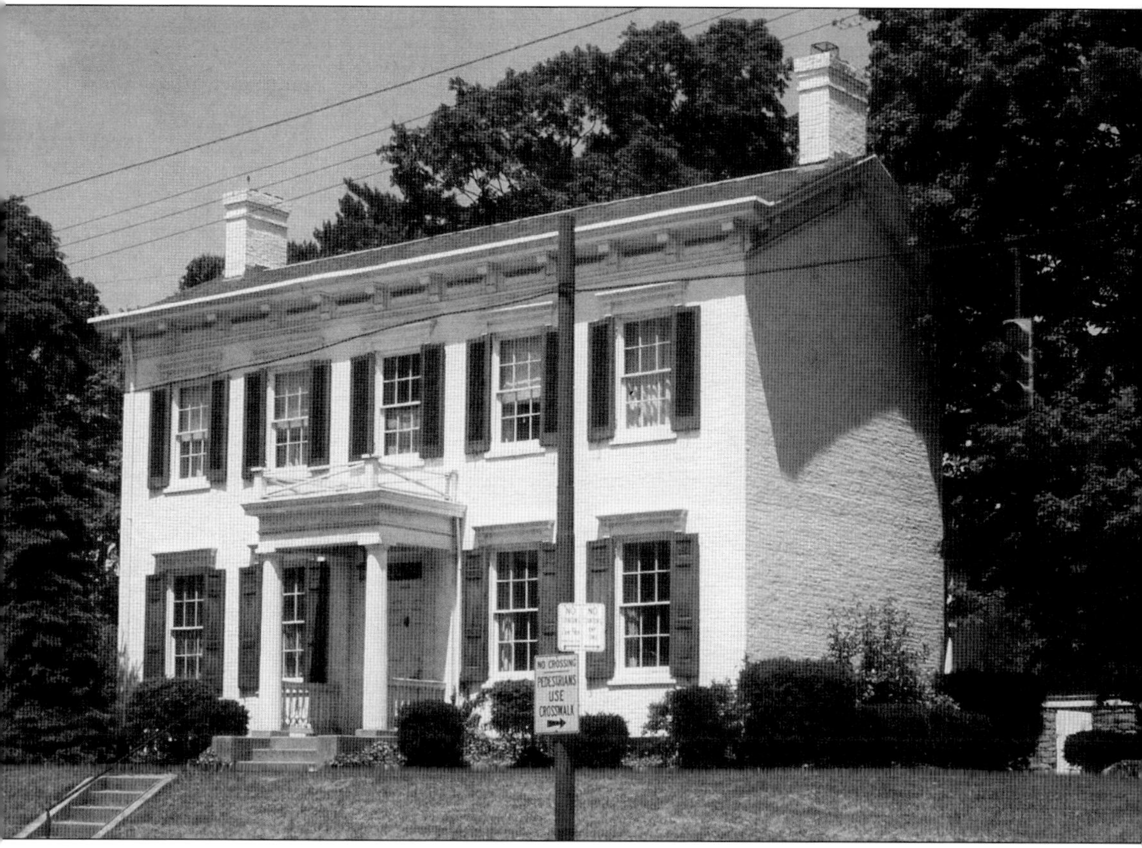

Benjamin Stewart (1780–1862) was born in New England and moved to Cincinnati in 1827. Two years later, he relocated to Madisonville, purchased a large tract of land, and began a lumber business. In 1838, he built this house on the property from lumber he had floated down the Ohio River on flatboats. His nephew designed the house at 5540 Madison Road, and it was the most prominent landmark in the district. Stewart was married three times and had a total of 10 children, including Benjamin M. Upon Benjamin M. Stewart's marriage in 1852, his father's nephew also designed a home for him. The existing building at 5524 Madison Road was originally the barn and carriage house on the estate, but it was converted to a residence several years ago. The main house is a classic example of the Greek Revival style and was put in the National Register of Historic Places in 1969 as part of the Madison-Stewart Historic District. The current owners, the Horstmeyers, have lived there since the 1980s and are the owners of Just Saab Cincinnati at 6323 Madison Road in Madisonville.

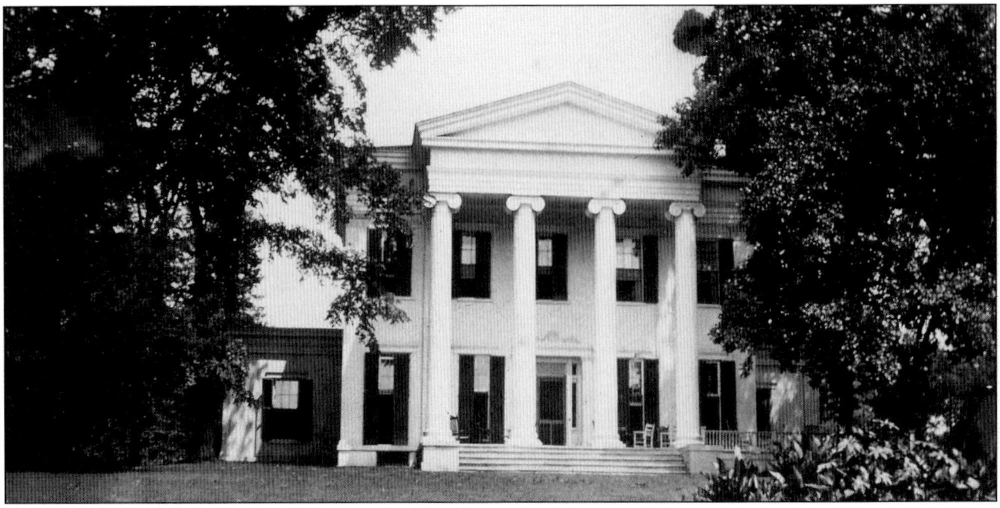

Around 1851, Dr. F.A. Parrish and his wife, Elizabeth Ferris Parrish, built this house, known as The Pillars because of its porch, as a country home on land inherited from Elizabeth's father, Andrew Ferris. The house, though beautifully located, was plagued by a series of misfortunes. About the time the home was completed, a pregnant Elizabeth Parrish was severely injured during a bus accident as she traveled to downtown Cincinnati to buy carpets for the house. She died soon after delivering a child who lived but one hour. After her death, a famous lawsuit took place between the heirs of the Parrish and Ferris families for the deed to the property.

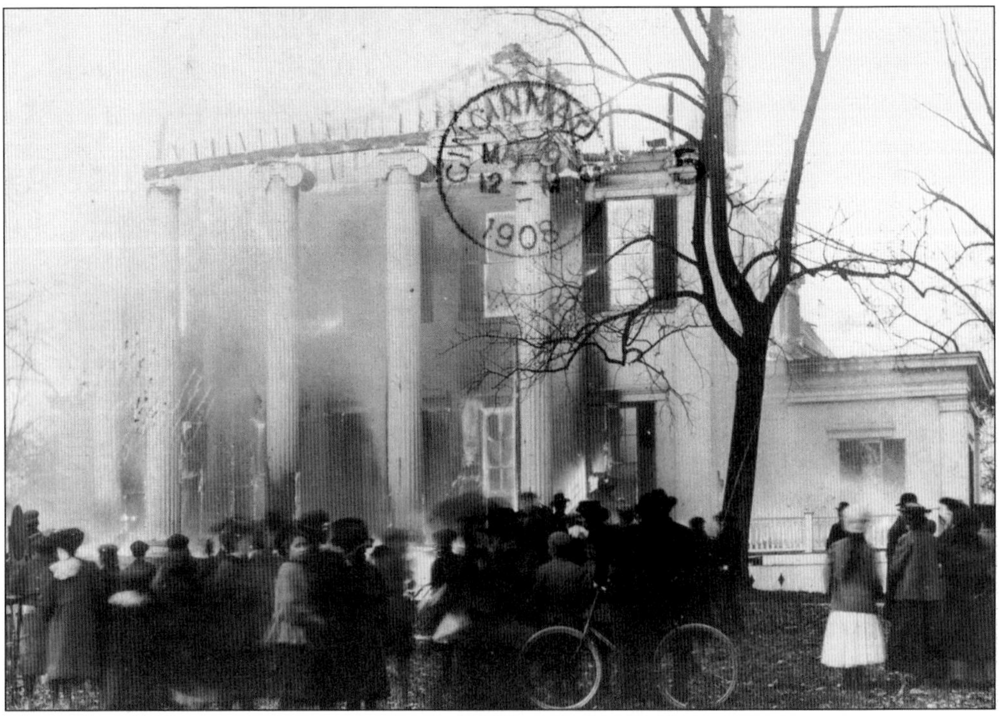

At some point, The Pillars was purchased by James T. Matthews, who leased it to a social organization. It became The Pillars Club and was the scene of spectacular gatherings. It remained as a club for 12 years before it was destroyed by fire in 1908. It was not rebuilt. The property at 5050 Madison Avenue is now owned by the Children's Home of Cincinnati.

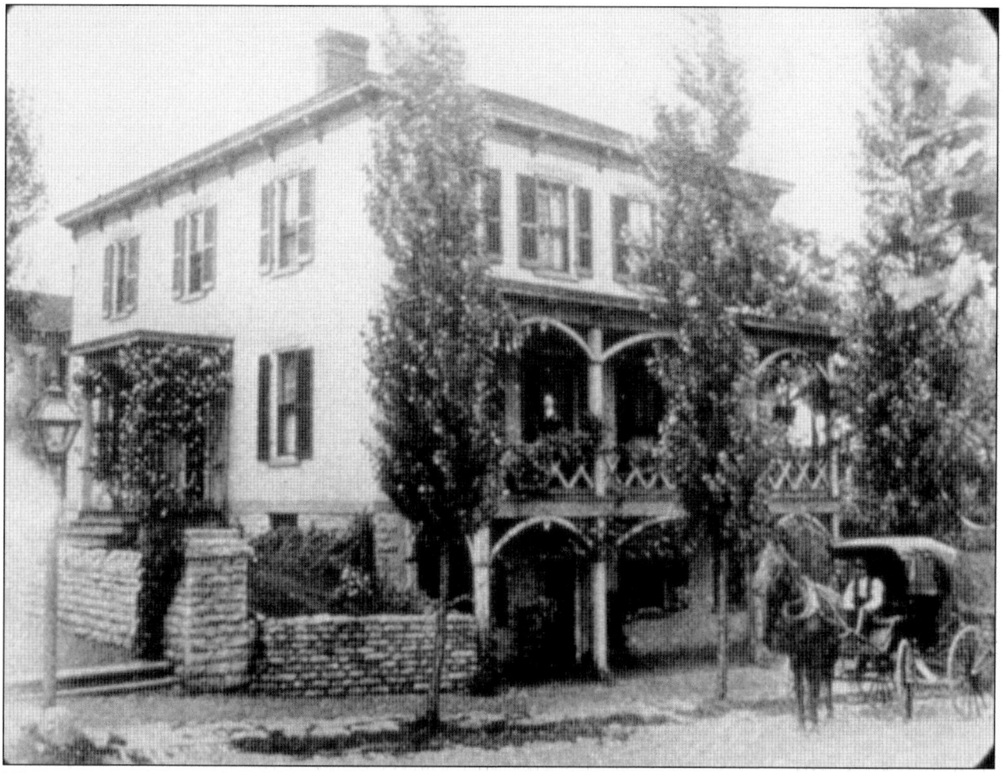

This impressive grey-brick house with a hitching post in front, known as the Covington House, stood at the northwest corner of Stewart Avenue and Covington Street. Annette Covington, the last descendant of the home's original owners, died in the 1950s. It was one of the earliest homes in the area and the scene of many gala festivities. Among Annette Covington's many accomplishments was painting. She once painted a portrait of little Ada Kelley, the sister of Mrs. Driehaus. The portrait was shown at the Woman's Art Club Exhibition at the Closson Galleries and was one of the exhibits from Cincinnati invited to the Ohio State Fair in August 1934.

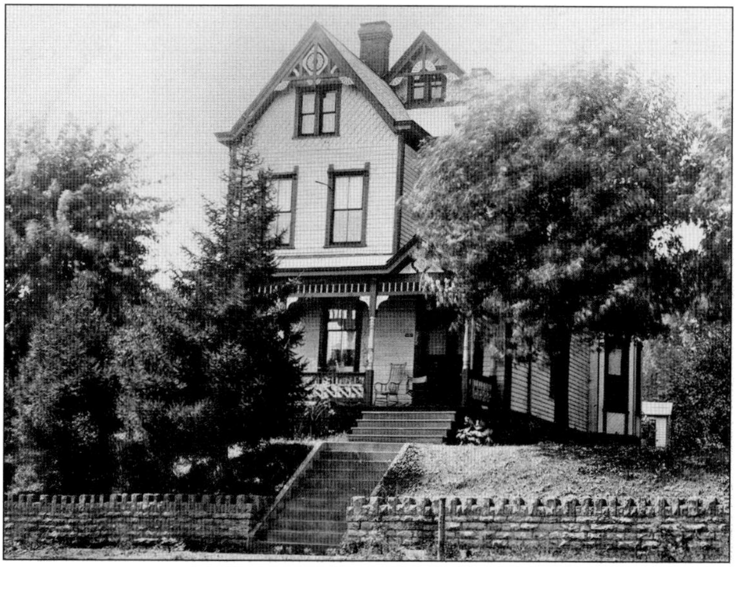

This Victorian house on East Ledge Street, with a sister house on Blaesi Street, is an excellent example of the Victorian influence in Madisonville. These turn-of-the-century houses can be lovingly restored before the wrecking ball gets to them, and many have been. They are worth saving.

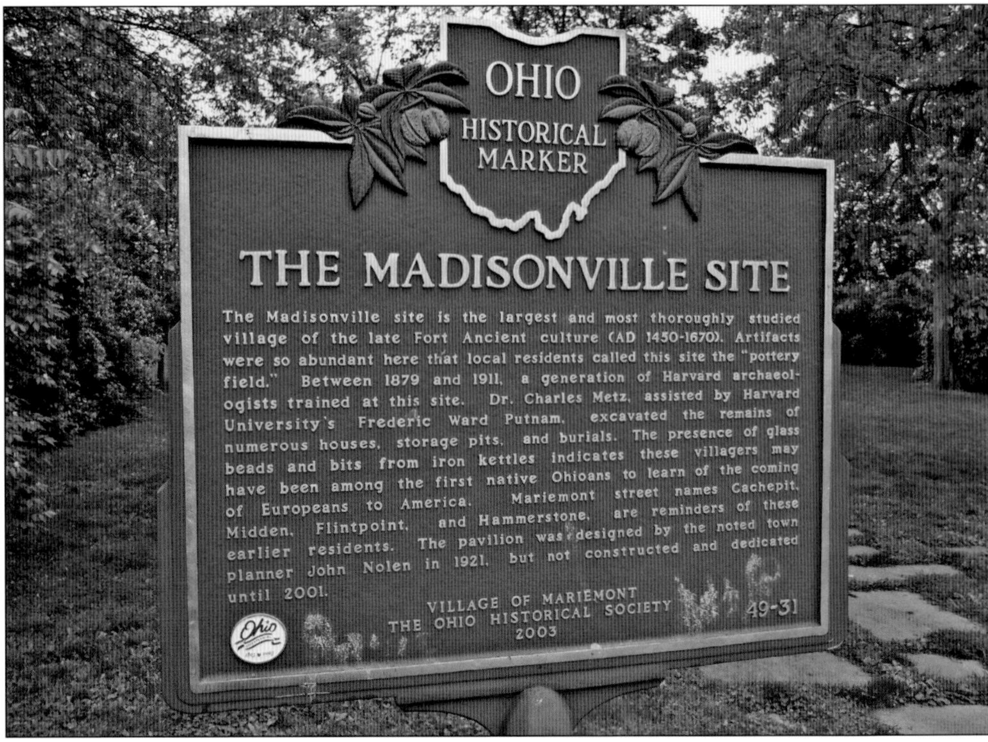

The Madisonville Site contained a treasure trove of artifacts from the Fort Ancient Peoples. This area was inhabited in the general time period between 1100 and 1670. It is known to have contained over 1,450 burials and 1,300 cache pits. Nearly one million artifacts were discovered and cataloged. Wes Cowan, of the television program *Antiques Roadshow*, considered the Madisonville Site "one of the 10 most important sites in eastern North America." Artifacts from the site are housed in museums across the world.

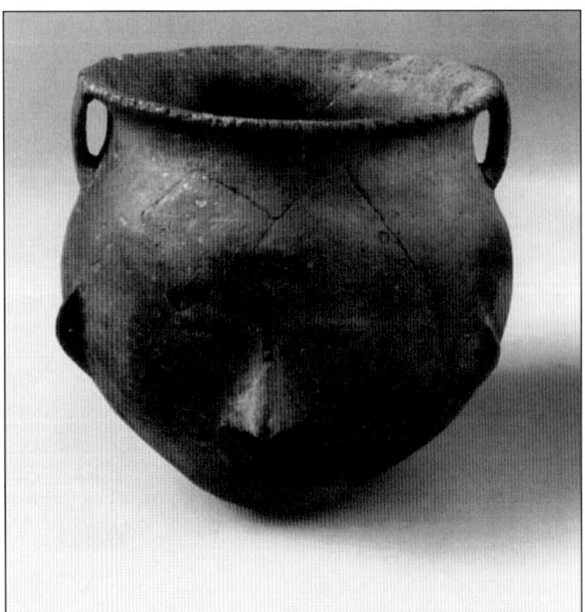

This human face effigy pot was dug by Dr. Charles Metz at the Madisonville Site and was the first piece donated to the Cincinnati Art Museum when the museum began in 1886. Today, the Cincinnati Art and Natural History Museums still own several artifacts from the Madisonville Site.

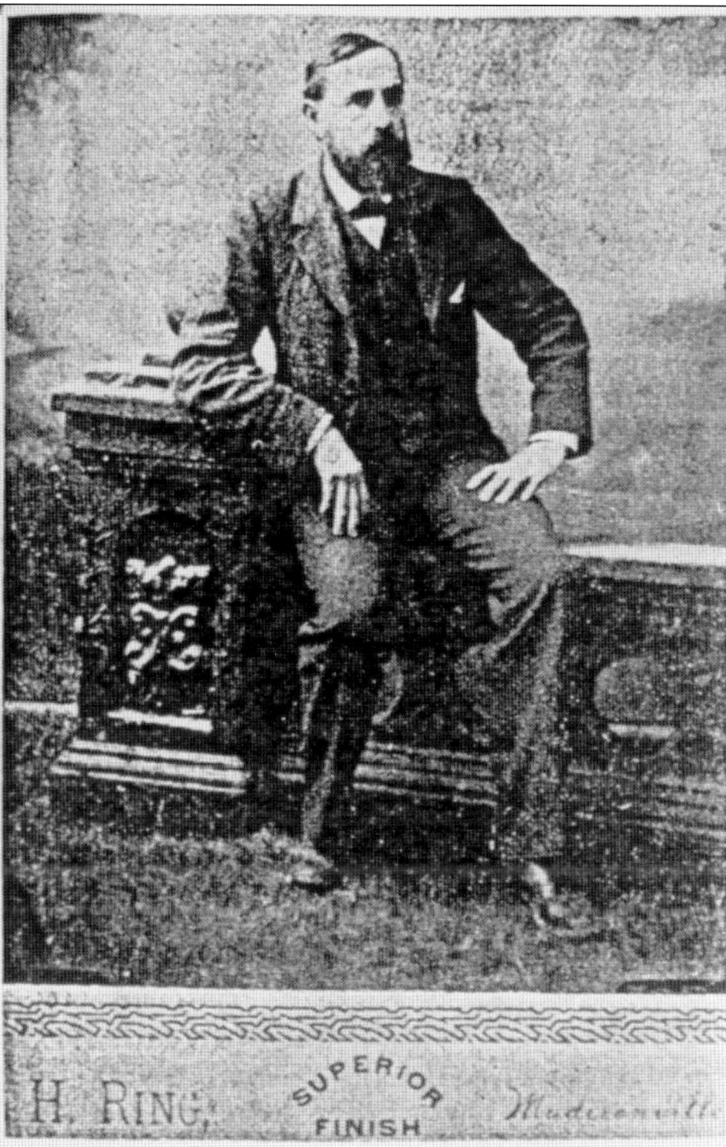

Dr. C.L. Metz, Mr. Madisonville

Dr. Charles Metz (1847–1926) earned his medical degree in 1871 from the Miami Medical College in Cincinnati and practiced medicine in Madisonville until just before his death. In addition to his practice, in which he delivered over 5,000 babies, Dr. Metz was heavily involved in the community. He helped establish the fire department in 1875, served on the school board, acted as the school physician, served as the first town health director, and facilitated the building of the Madisonville High School in 1903 and a new elementary school in 1909. His involvement earned him the nickname "Mr. Madisonville." In 1879, Dr. Metz established the Madisonville Literary and Scientific Society, which became the moving force behind the excavations at the site over the next five years. Soon, Harvard University's Peabody Museum and its curator, Fredrick Putnam, were interested in the site, and the museum excavated from 1882 to 1911. The site, known simply as the "Madisonville Site," is now world-famous due to Dr. Metz's initial detailing and excavation.

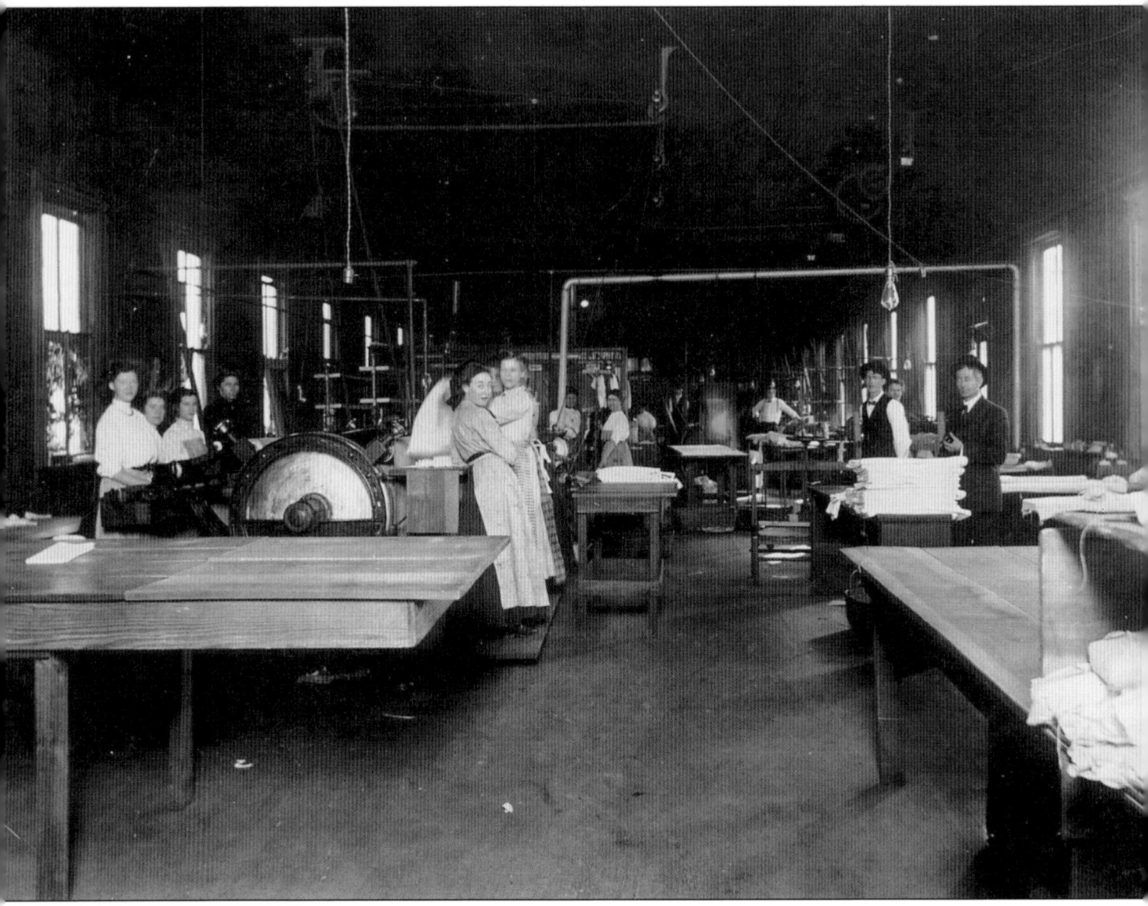

This interior photograph dated 1907 indicates that a laundry was in operation at 4709–4719 Central Avenue. However, a 1909 listing of Madisonville businesses indicates that the Madisonville Laundry Company was located at 6001–6003 Main Street. Around 1930, a company truck with the name "Model Laundry" was seen around town, and in January 1961, that laundry was sold to two brothers who had a chain of seven laundries across the country. In the newspaper article noting the sale, the laundry was said to have been in operation for 97 years, meaning it began in 1864. A 1960s addition, a large buff-colored structure, was built to better accommodate automobile customers bringing laundry to be washed. It prospered for the next 30 years, but in 1994, the laundry, a fixture in the community for almost 130 years, closed forever with little notice. In 2003, after several years of neglect, the aged structure was demolished by the city, leaving the 1960s addition standing.

Father and son Conrad and David Klein were druggists and operated a pharmacy in Madisonville. David joined his father's practice in 1878 after completing his education at Cincinnati Public Schools. David Klein also served as postmaster in Madisonville for many years and was an elected member of the board of education. As postmaster, David had a new post office erected on Madison Pike.

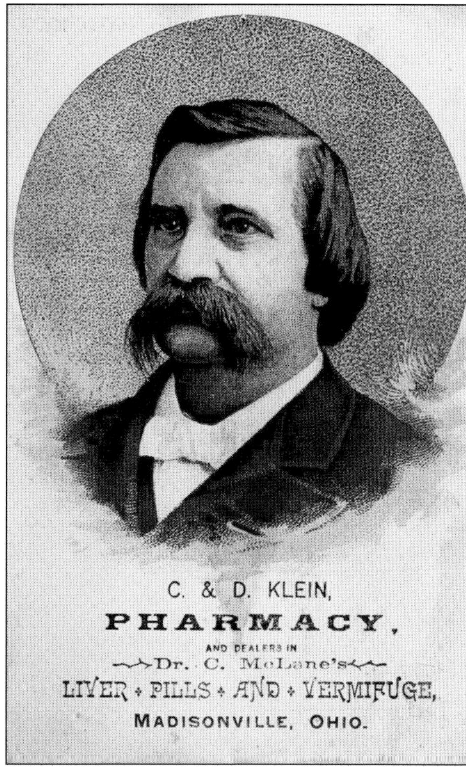

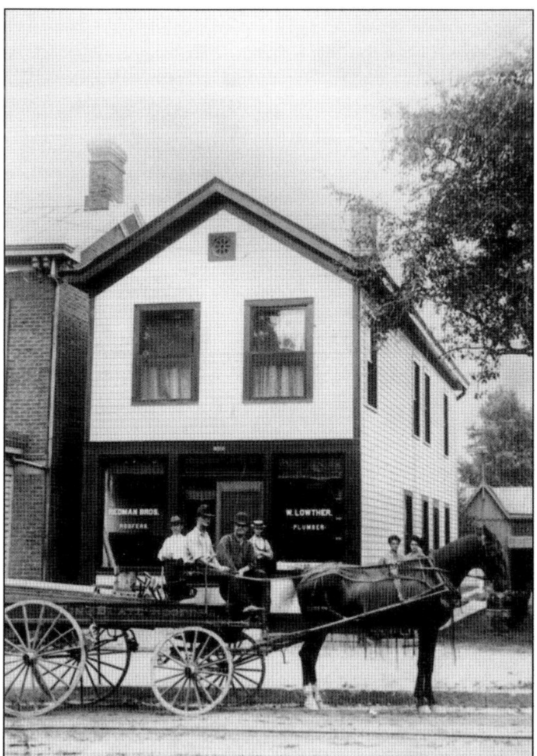

Pictured at left are two Madisonville businesses at 6010 Madison Road: Redman Brothers, Roofers, and W. Lowther, Plumber. The wagon in front reads, "Tin & Slate Roofers."

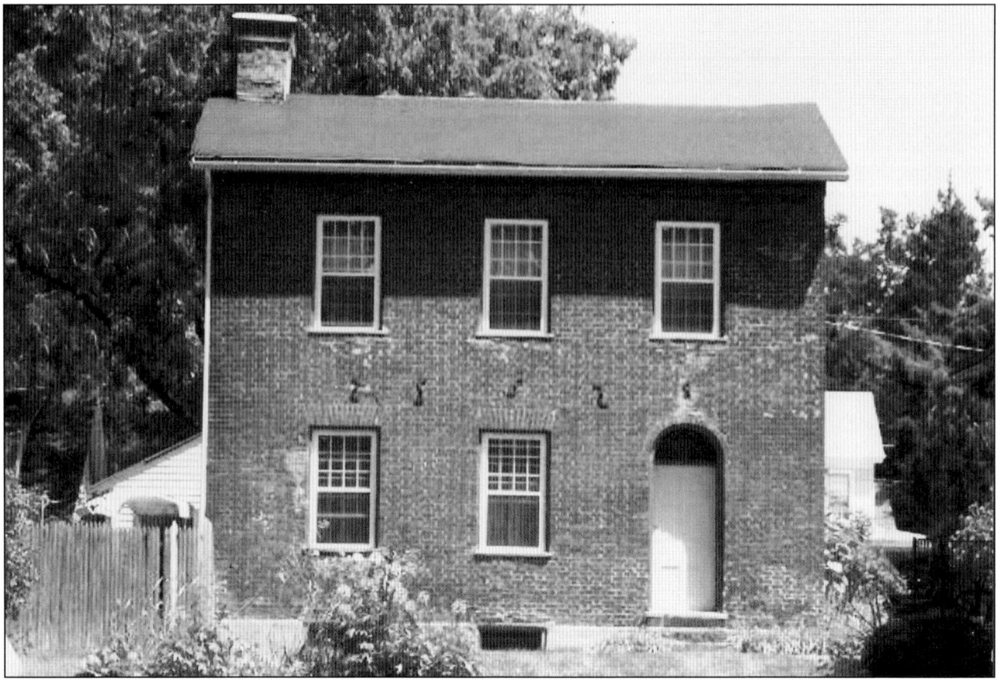

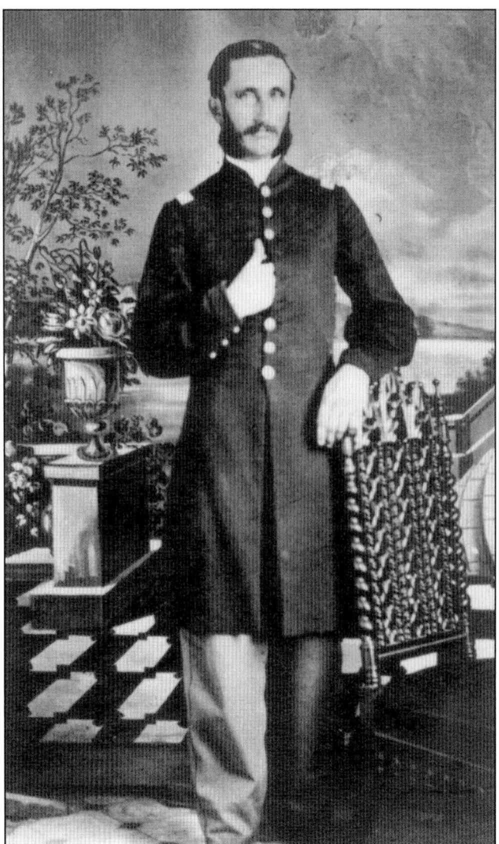

Joseph A. Morton's 72-acre estate on Morton Lane (now Ward Street) and Chandler Street included this homestead, built in the 1820s and still in existence. The oldest graveyard in Columbia Township was at the foot of West Indian Hill, on the premises of the Joseph Morton estate, where several members of the Ward family were buried. During construction of the King Towers apartment building in 1950, fill dirt was pushed over the hill, completely covering the area.

Capt. James T. DeMar, Company B, 88th Ohio Volunteers, seen here in his Civil War uniform, later became the first attorney for the Madison Building Association No. 2.

MADISON BUILDING ASSOCIATION,

No. 2.

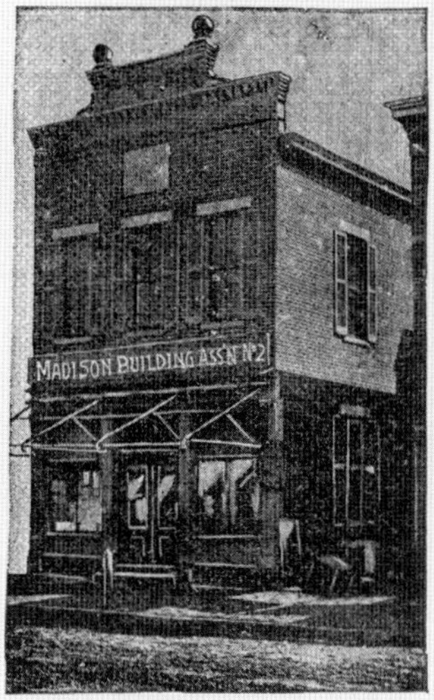

H. B. WHETSEL, PRESIDENT,
C. S. MUCHMORE, VICE-PRESIDENT.
C. B. CRUGAR, TREASURER.
G. TOMPKINS, SECRETARY.
A. J. NELSON, ASS'T SEC'Y

DIRECTORS.

JAS. JULIEN.
GEO. SAUER.
W. C. ROGERS.
T. A. MOORE.
J. ANDERSON WARD.
G. FISHER.
W. J. BEHYMER.
GEO. W. LOSH.
DR. C. L. METZ.
J. T. DEMAR, ATTORNEY.

MADISON BUILDING ASSOCIATION No. 2

Was Organized June 22, 1887.

Capital Stock, ...	$2,200,000.00
Receipts for the year 1890, . .	160,633.21
Net profits for the year 1890, . .	24,124.78
Dividend paid in cash, . . .	7 per cent.
Shares in force at close of year, . . .	1,810

Meets Monday Evening of each week.
Precedence in receiving loans sold at each meeting.
Money always ready when security is satisfactory.

SHARES, $500.00.

Weekly payment on borrowed share only $1.00; on depositors share 50 cents; but any larger amount may be paid at the option of the shareholder. The full amount paid credited as of that date.

Dividend paid to all shareholders.

Madisonville Lodge 419 F&AM, seen here about 1907, was built in 1886 and served the Masons for over 80 years. The building was vacated by the Masons around 1966, when they moved to another location. The structure was occupied by various groups over the years but had been vacant for 10 years and was in disrepair before its demolition in 2000. This picture shows the lower half of the structure, which housed a bank and the Madison Building Association No. 2. The Masons held their meetings in the top two floors. Madison Building Association No. 2 of Madisonville put this advertisement in the booklet for the opening of the waterworks in 1892.

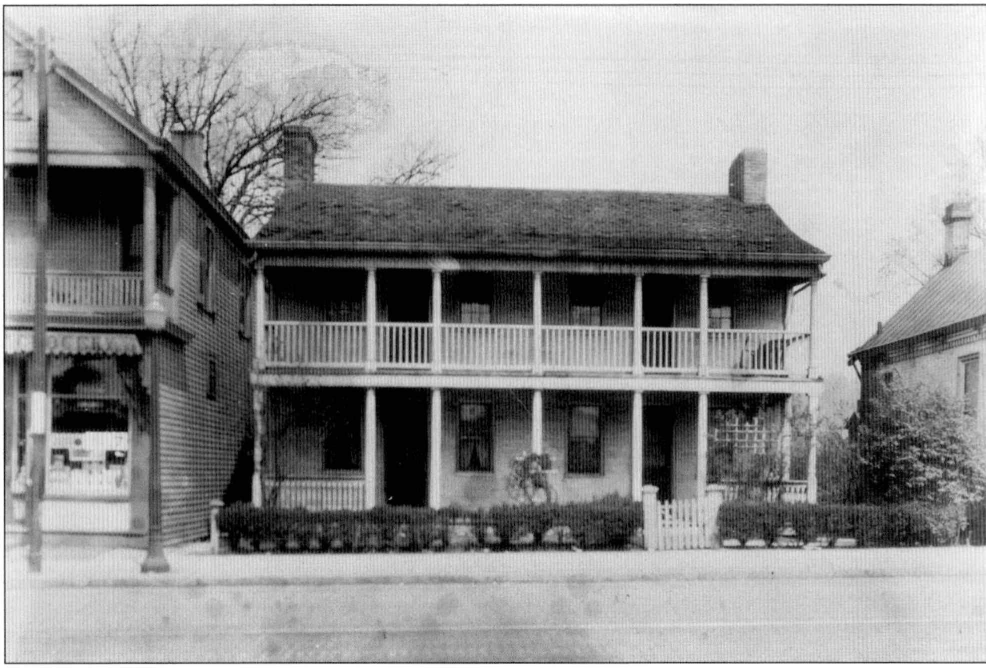

Dr. Jeffrys A. Black's two-family house at 6120 and 6122 Madison Road is pictured about 1890. Dr. Black owned considerable property in the vicinity, and he sold this and many more acres to Anthony Walburg in 1879. Walburg then established St. Anthony's Catholic Church on part of this land.

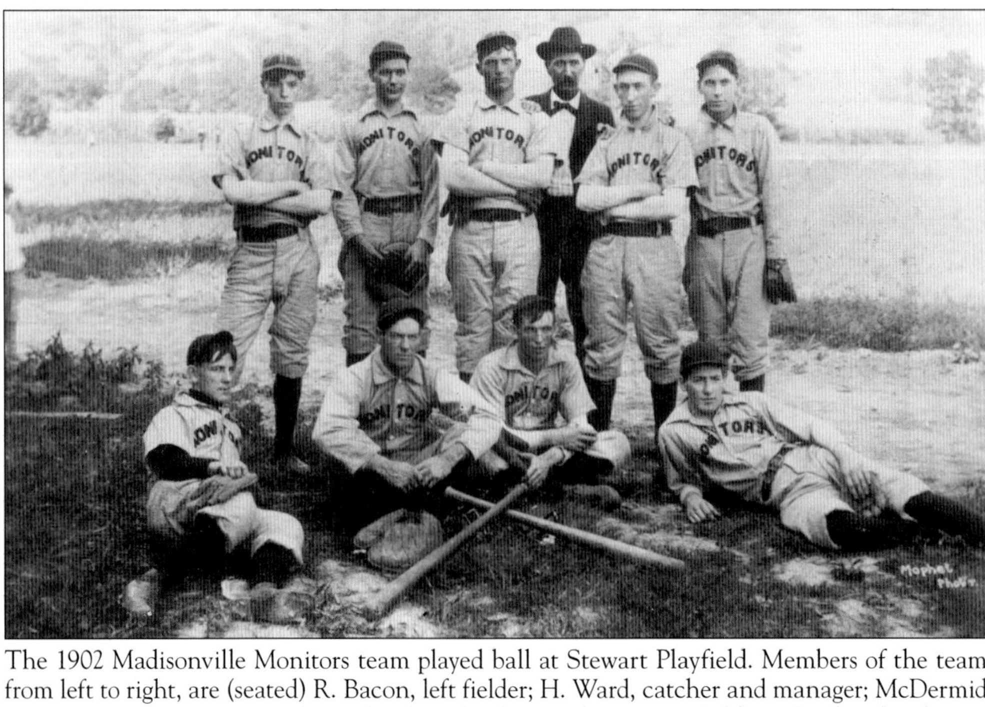

The 1902 Madisonville Monitors team played ball at Stewart Playfield. Members of the team, from left to right, are (seated) R. Bacon, left fielder; H. Ward, catcher and manager; McDermid, pitcher; and J. Henninger, right fielder; (standing) A.Fischer, center fielder; J. Fischer, first base; J. Wilson, second base; F. Kneipp, a faithful fan; F. Maphet, third base; and O. Fischer, shortstop.

Two

Life and Business Flourish after 1911 Incorporation

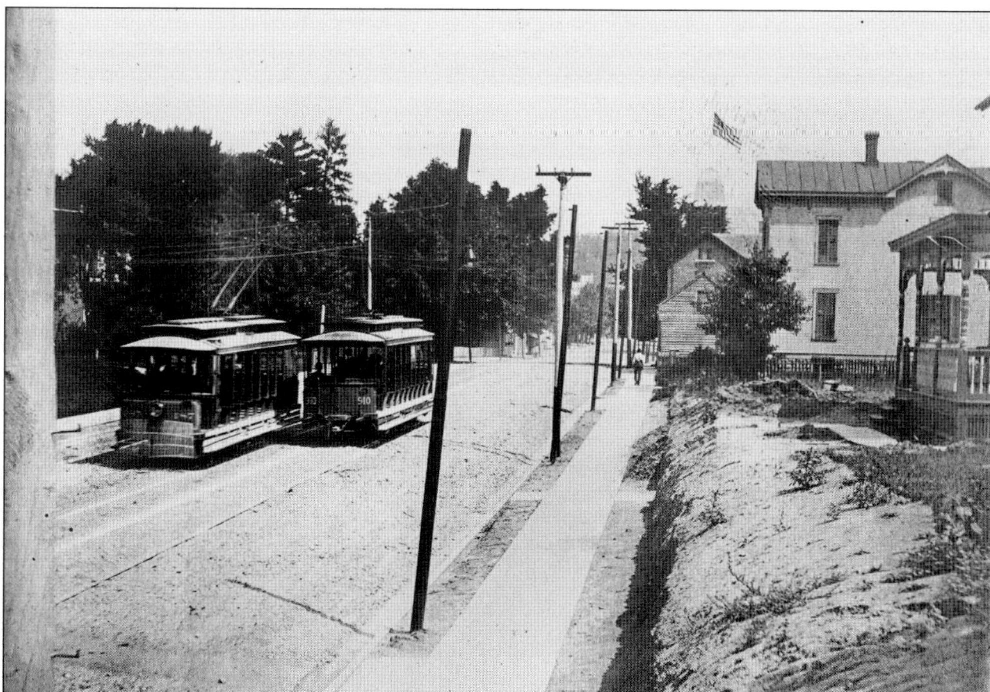

Tree-lined Whetsel Avenue is seen here with two trolley cars traveling south towards Bramble Avenue. In the background in the upper left is the town hall tower flagpole.

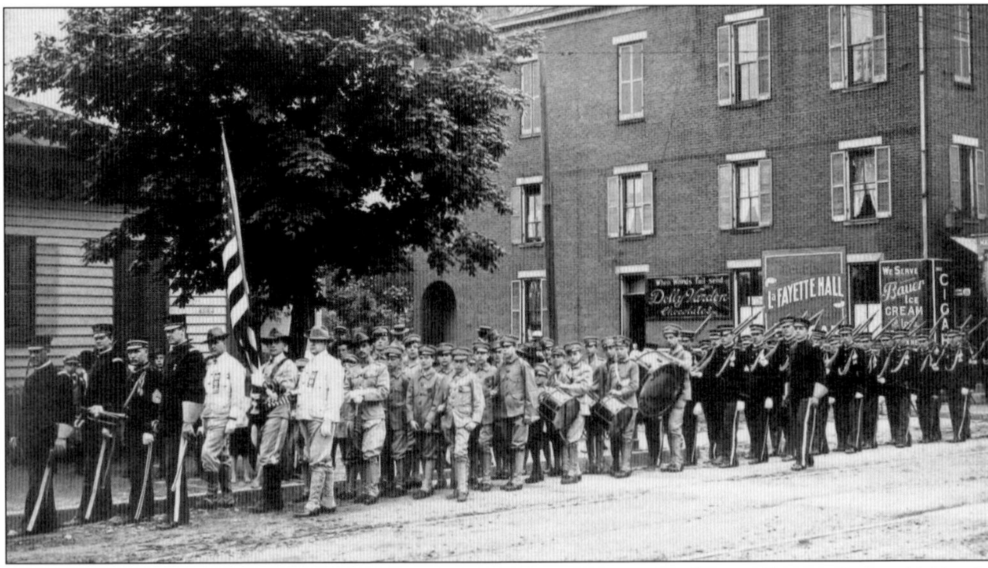

The Memorial Day Parade was a long-standing tradition in Madisonville until the 1960s. In 1915, the regalia are queued on Madison Road near Jamison Street, the start of the parade route. Women of the American Legion Auxiliary distributed poppies in honor of the World War dead and collected contributions for disabled veterans and families of fallen servicemen. In 1936, C.E. Baker, a 94-year-old Civil War veteran and Madisonville resident, was the honorary grand marshal.

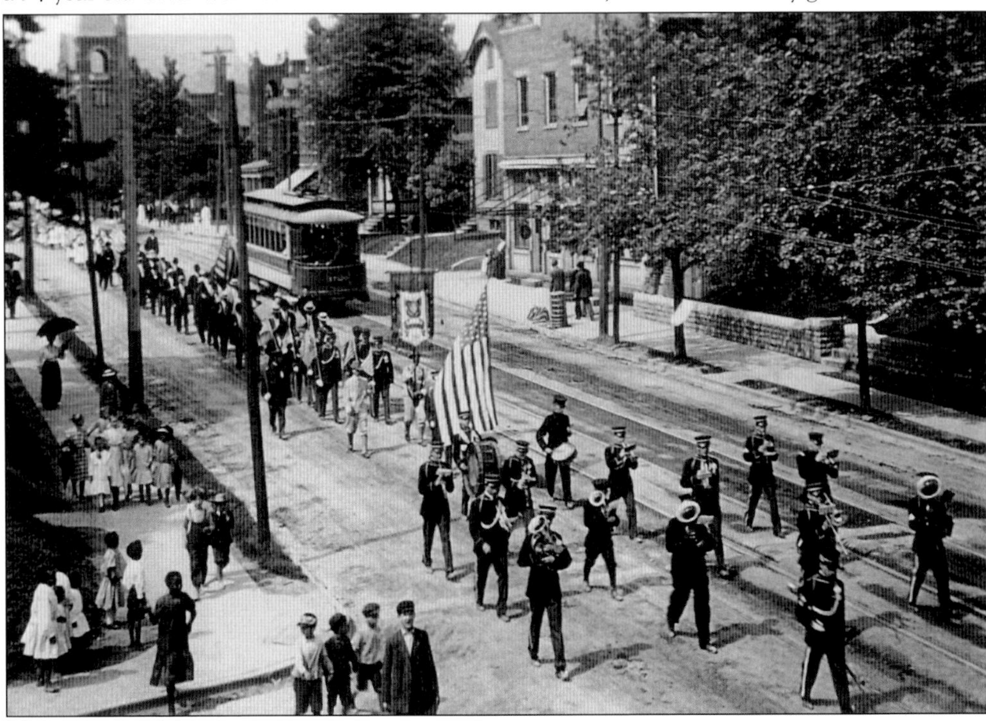

In another photograph from 1915, the parade moves south on Whetsel Avenue. The town hall and Settle Coal & Supply Co. are visible in the background on the south side of the street. Homes and merchants along the parade route were asked to proudly display an American flag. Schoolchildren ceremoniously marched and were also provided a place to watch all of the parade.

The Madisonville parade ended at Laurel Cemetery on Roe Street. Schoolchildren were the first to arrive in the cemetery so they could have an advantageous viewpoint. Veterans and fallen soldiers were honored in a service held with great ceremony. In this photograph, the Madison junior band, Madison council, and veterans pose for a formal photograph at the flagpole at Laurel Cemetery.

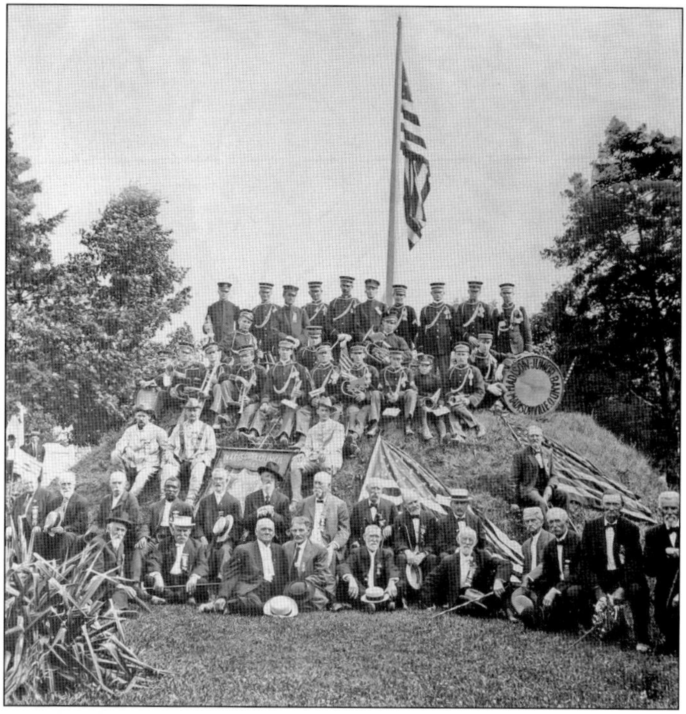

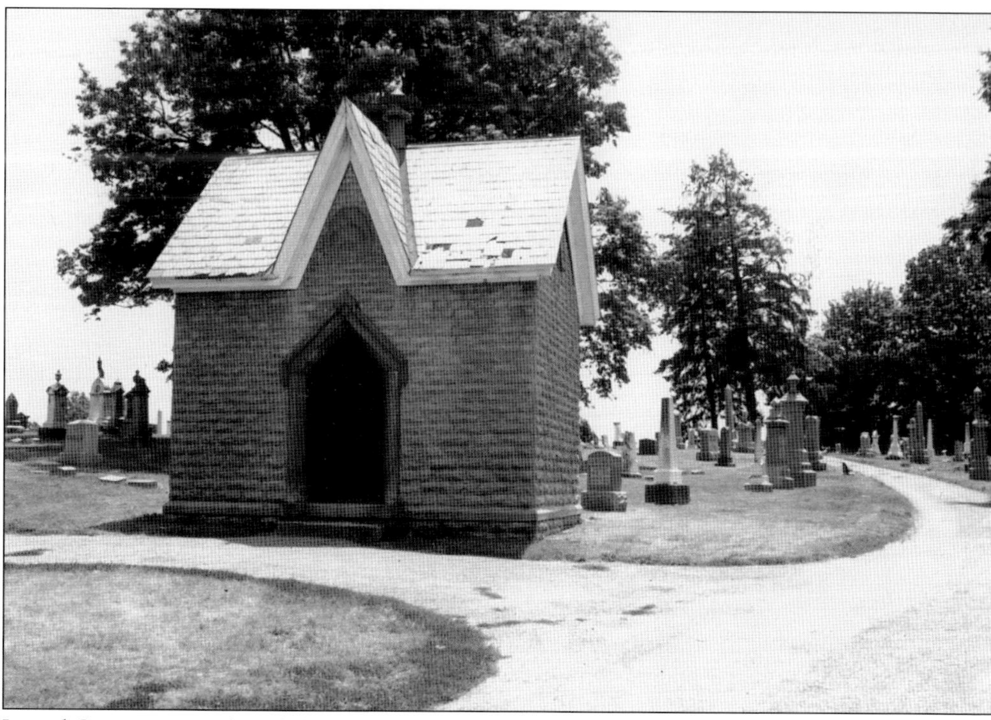

Laurel Cemetery was founded in 1863 by Laurel Lodge IOOF 191 at 5915 Roe Street at the corner of Whetsel Avenue and is still an active cemetery. There is a military section marking one War of 1812 veteran, 25 Civil War veterans, and four Spanish-American War veterans along with other prominent Madisonville citizens. The entrance gatehouse was built in 1878 with a marker.

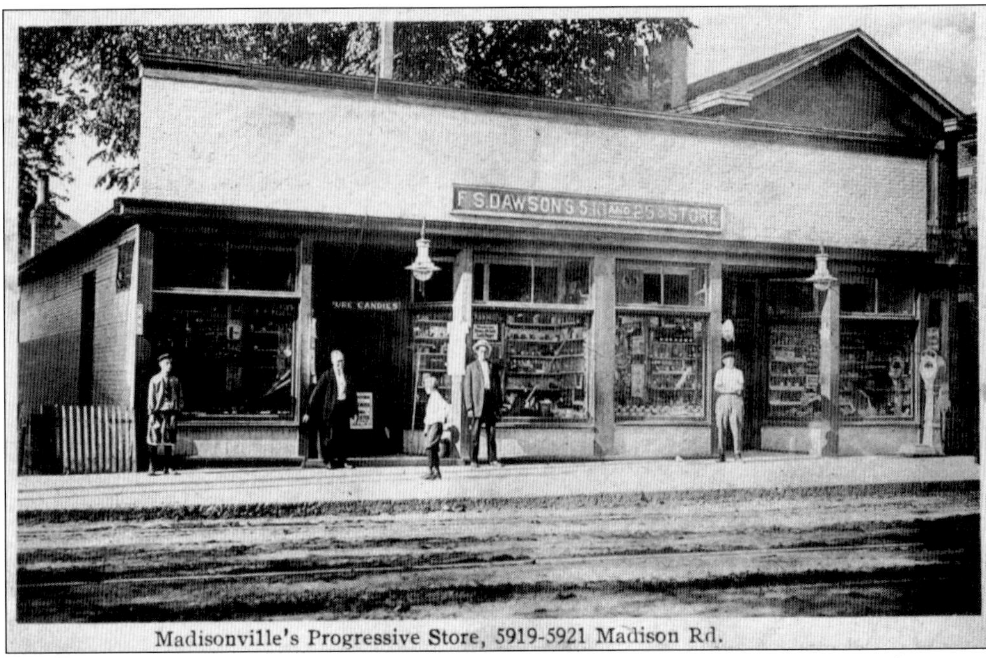

F.S. Dawson's 5&10¢ Store was built in the 1930s at 5919–5921 Madison Road. It became a Woolworth's in the 1950s.

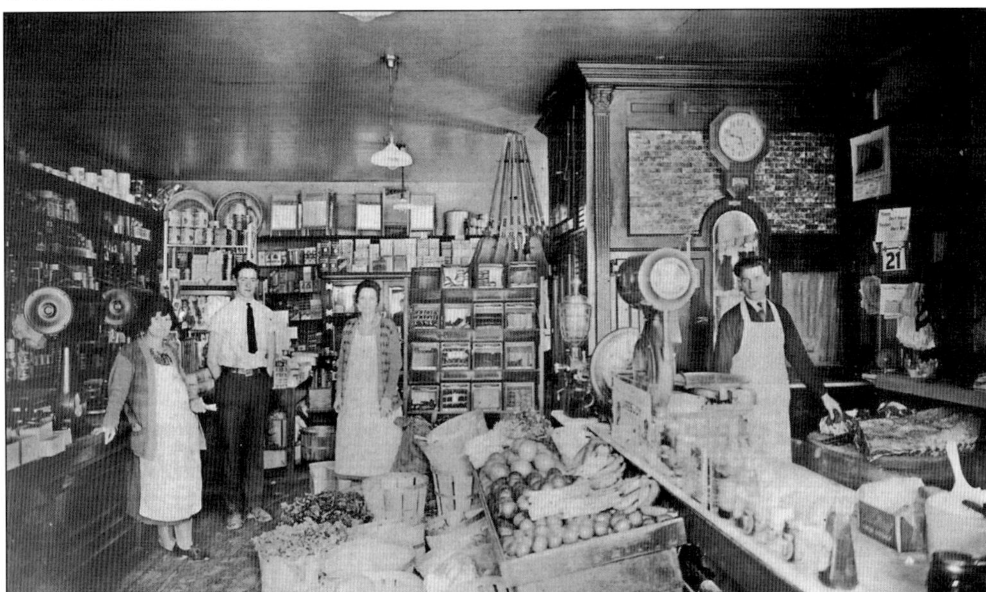

The Charles Glaser Grocery, seen here around 1920, was on the northwest corner of Chandler Street and Whetsel Avenue and was typical of the grocery stores of that era. Glaser (right) was the owner and butcher, enlisting the help of a deliveryman and two clerks. When a customer entered the store, he would ask the clerk for his desired items, and the clerk would then retrieve the requested items from the store shelves, cabinets, or produce areas. A succession of grocery stores followed after Glaser, with the last ceasing operation around 1975. The building was demolished in the 1980s.

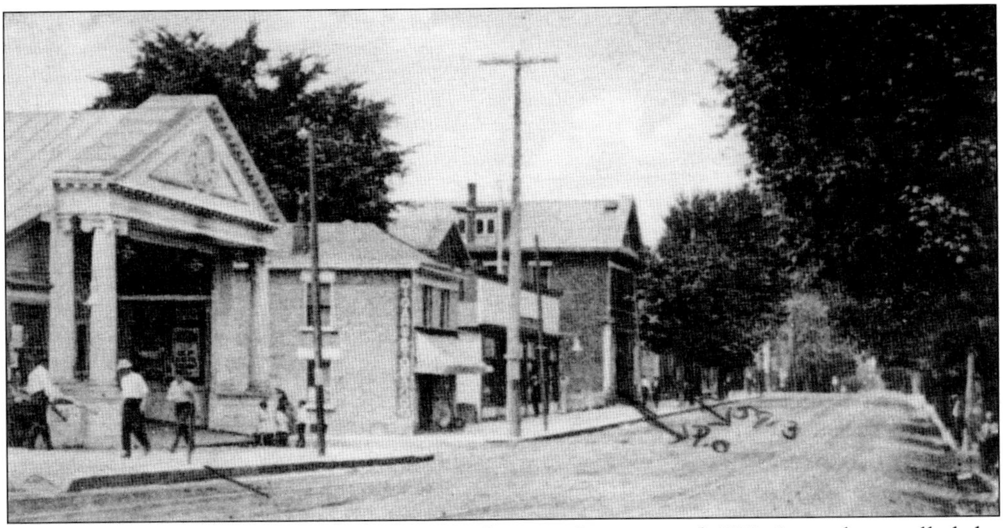

The Colonial Theater at 6003 Madison Road is seen here around 1911. It was later called the Madison Theater and closed on Saturday, February 2, 1952, after 43 years of local show business. The first show house, the Crystal Theater, was started in 1909 by Guy Cornish and John Tice and was located on the southwest corner of Ward and Sierra Streets but was subsequently moved to larger quarters and renamed Colonial Theater. It stood at the southeast corner of Ward Street and Madison Road, where a blacksmith shop, the first brick schoolhouse, a skating rink, and a laundry house all once stood.

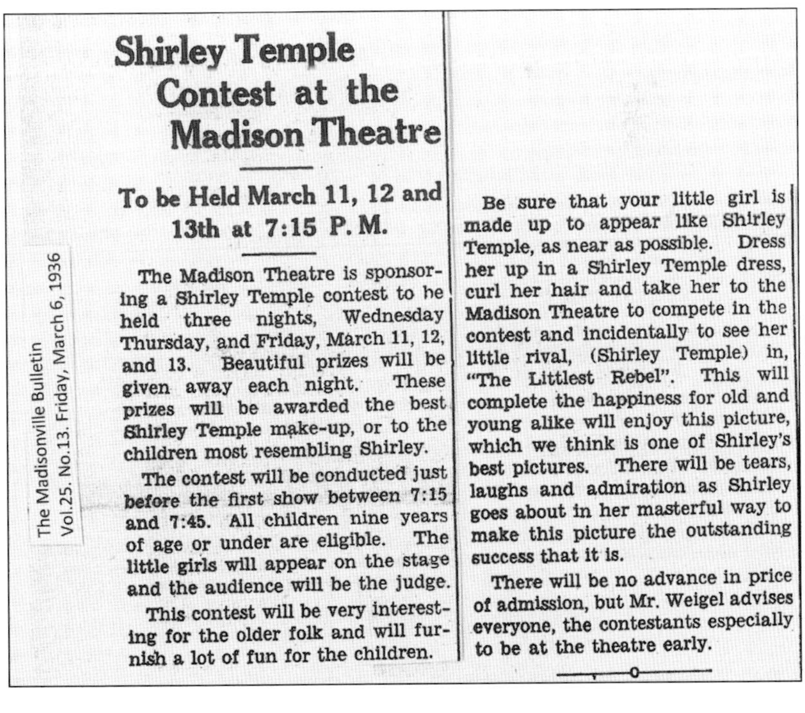

The Madisonville Bulletin
Vol.25. No.13. Friday, March 6, 1936

Shirley Temple Contest at the Madison Theatre

To be Held March 11, 12 and 13th at 7:15 P. M.

The Madison Theatre is sponsoring a Shirley Temple contest to be held three nights, Wednesday Thursday, and Friday, March 11, 12, and 13. Beautiful prizes will be given away each night. These prizes will be awarded the best Shirley Temple make-up, or to the children most resembling Shirley.

The contest will be conducted just before the first show between 7:15 and 7:45. All children nine years of age or under are eligible. The little girls will appear on the stage and the audience will be the judge.

This contest will be very interesting for the older folk and will furnish a lot of fun for the children.

Be sure that your little girl is made up to appear like Shirley Temple, as near as possible. Dress her up in a Shirley Temple dress, curl her hair and take her to the Madison Theatre to compete in the contest and incidentally to see her little rival, (Shirley Temple) in, "The Littlest Rebel". This will complete the happiness for old and young alike will enjoy this picture, which we think is one of Shirley's best pictures. There will be tears, laughs and admiration as Shirley goes about in her masterful way to make this picture the outstanding success that it is.

There will be no advance in price of admission, but Mr. Weigel advises everyone, the contestants especially to be at the theatre early.

This ad for the Madison Theater ran in the *Madisonville Bulletin* volume 25, number 13, on Friday, March 6, 1936.

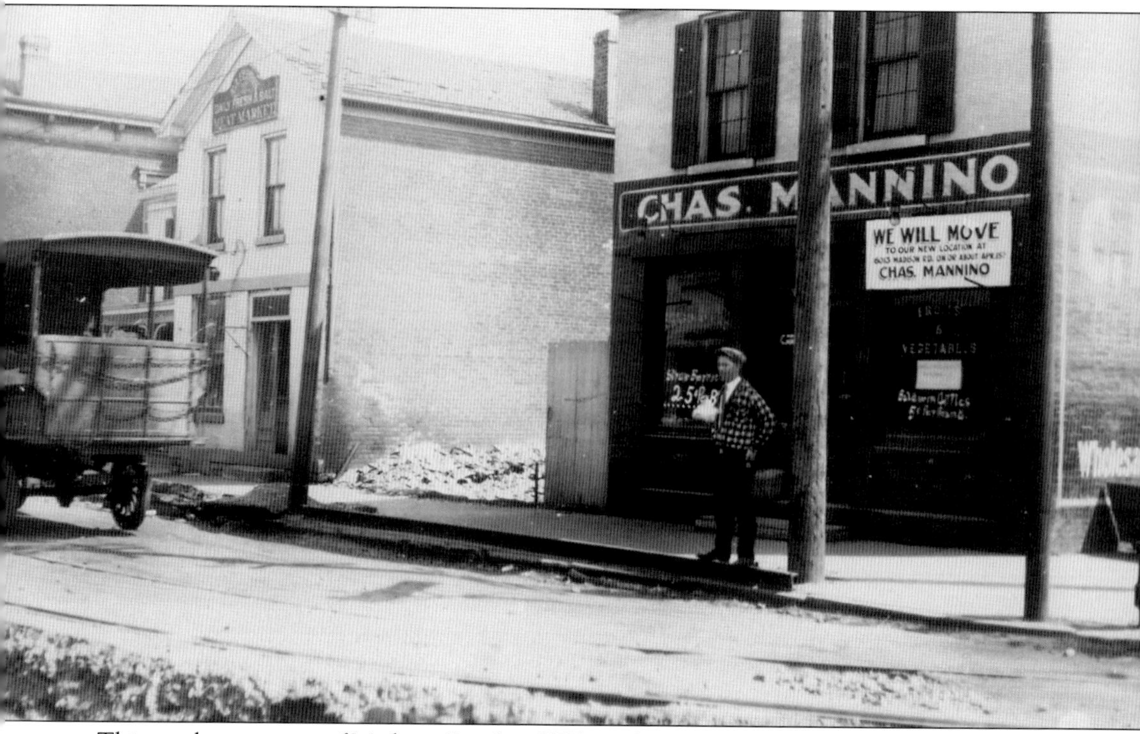

This southeast corner of Madison Road and Whetsel Avenue, pictured about 1925, was occupied by Charles Mannino's Market, and the sign out front read, "We will move to our new location at 6013 Madison Road on or about April 15th." The building next to Mannino's was A.F. Ferris Daily Fresh and Salt Meat Market. All would soon be demolished to make way for the construction

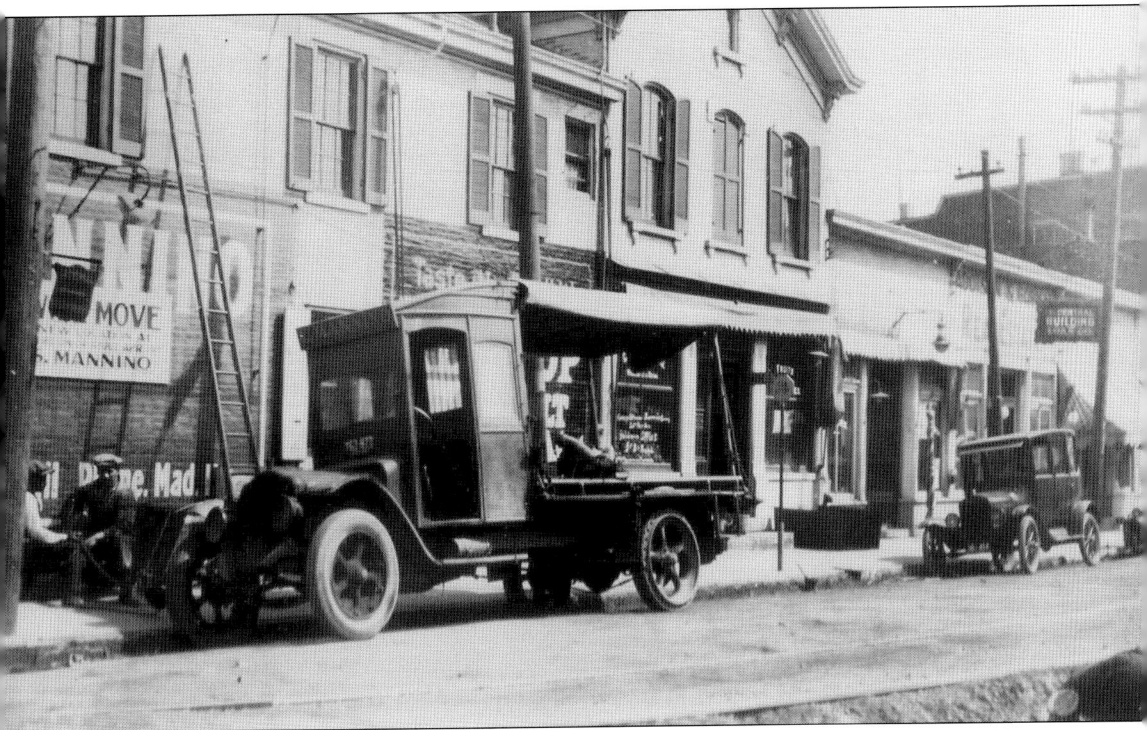

of a 28-unit apartment building with retail space on the first floor called the Madison Building. Along the east side of Whetsel Avenue, most of the block would be demolished to complete the Madison Building, which continued as a viable apartment and retail center through the 1950s. The building was completely demolished in 2010 to make way for a new Madison focal center.

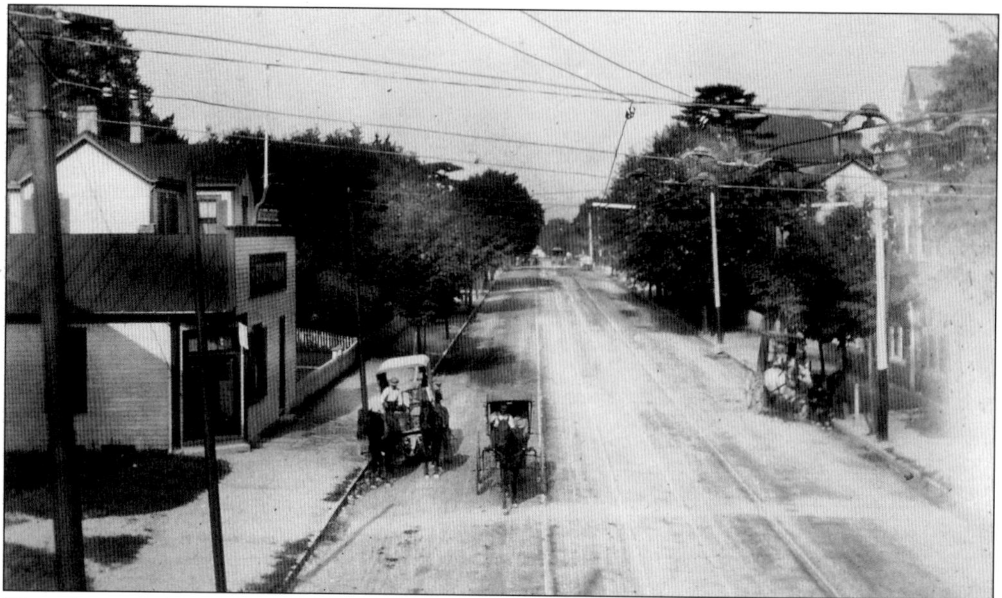

This photograph was taken around 1911 from the Kenwood Road and Madison Road railroad overpass looking west down Madison Road.

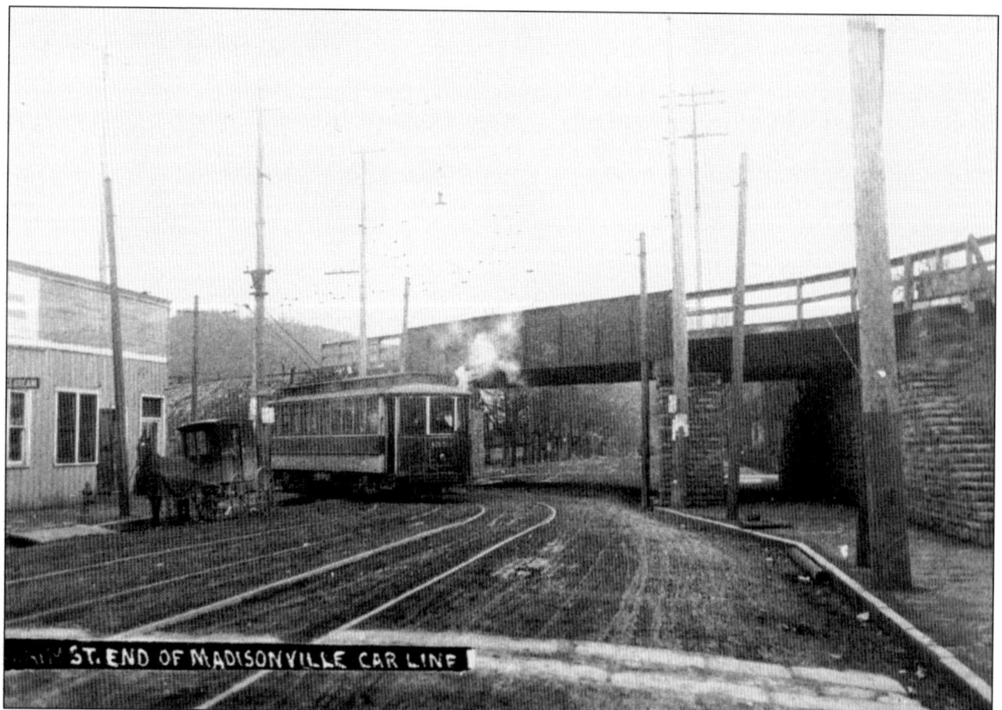

This 1911 photograph shows the corner of Madison and Kenwood Roads near the streetcar turnaround. The B&O overpass is above, and the east train station is off the photograph to the right. A streetcar can be seen turning onto Madison Road to begin its route back to the city. The turnaround was constructed about 1905, when the first streetcars came to the business area of Madisonville and needed a place to turn around. Today, it is used by the bus system serving Madisonville.

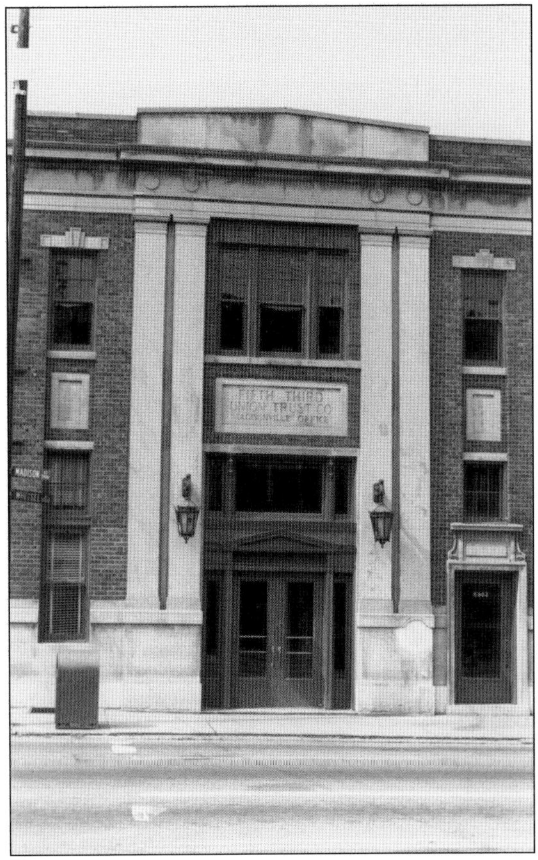

The newly constructed Fifth-Third Bank building at the northeast corner of Madison Road and Whetsel Avenue is seen here in 1927. The bank thrived in this location until 1982, when it moved farther down Madison Road to the location where it still serves Madisonville residents. The bank building was the fourth structure on this corner, after Perry's Taverns in 1809, Goggin House in 1830, Maphet's Grocery in the 1880s, and Bainum's Drug Store in the 1910s. This building is still standing and is being rehabilitated in 2012.

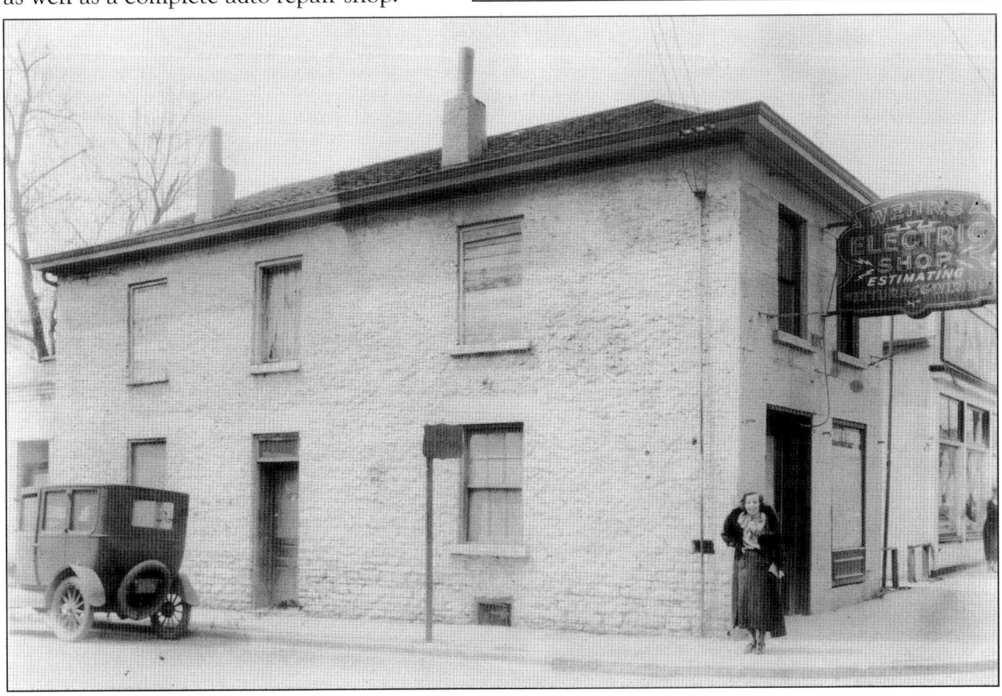

Herb Mayer's Radio and Auto Supply Store was remodeled to accommodate Martin Wehr's Electric Shop on Madison Road near Mathis Road, according to the January 27, 1933, issue of the *Madisonville Bulletin*. The two stores combined into one large place of business handling radios, refrigerators, auto supplies, electric lamps, washing machines, and all electric equipment. In addition to the line of goods they carried and displayed, they also maintained shops for the repair of goods and the recharging of batteries, as well as a complete auto repair shop.

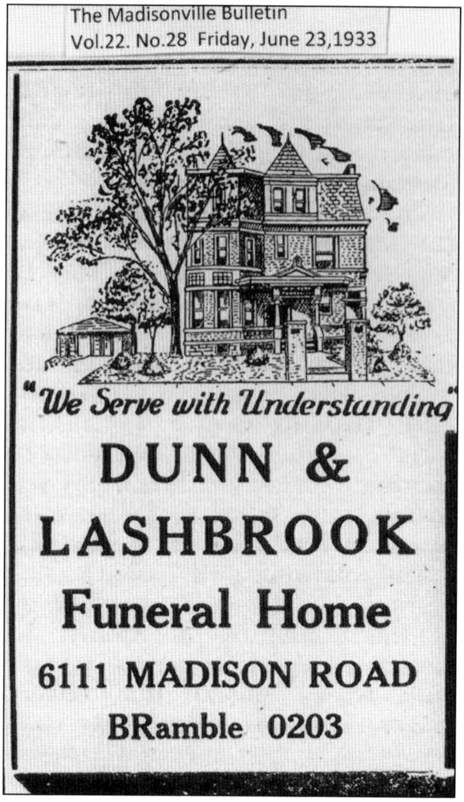

The Dunn & Lashbrook Funeral Home on Madison Road occupies the house built by Dr. Charles Metz in the 1890s as his home and office. After his death, the home was purchased and repurposed for a funeral home. In 1934, the funeral home was renovated and the owners held an open house, showcasing the exquisite Colonial-style decorations, furniture, crystal light fixtures, and modern laboratory. The funeral home was in operation until the 1970s.

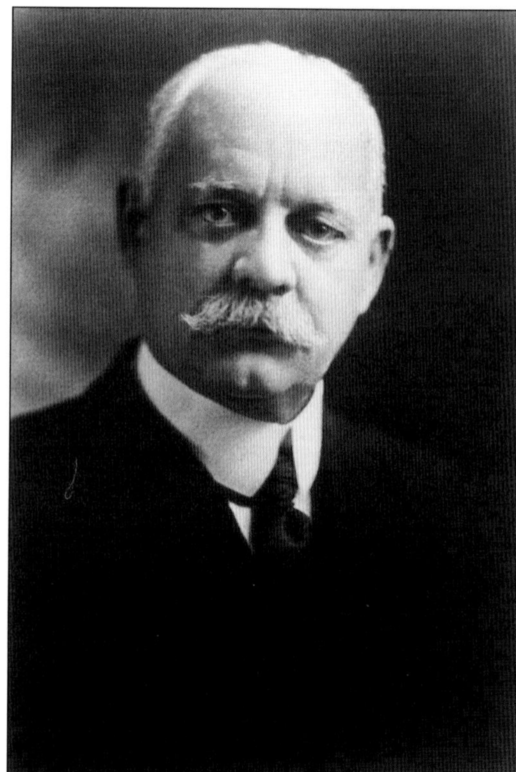

Judge Oliver B. Jones, seen here in 1935, owned considerable property in Madisonville. He was a founder of the Cottage Building and Loan Company, an early financial institution in Madisonville.

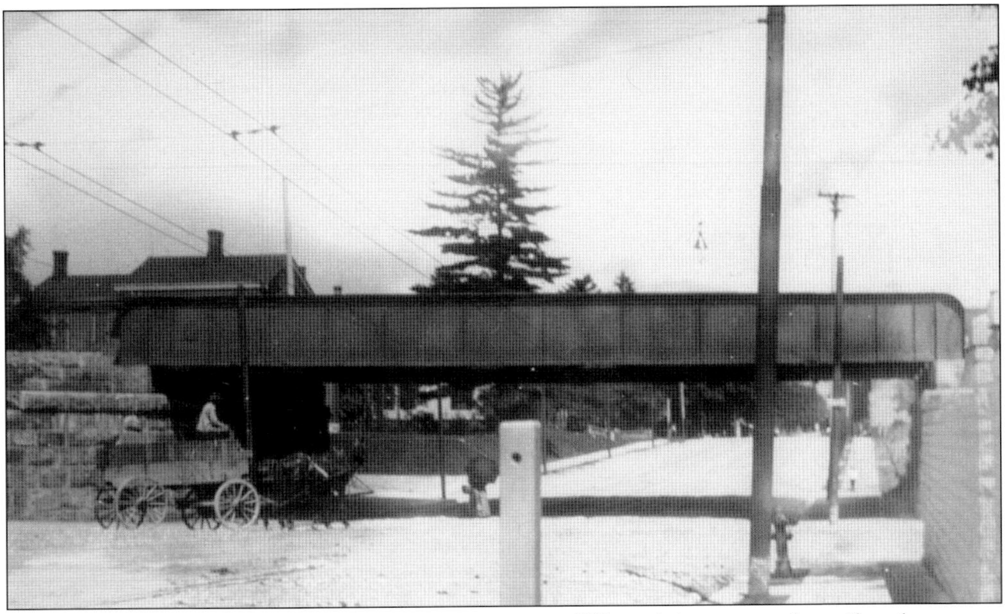

This horse-drawn wagon comes off Erie Avenue onto Whetsel Avenue at the railroad overpass that W.H. Settle constructed to connect the trolley line.

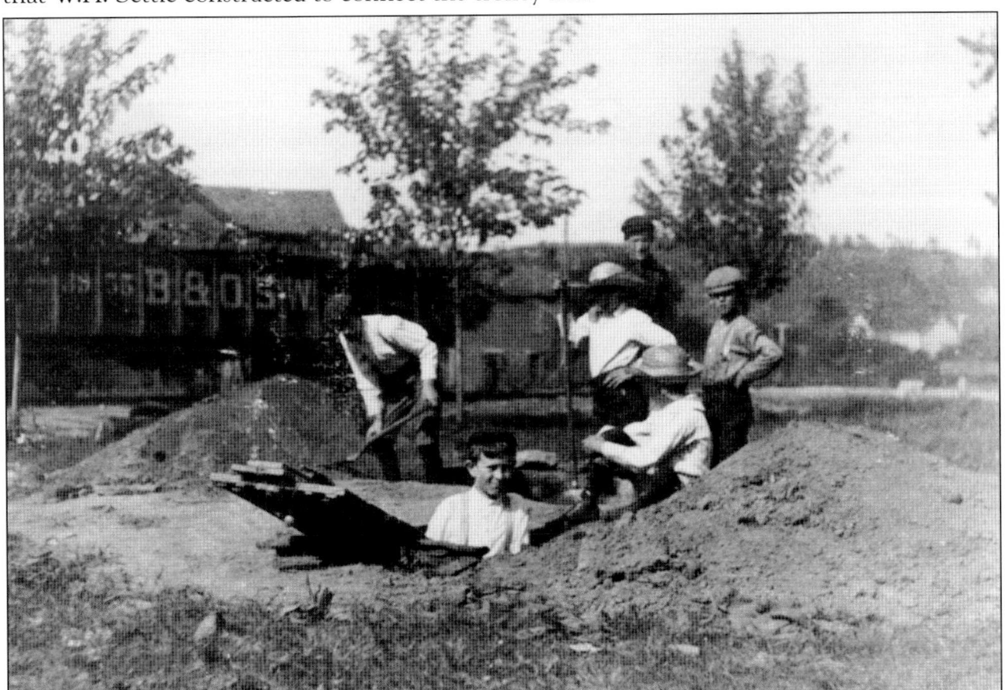

These boys dig a hole on a triangular lot owned by the railroad on the north side of Erie Avenue between Simpson and Mathis Streets. They said they were building a tunnel. The boy standing down in the hole is Charles W. Sawyer, who would go on to become secretary of commerce under President Truman and at one time served as the US ambassador to Belgium. Robert Miller, with the large straw hat, later worked on the engineering crews that bored the great Moffat Railroad Tunnel on the Denver & Rio Grande Western Railroad. Burnet Creed is on the far right.

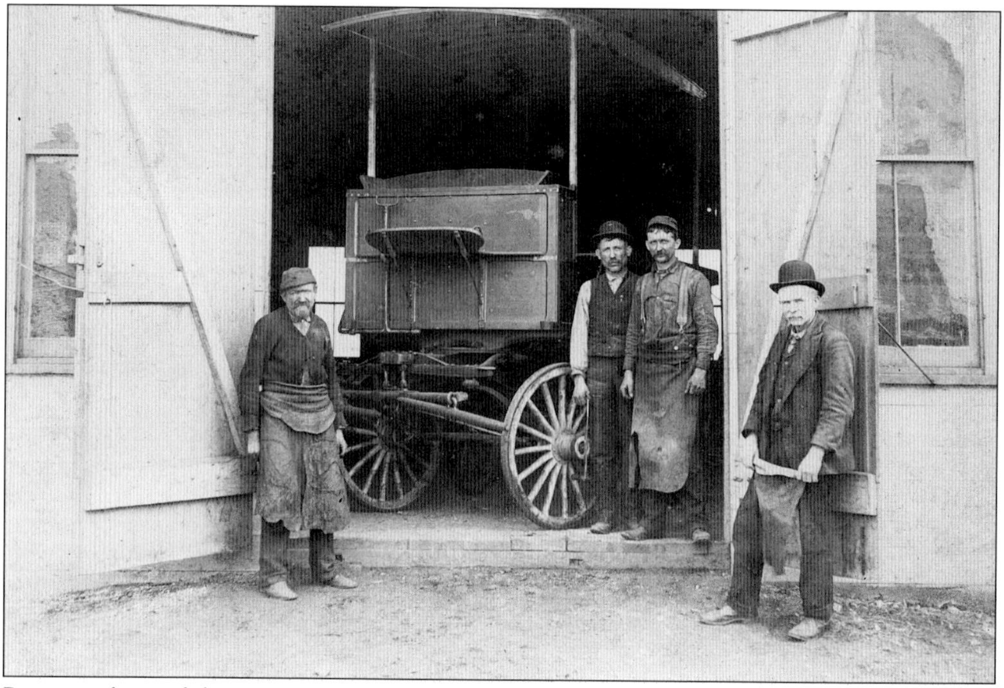

Posing in front of the wagon shop on Whetsel Avenue around 1900 are, from right to left, Pat Kelly, John Lay, John Hanee, and an unidentified man.

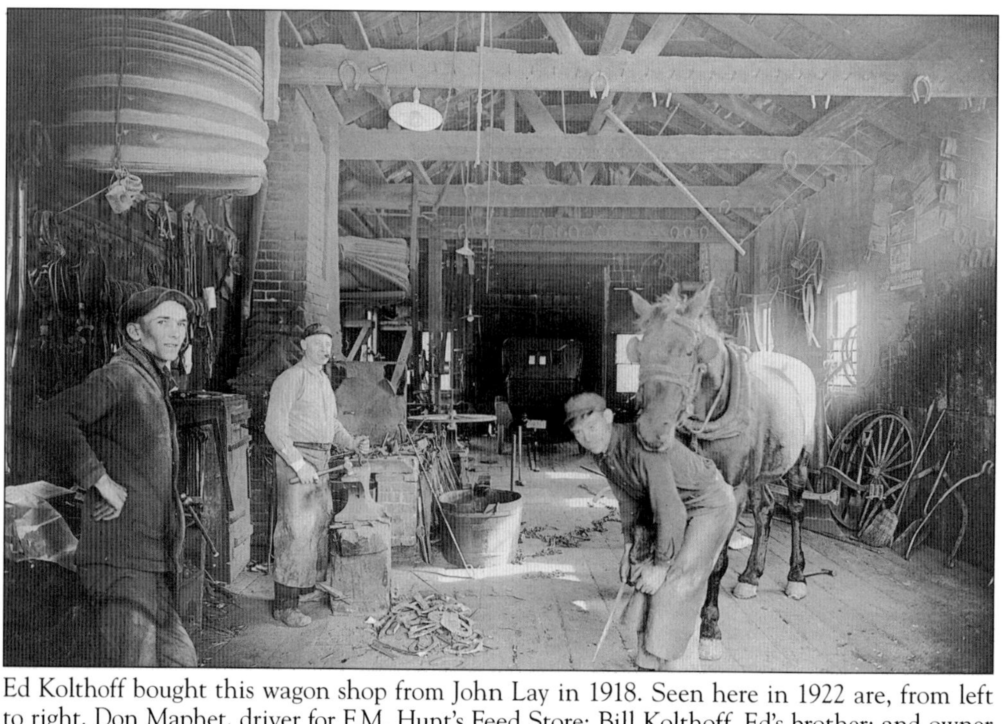

Ed Kolthoff bought this wagon shop from John Lay in 1918. Seen here in 1922 are, from left to right, Don Maphet, driver for F.M. Hunt's Feed Store; Bill Kolthoff, Ed's brother; and owner Ed Kolthoff.

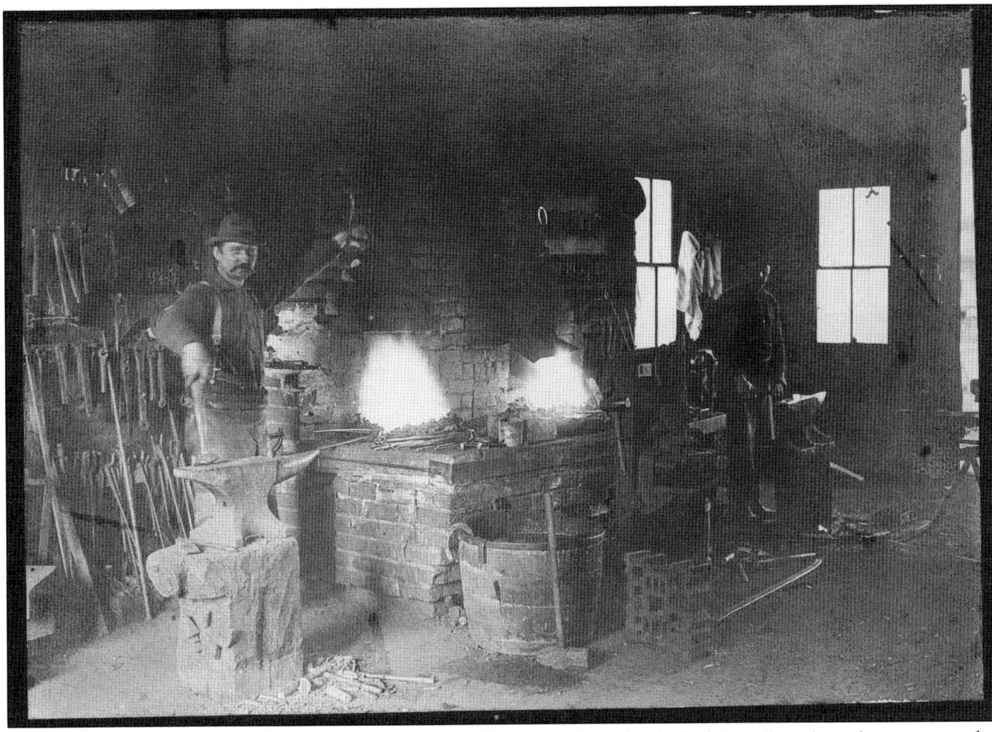

Here, John Lay holds a hammer on the anvil in one hand while his other hand operates the bellows in his blacksmith shop. The shop was first located on Madison Road and Ward Street and later relocated to Whetsel Avenue.

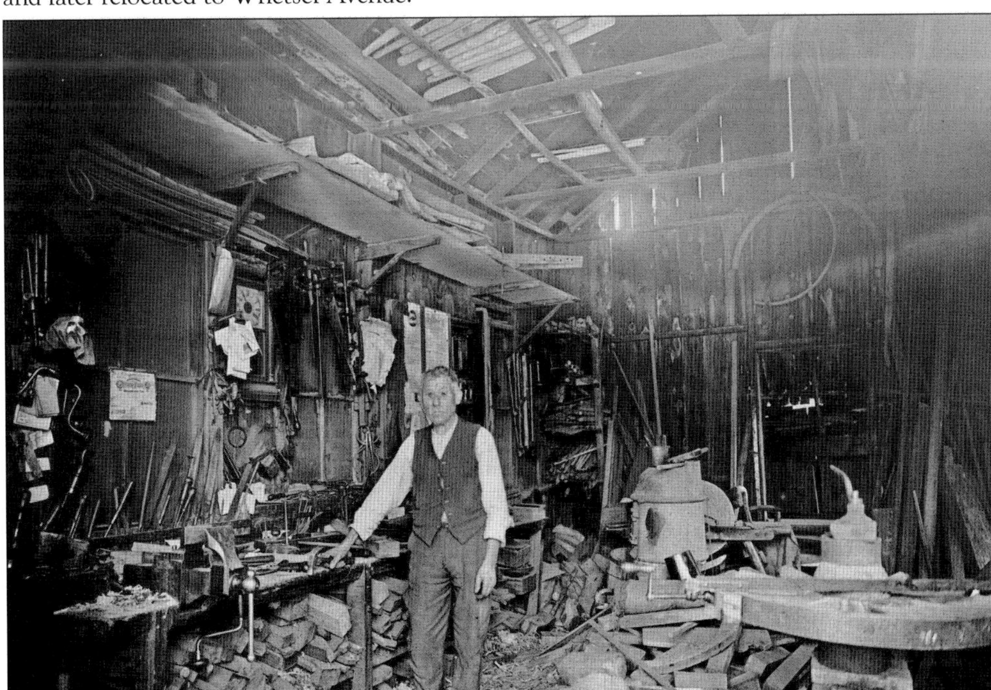

John Hanee, in his later years in 1922, poses amongst his tools at the wagon shop.

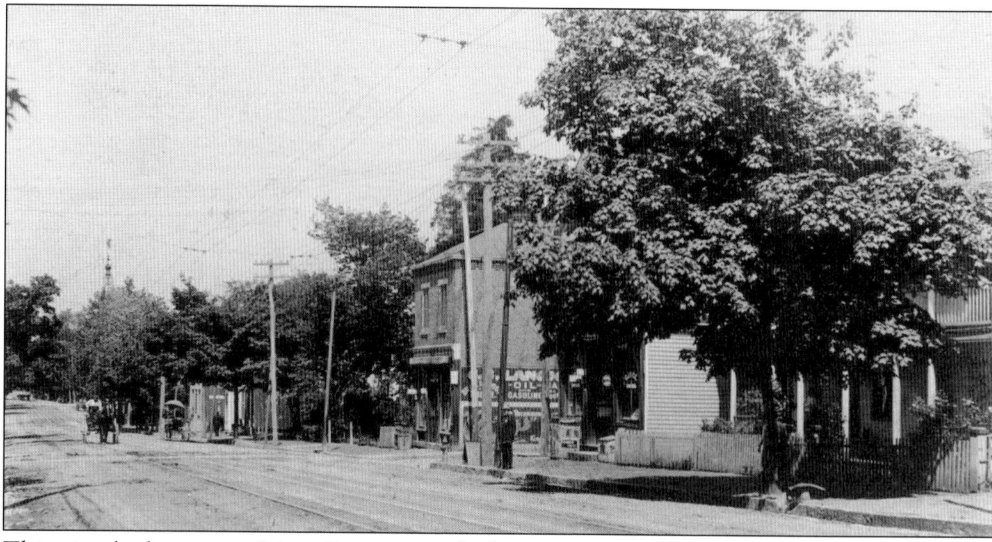

This view looks west on Main Street towards the corner of Mathis Street. The building on the far corner is Langdon's Grocery Store, which sold oil and gasoline as well as groceries. The means of transportation at the time was the horse and buggy, two of which are seen here. In front of the near store, a policeman wears the dome-shaped helmet used at the time. Kramer's Grocery Store was next on that corner.

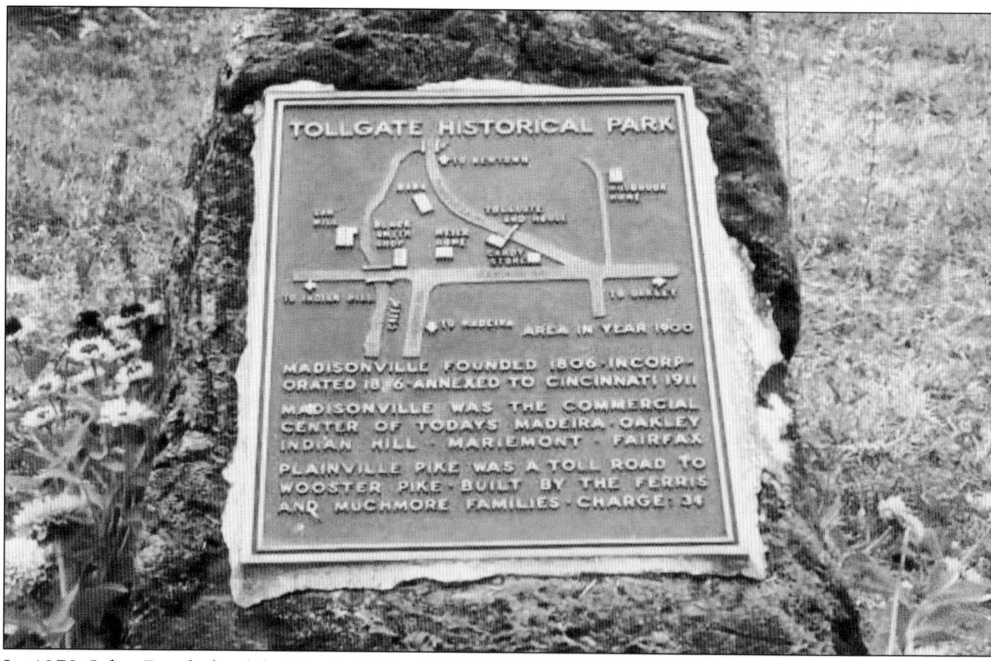

In 1973, John Burdick of the Burdick & Bauer-Nilson Architecture Firm purchased the triangular parcel of land at Madison Avenue and Plainville and Camargo Roads in order to return the land to the Cincinnati park board. This parcel was once the site of a tollgate and tollhouse, as well as a cow pasture, blacksmith shop, and sawmill. Tollgate Park was dedicated in October 1974 with a granite stone. The sign reads, "Madisonville was the commercial center of today's Maderia, Oakley, Indian Hill, Mariemont and Fairfax." This was true because of the easy access from Plainville Pike to Wooster Pike leading to downtown Cincinnati.

The Ackermann family stands in front of the Confectionery Bakery on Ackermann's Corner around 1911.

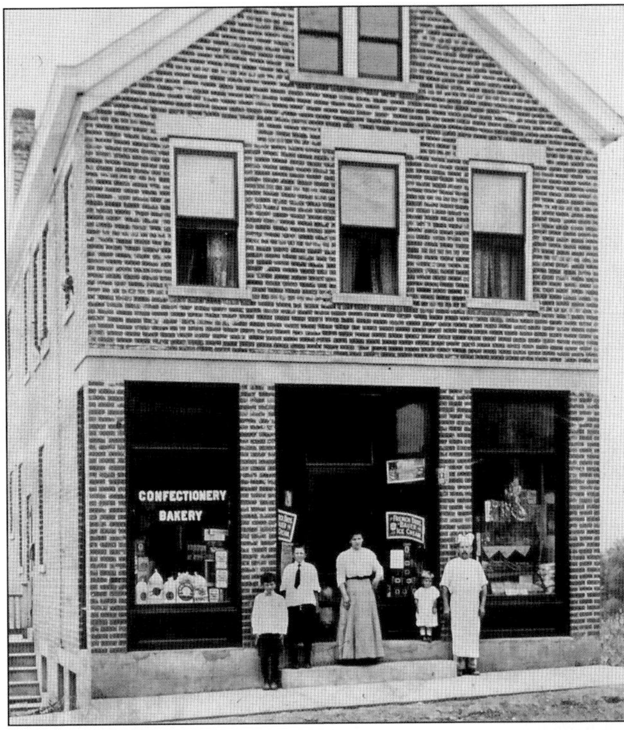

Ackermann's Corner, at 5909–5911 Bramble Avenue, had been a family business since 1911, first as Confectionery Bakery. By 1959, they had expanded and remodeled three times into Ackermann's Parkview Super Market. Today, Ackermann's Corner still houses a supermarket. The demolished foundation in the forefront of this photograph was the old Kroger's building.

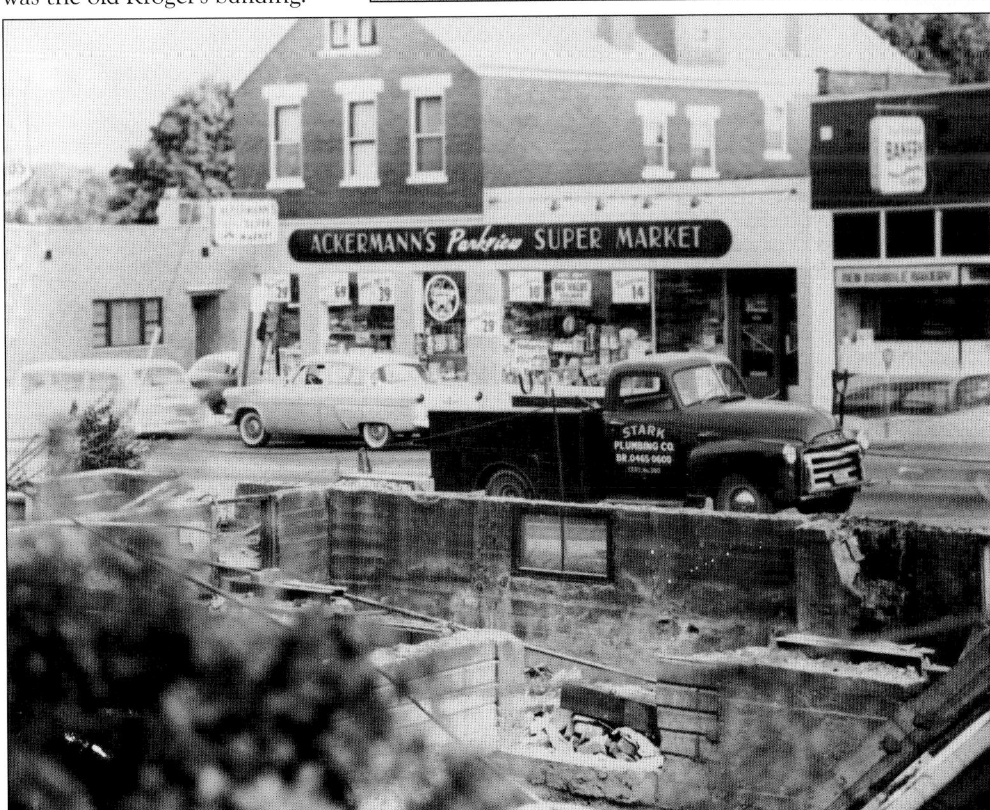

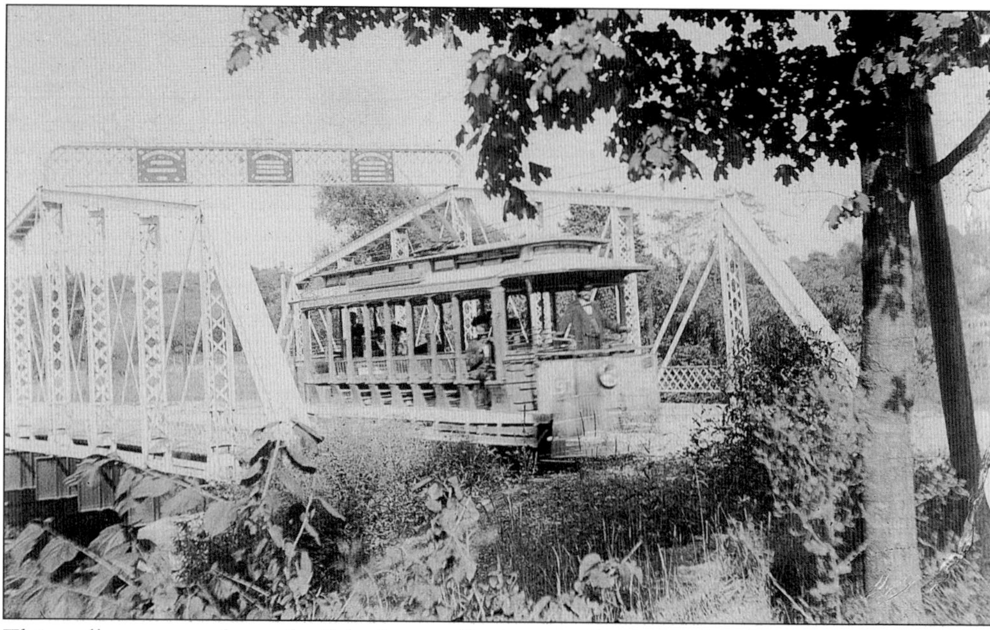

This trolley car travels on the Erie Avenue Bridge over Duck Creek. The *Madisonville Bulletin* on Friday, February 15, 1935 read: "Erie Avenue grade crossing elimination, a familiar figure in the last 20 councilmanic years, plan will probably be carried out. The inability of railroads to go ahead with their 65 percent had prevented action. This old issue is again before council, this oft-debated project was revived by the recent accident which took two lives. Gates may be installed and watchmen put on duty as a temporary precaution."

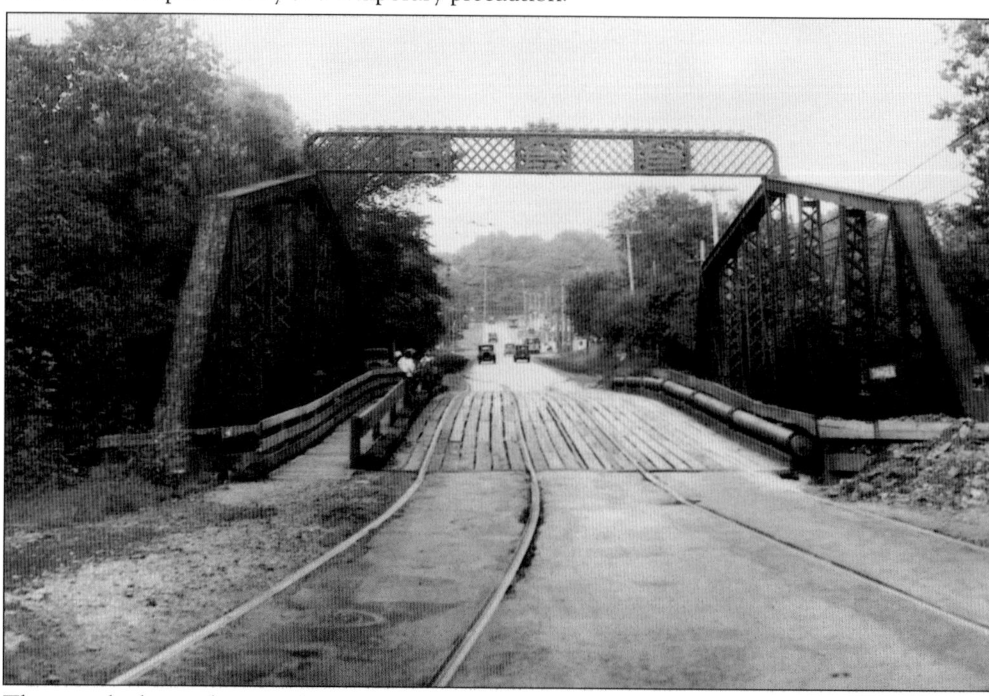

This view looks northeast at the Erie Avenue Bridge over Duck Creek before the grade-separation improvement was made at Erie Avenue and Red Bank Road in September 1931.

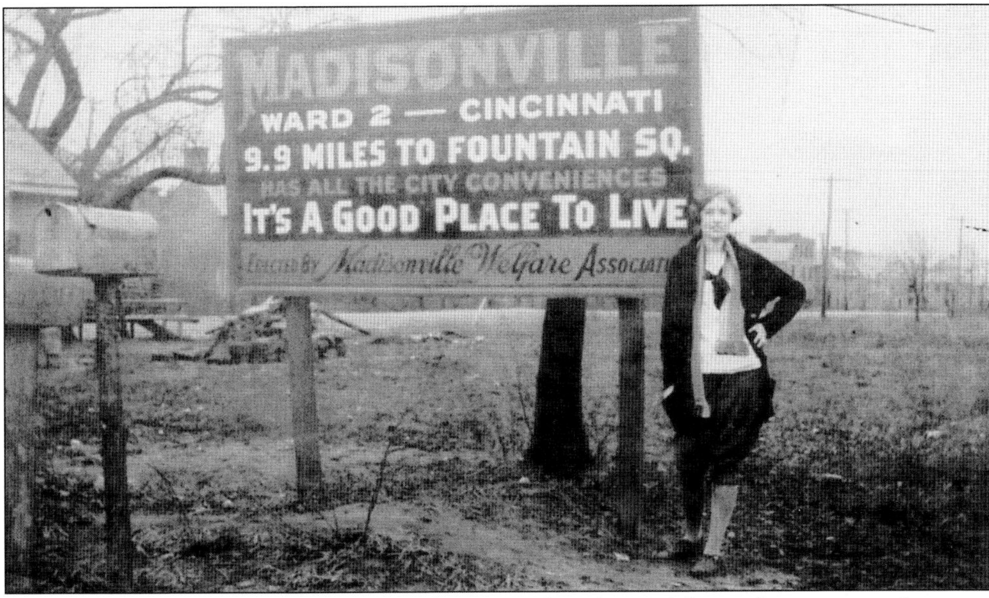

Bramble Avenue resident Dorothy Humphries stands in front of this real estate sign advertising Madisonville's qualities in 1925.

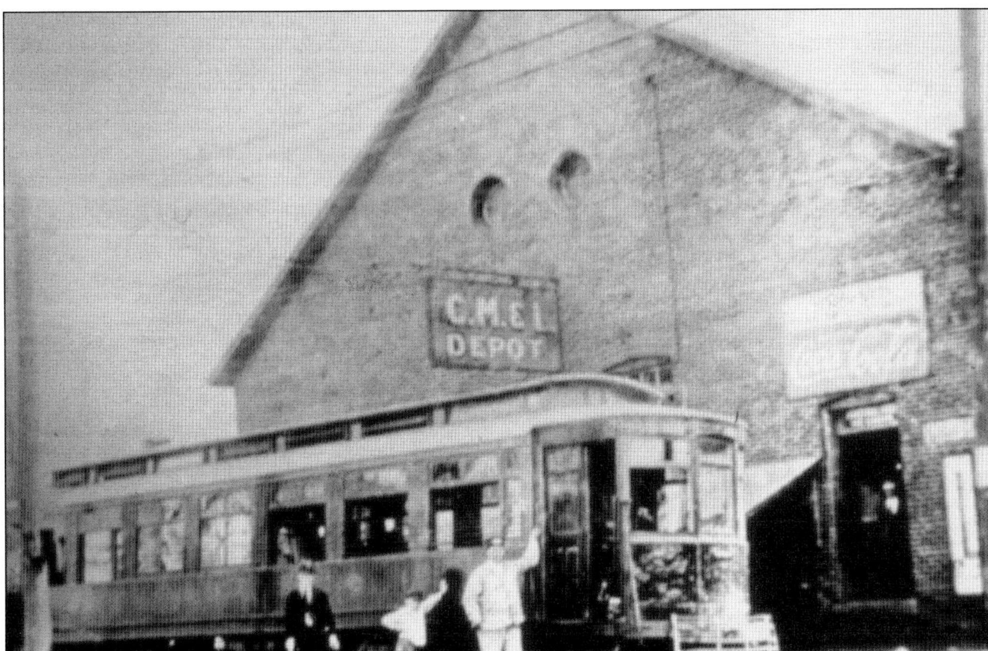

In front of the Milford Junction carbarn is one of the interurban cars, which traveled between the junction and Blanchester on the SM&B interurban line beginning in 1904. The barn, located off of Erie Avenue, included a ticket office, a waiting room, and a lunchroom. The interurban route had a short run. Service was cut back to Milford after only a few years, and by 1936, service to Mariemont was discontinued. The barn was demolished in 1941 in the midst of a major renovation of the area.

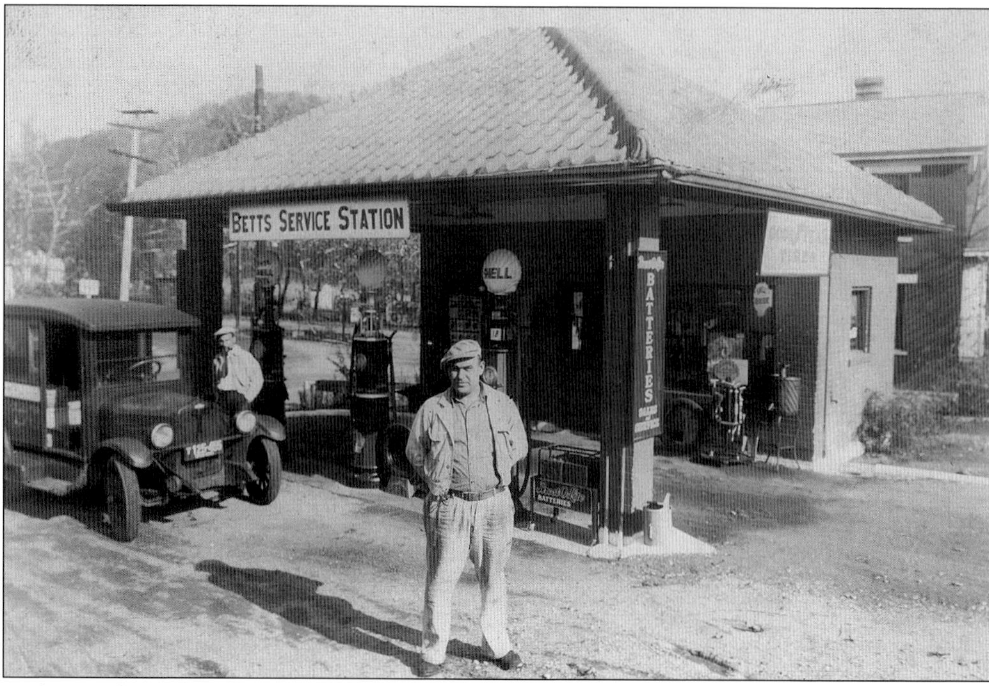

Walter Beckman poses in front of Betts Service Station while his butter and egg truck fills up at the pump around 1926. The station was at the triangle corner of Madison, Plainville, and Camargo Roads. This same building became a "pony keg," a small drive-through convenience store, before it was torn down.

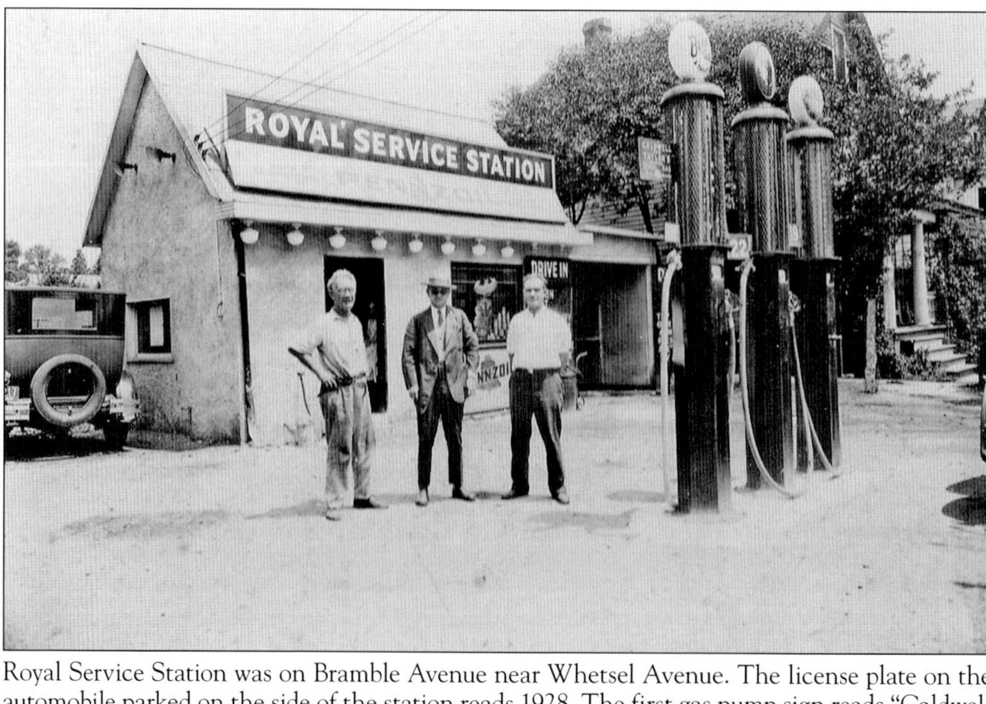

Royal Service Station was on Bramble Avenue near Whetsel Avenue. The license plate on the automobile parked on the side of the station reads 1928. The first gas pump sign reads "Caldwell and Taylor's Original Benzol Gas."

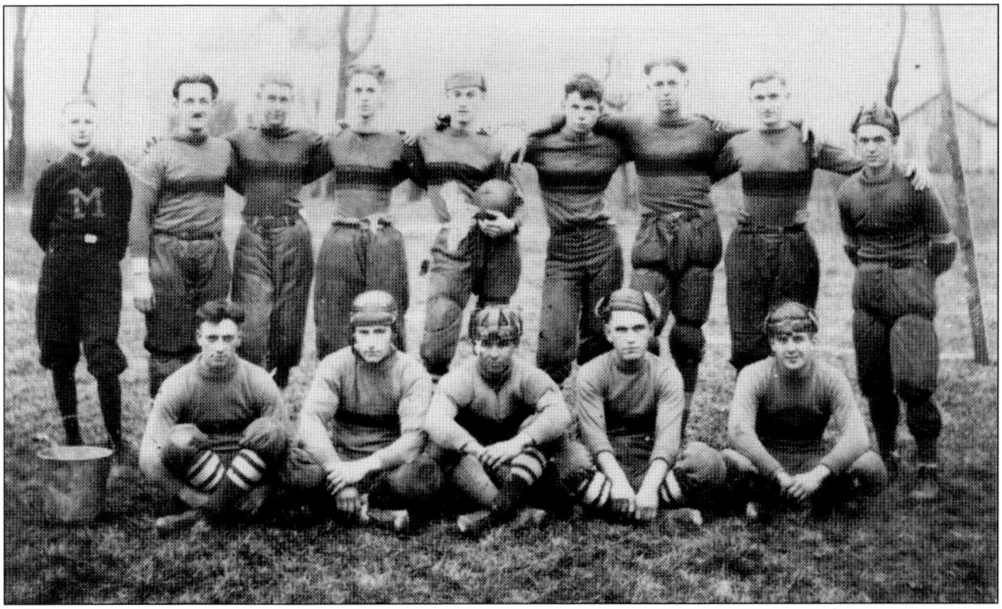

The Milo A.C. team poses for a team photograph at Stewart Playfield during their 1915–1916 season. They are, from left to right, (seated) Frank Shaffner, Babe Schafer, Toad Jordan, Les "Fat" Davis, and Babe Dewire; (standing) Art "Flip" Andriot, Lloyd "Dizzy" Bryan, Bert Trout, Don Aubrey, Syd "Cannonball" Bailey, Horace "Mose" Rice, Gus Lewin, Lloyd Bailey, and Toy Jordan.

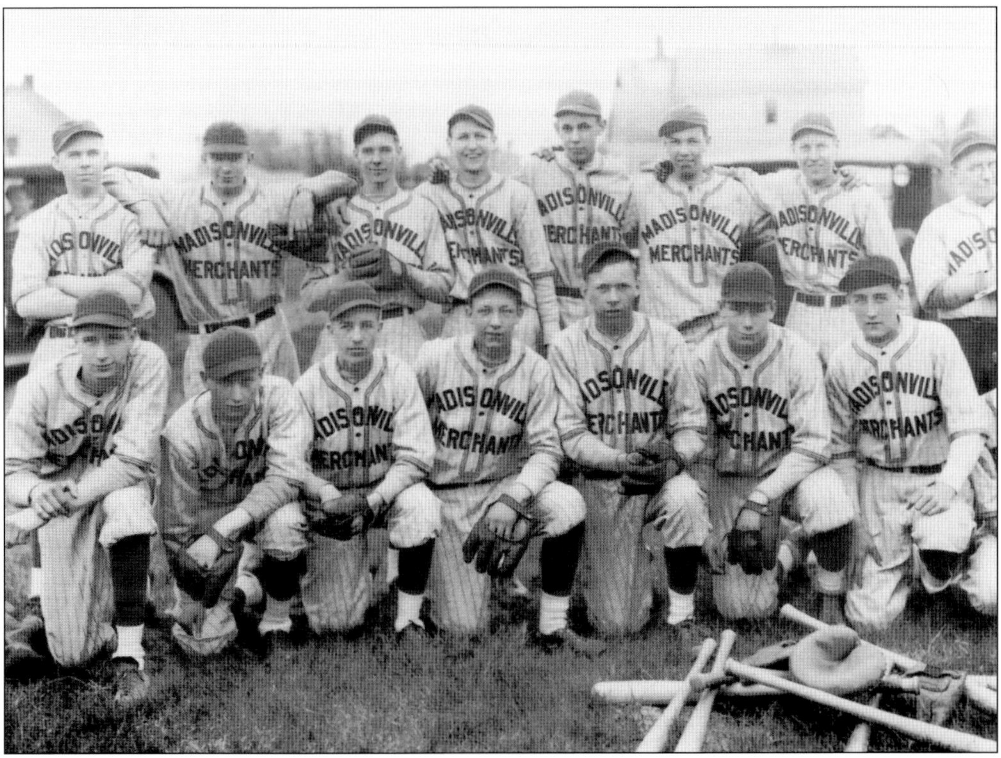

The 1902 Madisonville Monitors baseball team who played at Stewart Playfield were the predecessors for this Madisonville Merchants baseball team in the 1930s.

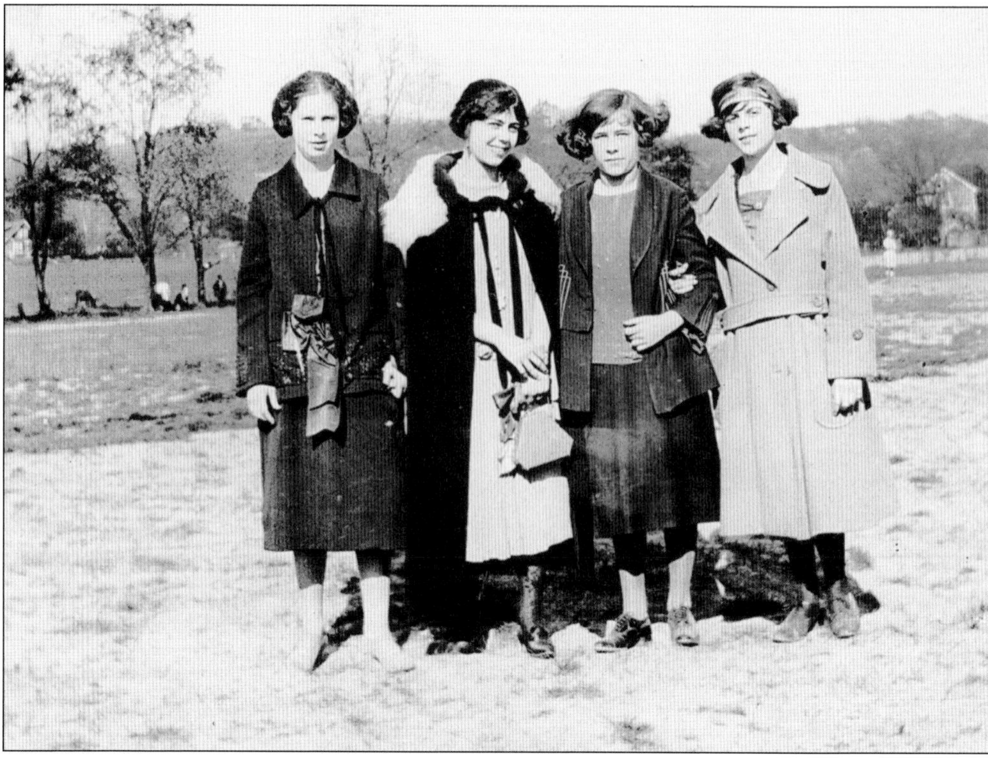

These young ladies of Madisonville are enjoying the day at Stewart Playfield in the 1920s.

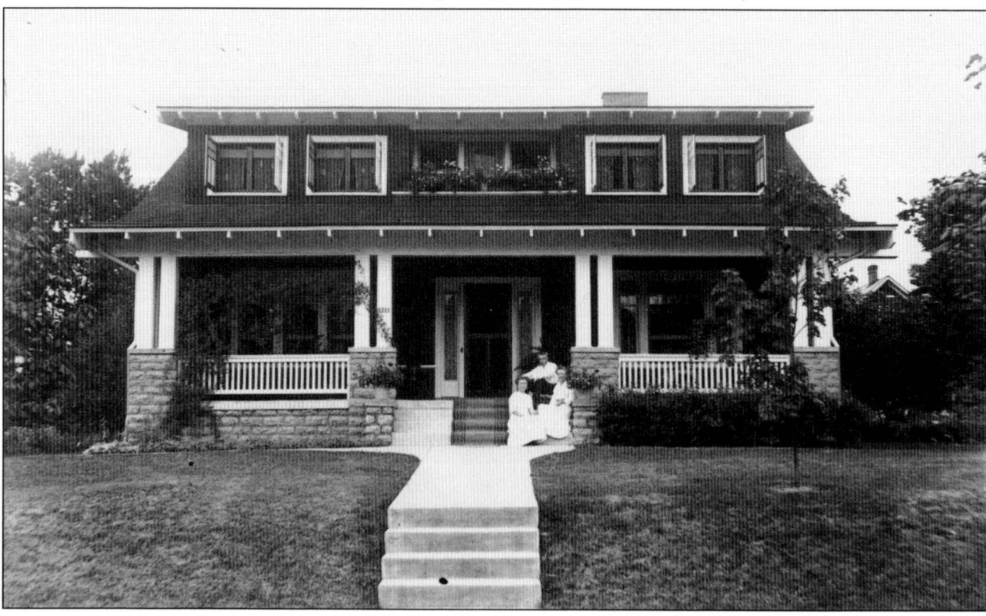

This beautiful 1906 Craftsman-style house at 5536 Arnsby Place was the home of Robert Miller, the son of B&O Railroad paymaster Frank Miller. Bob Miller became a civil engineer and helped build tunnels in the Rocky Mountains for the Denver & Rio Grande Western Railroad. He worked with Charles Taft in the building of Laure Homes in Cincinnati. When Bob became well-established, he moved to a larger, more prestigious home on Kenwood Road.

Three

Influential Educators, Public Schools

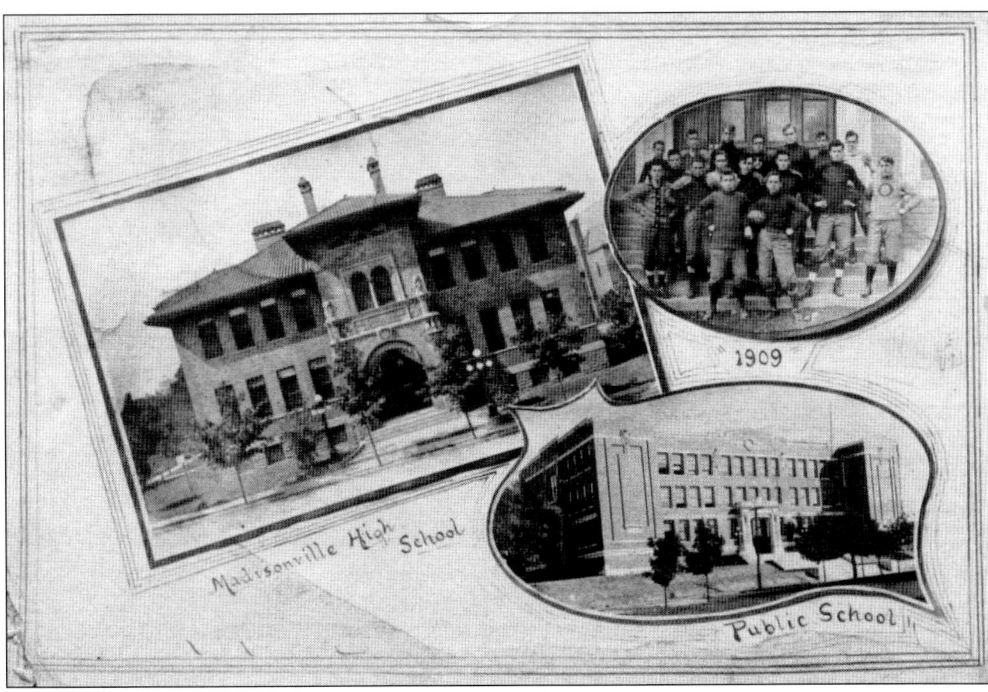

This 1909 postcard shows Madisonville High School and its football team as well as the public school.

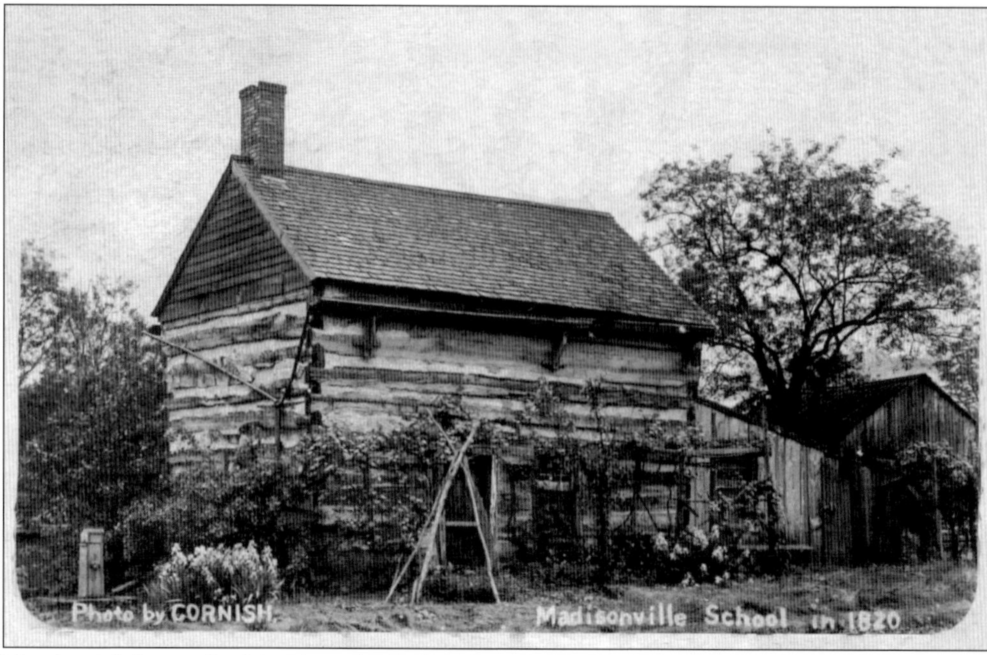

The first Madisonville School was built about 1810. The log school, pictured in an 1870 postcard, was 15 feet by 20 feet with a large fireplace at the west end. It continued to serve the community long after a new brick structure was built in 1832 on the southeast corner of Ward Street and Madison Road. In 1840, a second story was added to the brick building, and it served the area until another new school was built in 1872.

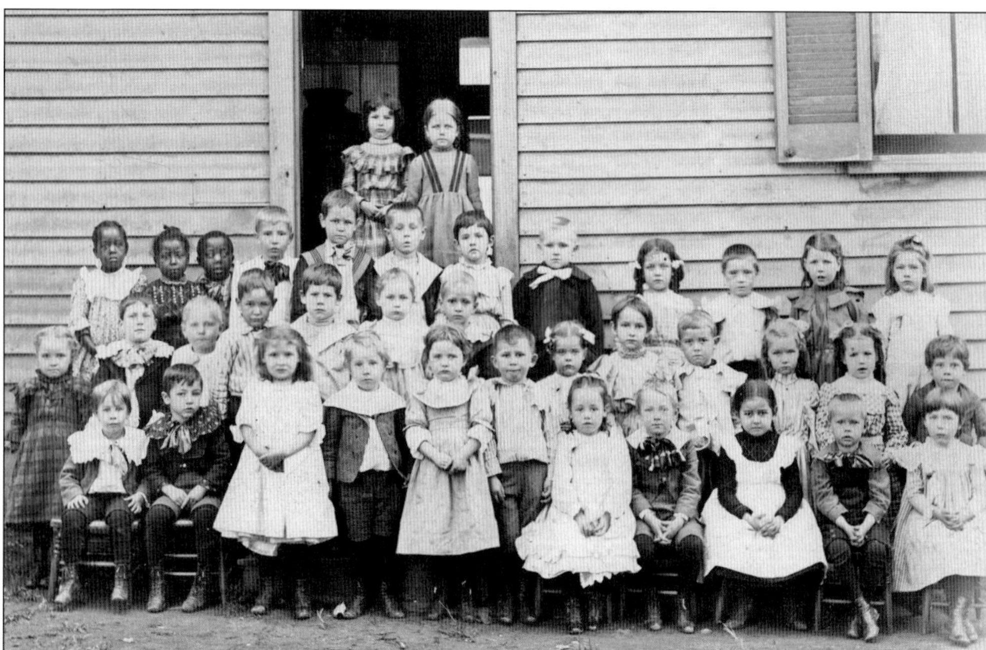

Miss Levoy's 1905 kindergarten class poses at the northeast corner of Madison Road and Mathis Street for a class photograph.

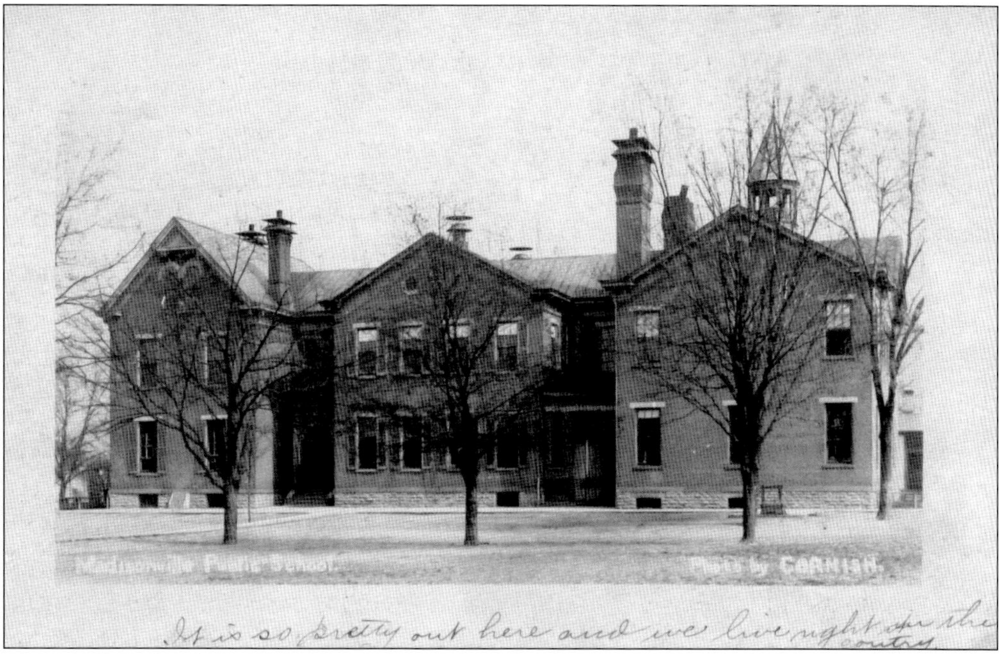

This public school building was a brick structure with 12 large, ventilated, and heated rooms supplied with all the modern conveniences. The schoolhouse had primary, intermediate, and high school departments. It was built on Lot No. 7, bounded by Ward Street, Prentice Street, and Mathis Street. The Cincinnati & Marietta Railroad (later part of the B&O), which came through Madisonville in 1866, formed the south border of the school. Classes began in 1872. The school was actually constructed in three sections over a long period of time, with the last section completed around 1889.

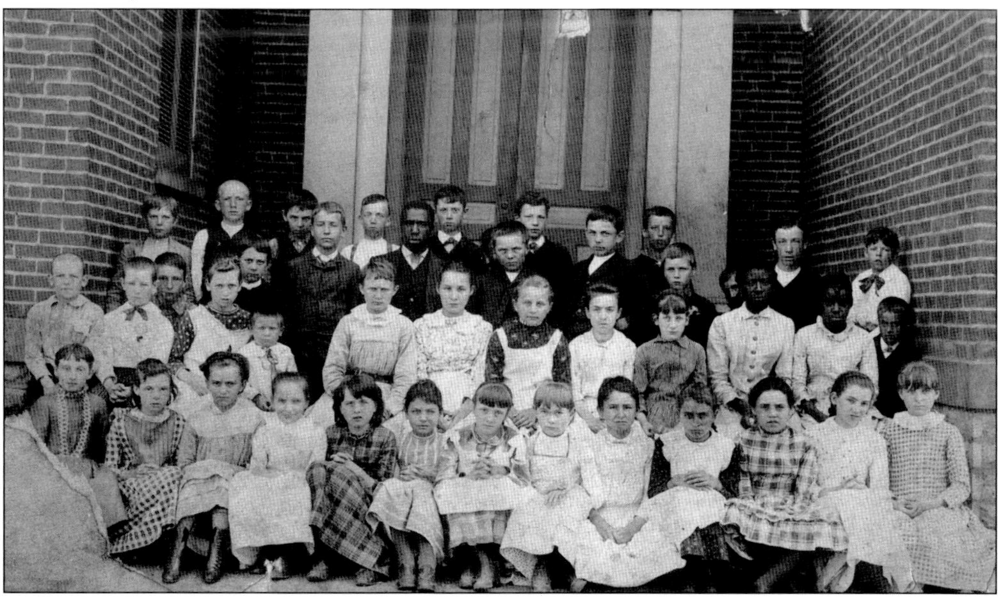

Madisonville Elementary school children are posed in front of the school building on October 31, 1895. The children would have likely that evening been engaged in local Halloween festivities, including wearing costumes and begging for treats in the local community.

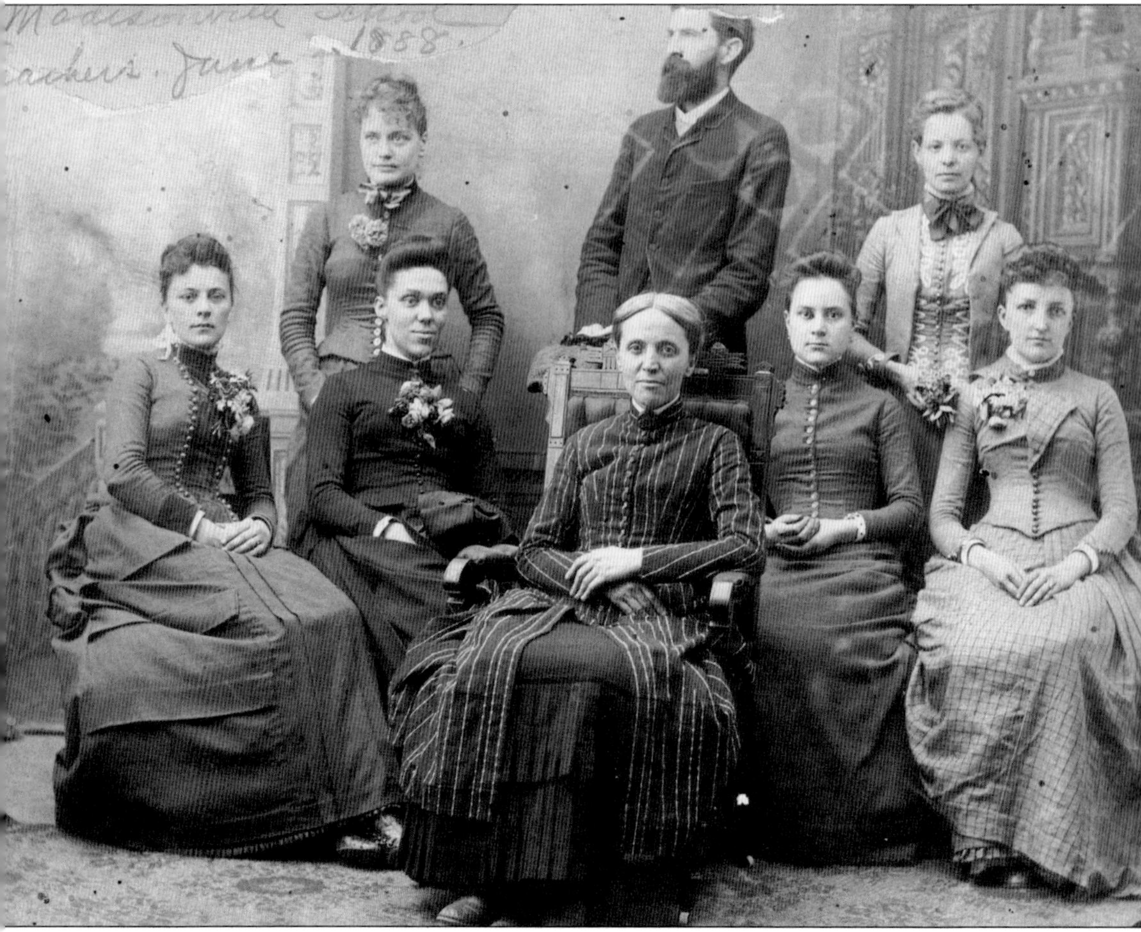

This photograph was taken in June 1888 of the Madisonville School teachers. Jeannie Bryan (first row, second from left) was an early African American educator in Madisonville. She appears in three graduation pictures in the authors' possession and signed graduation diplomas as assistant to the principal. She taught French, Latin, and English. Though Madisonville schools were not segregated, nor were Cincinnati public schools, several black schools were opened in Cincinnati, including the Douglass School in 1850 and the Colored Industrial School of Cincinnati in 1919. The later was open for nearly 50 years, closing in 1962.

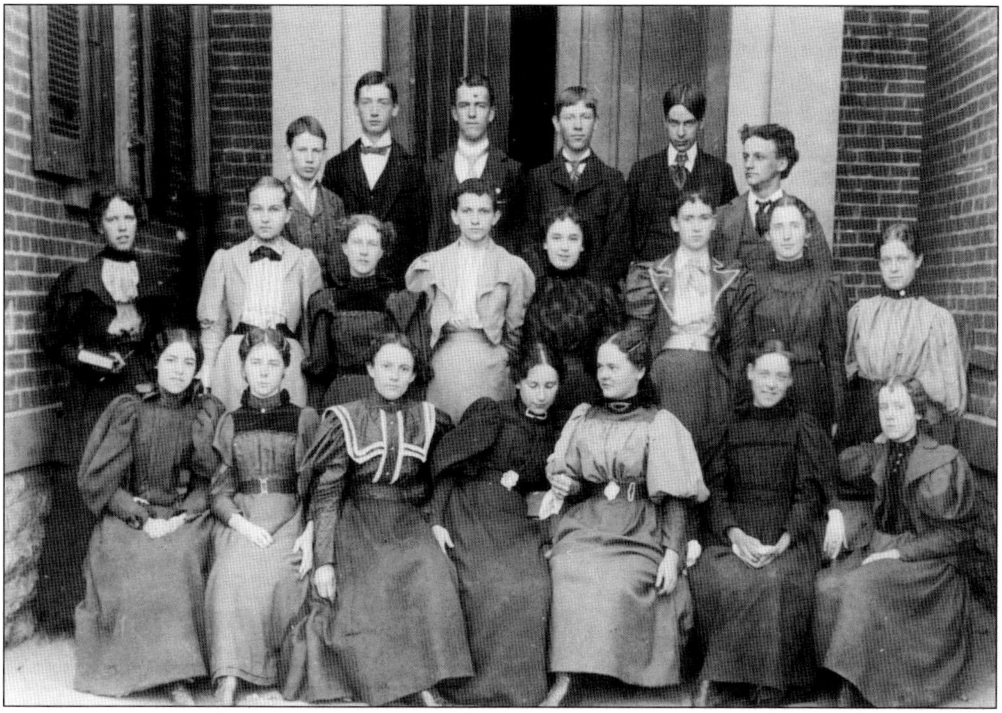

Madisonville's school systems were considered second to none, and the original high school, built in 1872, was the envy of the surrounding area. Pictured above is the Madisonville High School graduating class of 1898 in front of the original high school building. Of note in this graduating class is Clara Metz, the daughter of Dr. Charles Metz, who was instrumental in the excavation of the Madisonville Site and was nicknamed "Mr. Madisonville" for all of his contributions to the community. From left to right are (first row) Viva Losh, Bess Woodward, Allie Printy, Mary Finch, Grace Guilford, Jessie Brunson, and Nellie Finch; (second row) Ruth ?, Clara Metz, Anna Gomien, Eva McGrew, Helen DeMar, Ada Champlin, Viola Spangler, and Bess Bragdon; (third row) Shipley Fry, Frank Gorman, George Spangler, Elbert Nash, Allen Conkling, and Fritz Powell.

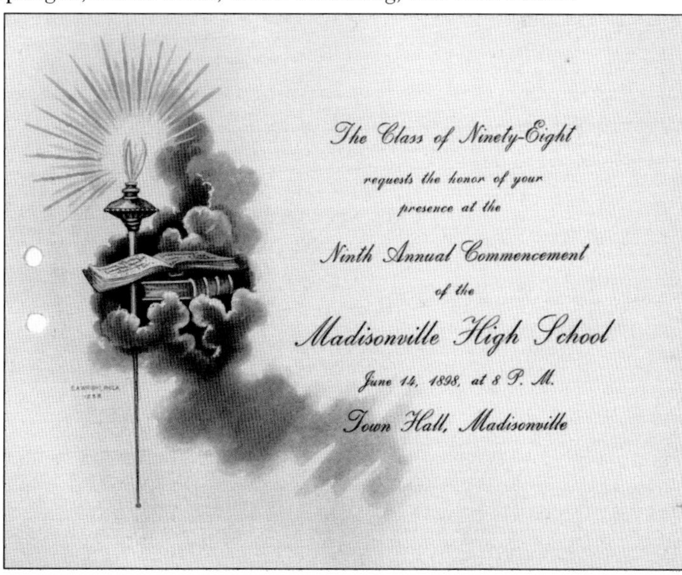

Madisonville High School held its ninth annual commencement on June 14, 1898, in the Madisonville Town Hall auditorium.

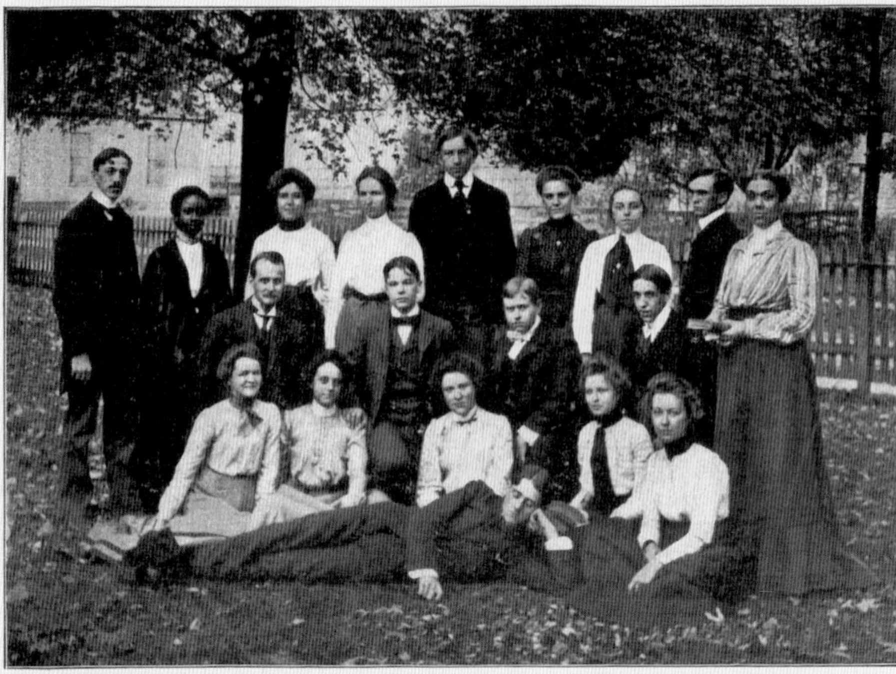

THE CLASS OF 1902.

Prof. I. W. Driehaus. Martha Mundy. Mary Wood. Margaret Ingersoll. Dawson Woodward. Lulu Strate. Hattie Agin. Osborne Rogers.
Prof. E. D. Lyon. Stanley Goff. Chas. Marchmann. Wilbur Metz. Mrs. J. M. Bryan.
Ethel Hier. Rose Wirthlin. Blanche Bush May C. Hessler. Edua Dawson.
George B. Lindsley.

The Madisonville High School graduating class of 1902 is shown in the above photograph. From left to right are (first row) George B. Lindsley (reclining), Ethel Hier, Rose Wirthlin, Blanche Bush, May C. Hessler, and Edna Dawson; (second row) Prof. E.D. Lyon, Stanley Goff, Charles Marchmann, Wilbur Metz, and teacher Jennie M. Bryan; (third row) Prof. I.W. Driehaus, Martha Mundy, Mary Wood, Margaret Ingersoll, Dawson Woodward, Lulu Strate, Hattie Agin, and Osborne Rogers. There were no segregated schools in Madisonville. Male and female students of all races and creeds attended together.

PROGRAMME OF

THE DEDICATION

— OF —

THE NEW HIGH SCHOOL BUILDING,

MADISONVILLE, OHIO.,

Saturday, February, 22nd, 1902.

9 A. M. to 12 M.

School House open for Inspection.

AFTERNOON.

Exercises begin promptly at 1:30 o'clock.

1. SONG—"America" - - - - - ALL
2. Presentation of Flag, MADISONVILLE COUNCIL No. 17, JR. O. U. A. M.
3. Response, - - - - PROF. GEO. F. SANDS, Pres. B. of E.
4. Hoisting of Flag on Staff, - - - - - FLAG COMMITTEE
5. Flag Salute, - - - - - LYTLE GREYS
6. Exhibition Drill, - - - - - LYTLE GREYS
7. Presentation of H. S. Building to the Public, PROF. GEO. F. SANDS, Pres. B. of E.
8. Response, - - - - - MAYOR DITTGEN
9. Address, - - - - - CAPT. W. W. PEABODY
10. Address - - - - L. D. BONEBRAKE, State Supt. of Schools
11. Address, - - - - - DR. R. D. BOONE
12. Address, - - - - - PROF. F. B. DYER
13. Address, - - - - - JUDGE HOWARD FERRIS

The new high school building was dedicated on Saturday, February 22, 1902.

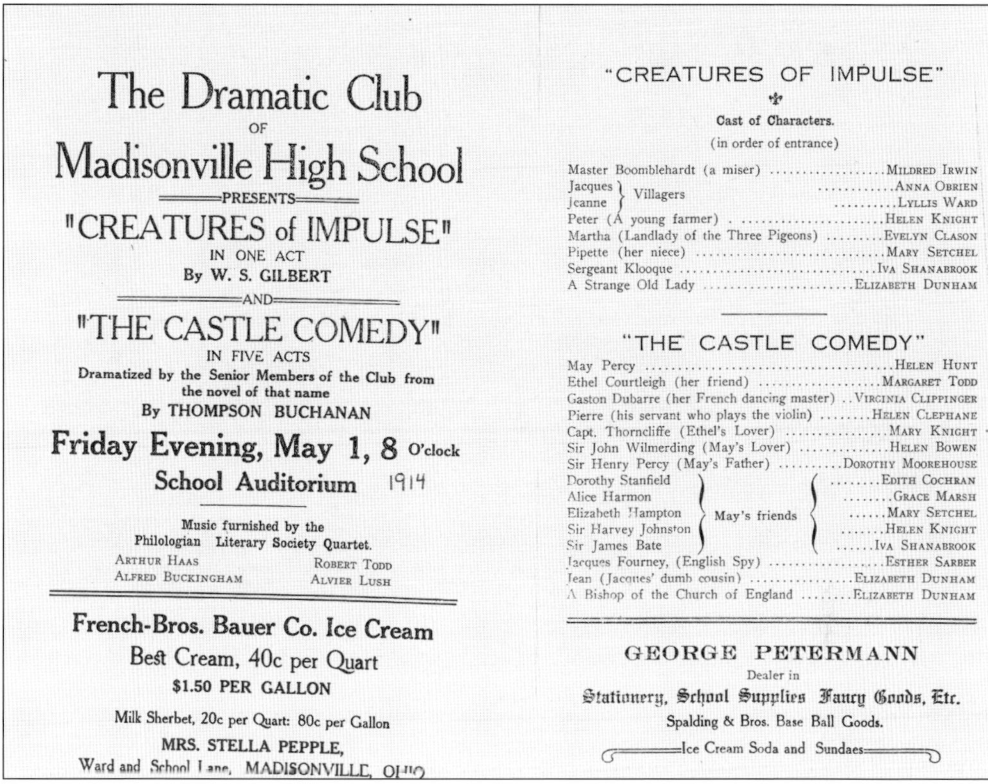

The Dramatic Club
OF
Madisonville High School

PRESENTS

"CREATURES of IMPULSE"
IN ONE ACT
By W. S. GILBERT

AND

"THE CASTLE COMEDY"
IN FIVE ACTS
Dramatized by the Senior Members of the Club from the novel of that name
By THOMPSON BUCHANAN

Friday Evening, May 1, 8 O'clock
School Auditorium 1914

Music furnished by the Philologian Literary Society Quartet.

Arthur Haas — Robert Todd
Alfred Buckingham — Alvier Lush

French-Bros. Bauer Co. Ice Cream
Best Cream, 40c per Quart
$1.50 PER GALLON
Milk Sherbet, 20c per Quart: 80c per Gallon
MRS. STELLA PEPPLE,
Ward and School Lane, MADISONVILLE, OHIO

"CREATURES OF IMPULSE"
Cast of Characters.
(in order of entrance)

Master Boomblehardt (a miser) .... Mildred Irwin
Jacques } Villagers .... Anna Obrien
Jeanne } Villagers .... Lyllis Ward
Peter (A young farmer) .... Helen Knight
Martha (Landlady of the Three Pigeons) .... Evelyn Clason
Pipette (her niece) .... Mary Setchel
Sergeant Klooque .... Iva Shanabrook
A Strange Old Lady .... Elizabeth Dunham

"THE CASTLE COMEDY"

May Percy .... Helen Hunt
Ethel Courtleigh (her friend) .... Margaret Todd
Gaston Dubarre (her French dancing master) .. Virginia Clippinger
Pierre (his servant who plays the violin) .... Helen Clephane
Capt. Thorncliffe (Ethel's Lover) .... Mary Knight
Sir John Wilmerding (May's Lover) .... Helen Bowen
Sir Henry Percy (May's Father) .... Dorothy Moorehouse
Dorothy Stanfield } May's friends .... Edith Cochran
Alice Harmon } May's friends .... Grace Marsh
Elizabeth Hampton } May's friends .... Mary Setchel
Sir Harvey Johnston } May's friends .... Helen Knight
Sir James Bate } May's friends .... Iva Shanabrook
Jacques Fourney, (English Spy) .... Esther Sarber
Jean (Jacques' dumb cousin) .... Elizabeth Dunham
A Bishop of the Church of England .... Elizabeth Dunham

GEORGE PETERMANN
Dealer in
Stationery, School Supplies Fancy Goods, Etc.
Spalding & Bros. Base Ball Goods.
Ice Cream Soda and Sundaes

The Madisonville High School Dramatic Club performed *The Castle Comedy* on Friday evening, May 1, 1914.

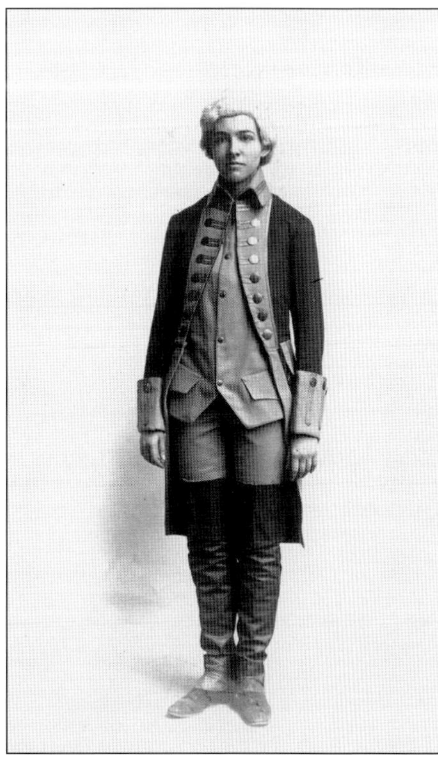

Mary Knight poses in her Captain Thorncliffe costume for the Dramatic Club of Madisonville High School in the play *The Castle Comedy*, held in the school auditorium. Mary Knight Asbury, the daughter of Dr. Arthur Knight and Anna Metz Knight, became the first woman ophthalmologist in Cincinnati, graduating from the University of Cincinnati College of Medicine. Shortly after her death in 1986, the college established the Mary Knight Asbury Chair of Ophthalmic Pathology.

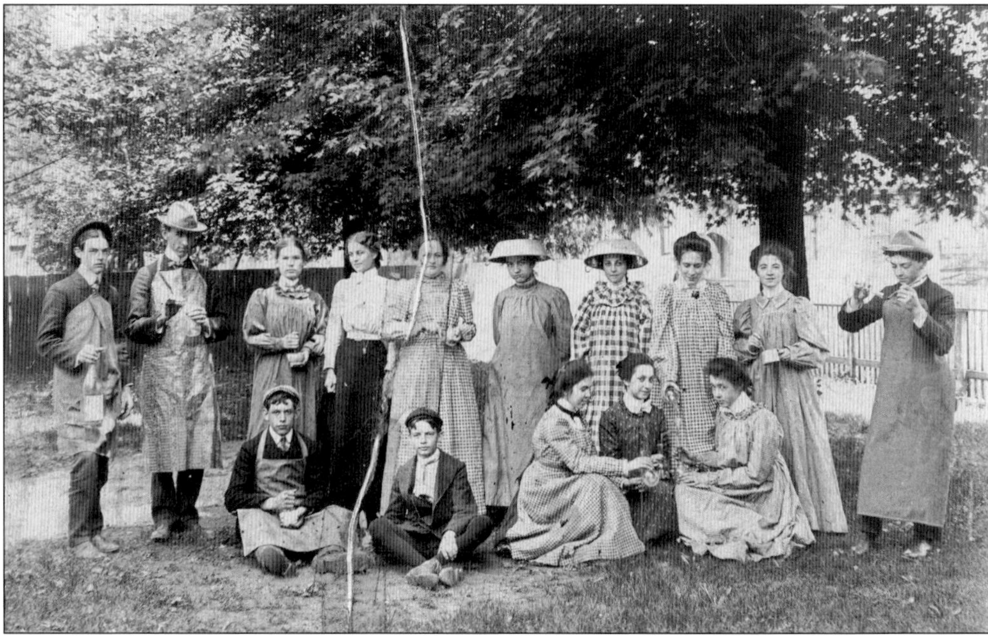

The sciences were considered an important part of education at the beginning of the 20th century. In the immediate area, residents of Madisonville, led by Dr. Charles Metz, were engaged in amateur archeological excavation of the earthen mounds built by prehistoric Native Americans. Madisonville High School had an excellent science curriculum. Pictured above is the Madisonville High School laboratory class outdoors on the school grounds in 1901.

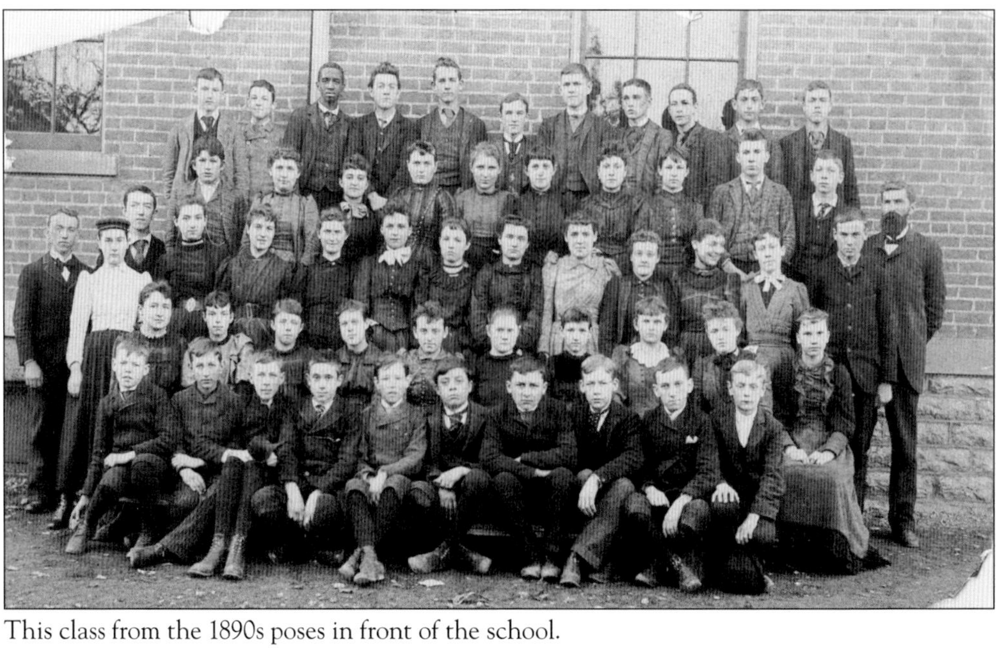

This class from the 1890s poses in front of the school.

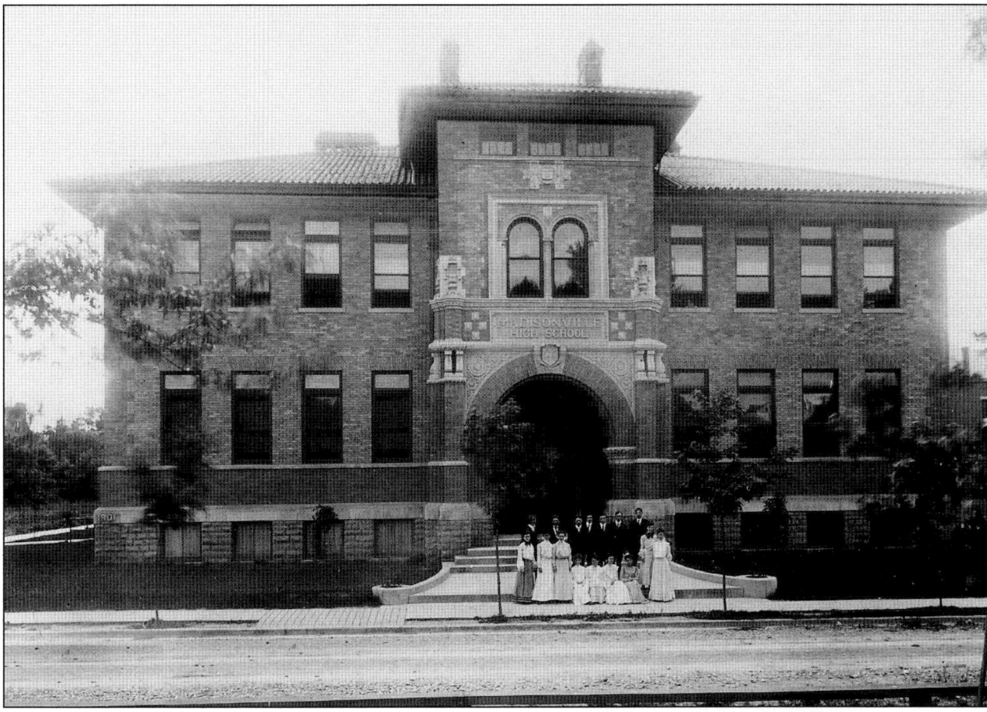

Madisonville High School was established in 1886, with classes first held in the elementary school building. In 1903, the school moved into its new building, designed by famous architect Henry Hake. This photograph is of an early graduating class. The building served as the high school until 1919, when East High, later Withrow High School, was completed, at which time Madisonville students were sent there. This building continued to be used as part of Madisonville Elementary School. With the closing of the elementary school in 1980, the building was sold, renovated by a development group, and later purchased by New Life Temple, which now has a Christian school.

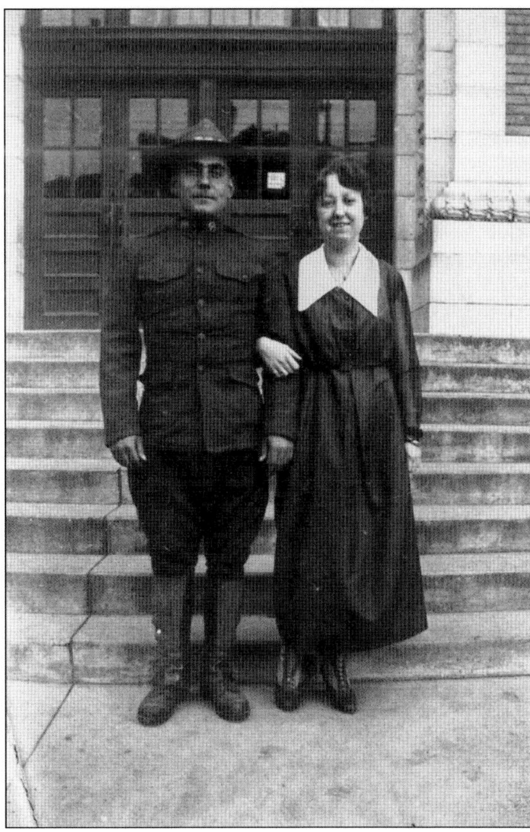

World War I high school sweethearts George Busald and Nelda Kistner pose in front of the school in 1917.

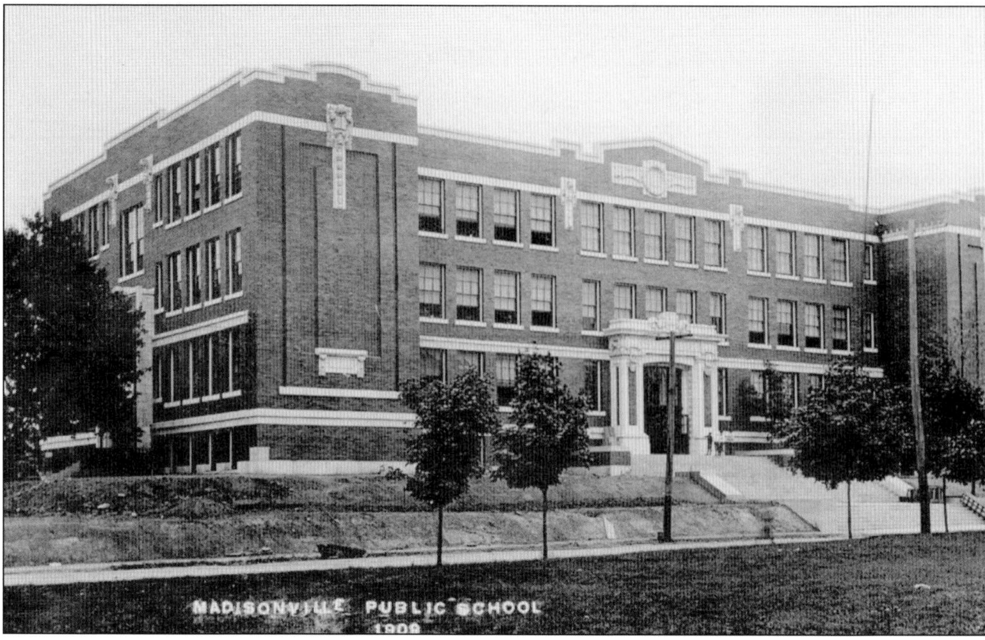

In the early 1900s, it became evident that a new elementary school was needed to serve the increasing population of Madisonville, and a new building was constructed toward the Prentice Street side of the property. The main entrance to this building faced Ward Street, just across the street from the high school. The cornerstone was laid on August 22, 1908, and the building was dedicated on October 9, 1909.

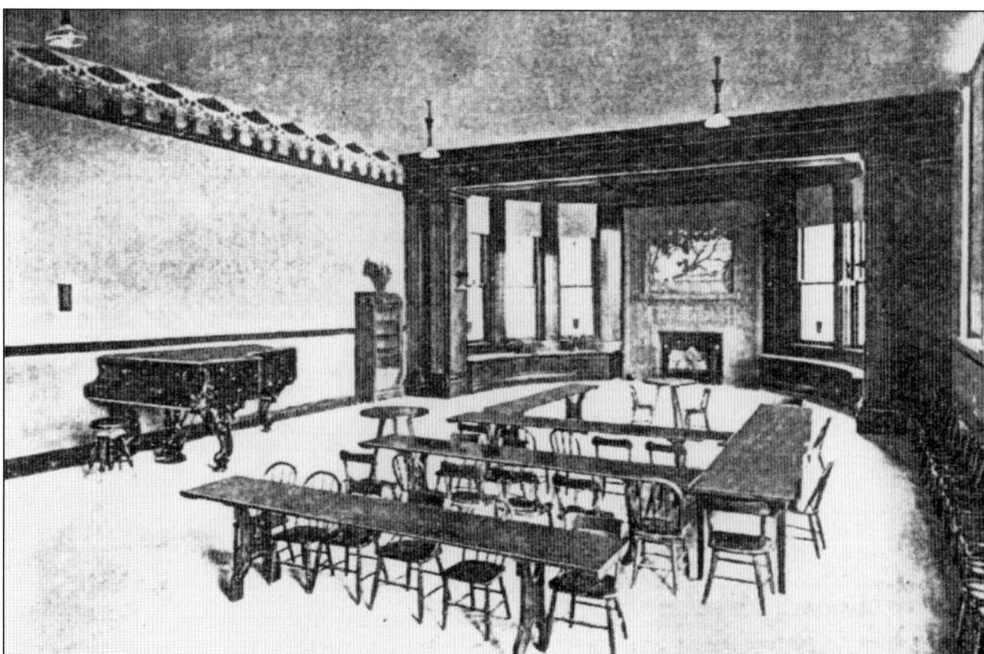

The kindergarten room in the new 1909 Madisonville Elementary School featured a faience mantel in colored matte glazes made by the Rookwood Pottery Company of Cincinnati and a Rookwood mural of a little boy on a rope swing.

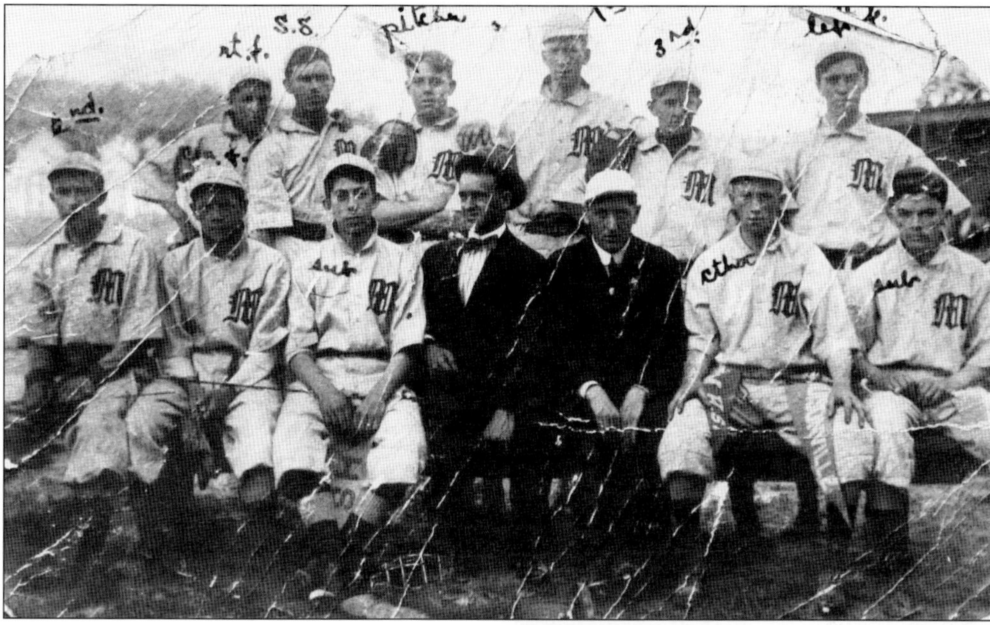

The Madisonville High School baseball team poses for this photograph around 1900. The picture was probably taken on the field located along today's Stewart Road. From its earliest days as a community, Madisonville had the advantage of being able to use a large, fairly well-developed field within easy walking distance of the center of Madisonville's population. The field, in use since the late 1800s, was so large and adaptable that many sports could be played there simultaneously. Today, it is the site of Stewart Park and the Madisonville Recreation Center.

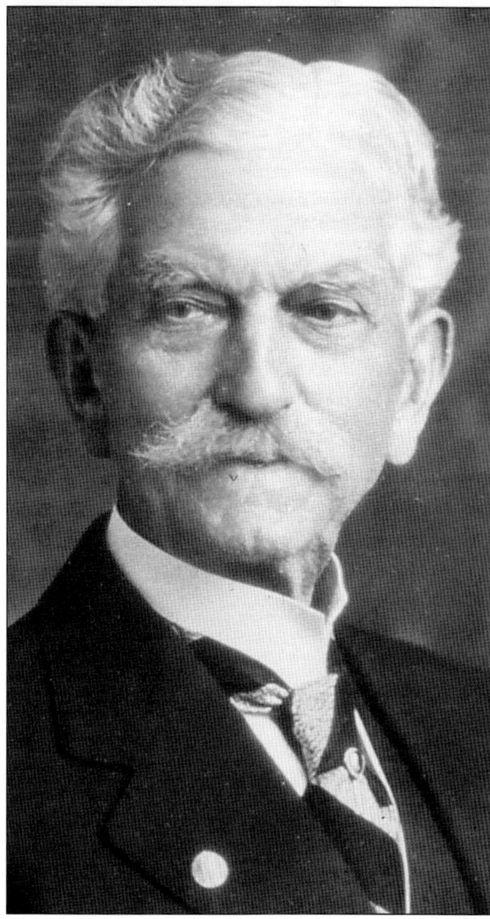

Educator George F. Sands, president of the Cincinnati Board of Education, was also president of the National Baseball Association in 1867–1868 and lived on Tompkins Avenue. In 1860, townball was introduced to Cincinnati with the Excelsior Townball Club. The game was similar to baseball. It was organized in Madisonville in 1863 as the Cincinnati Buckeye Townball Club, with George F. Sands as president and second baseman. Games were played until 1866, when it was reorganized as the Buckeye Baseball Club. It competed around town and in neighboring states with other organized clubs, including the Cincinnati Red Stockings. The club fell into debt and disbanded in 1869.

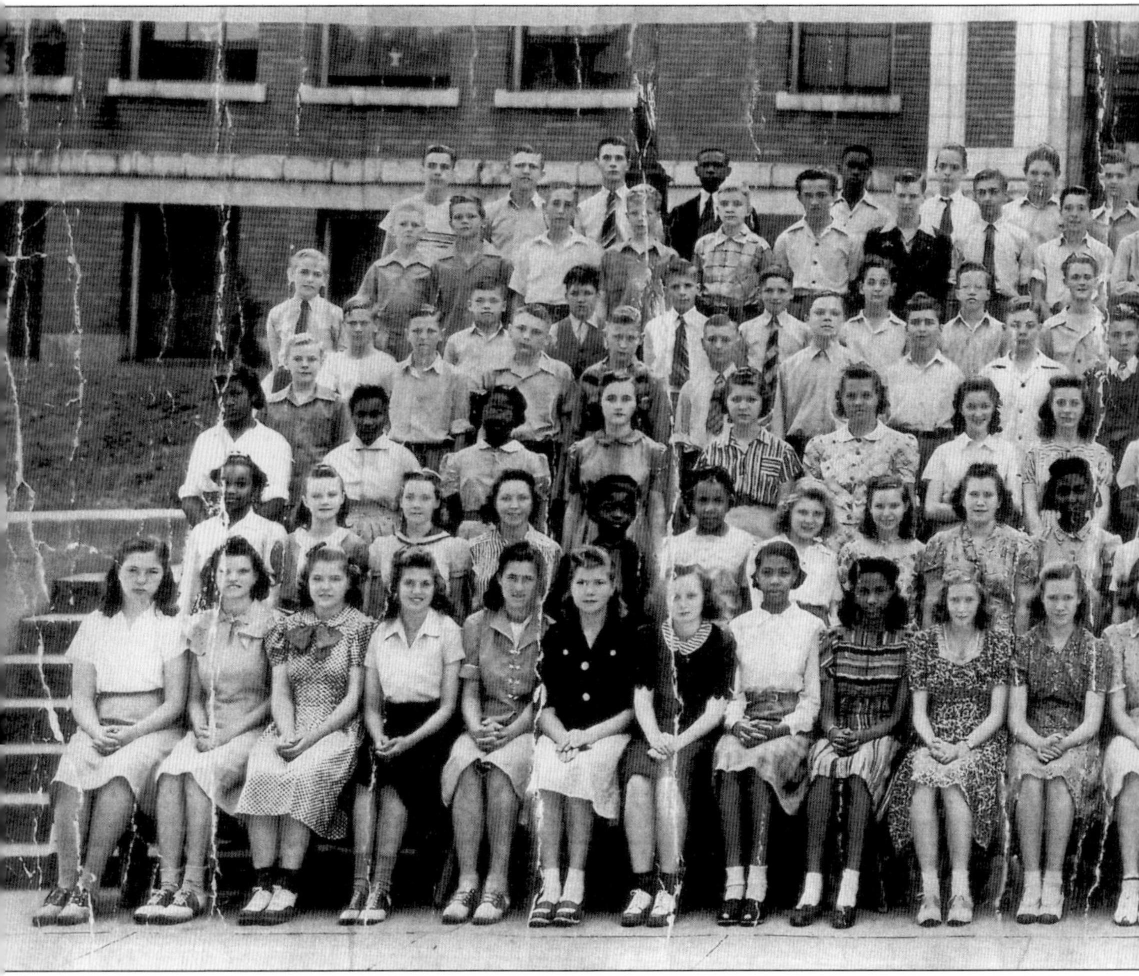

The 1941 eighth-grade graduation class of 147 pupils received certificates of promotion from Principal W.A. Justice. They were A. Aerni, B. Ainsley, M. Amos, E. Anderson, L. Arnold, R. Baker, N. Beiser, C. Bennett, R. Bennett, R. Berry, M. Blow, P. Bogart, T. Bomar, G. Brandt, R. Brueckner, E. Bryan, R. Busald, J. Bush, O. Bush, M. Campbell, D. Carter, J. Casey, R. Collier, E. Collins, M. Cooper, E. Cordry, F. Cox, S. Crawford, H. Creel, M. Davis, G. Dean, F. Decker, J. Dollenmeyer, M. Dolph, J. Earhart, O. Edmonson, E. Edwards, M. Fancher, Y. Embry, J. Fille, B. Frederick, R. Fritz, G. Frye, R. Gallagher, I. Gans, W. Gosc, B. Glancy, V. Green, M. Gronauer, D. Hall, V. Hall, R. Harrison, M. Hartman, V. Heiden, R. Hein, J. Henderson, S. Herman, C. Hickman, S. Hess, W. Hicks, G. Hill, H. Hutchinson, J. Johnson, M. Johnson, P. Jones, P. Jones, W. Jones, G. Judkins, K. Kagrise, E. Kattelman, C. Keel, C. Lammers, A. Lapthorn, A. Lec,

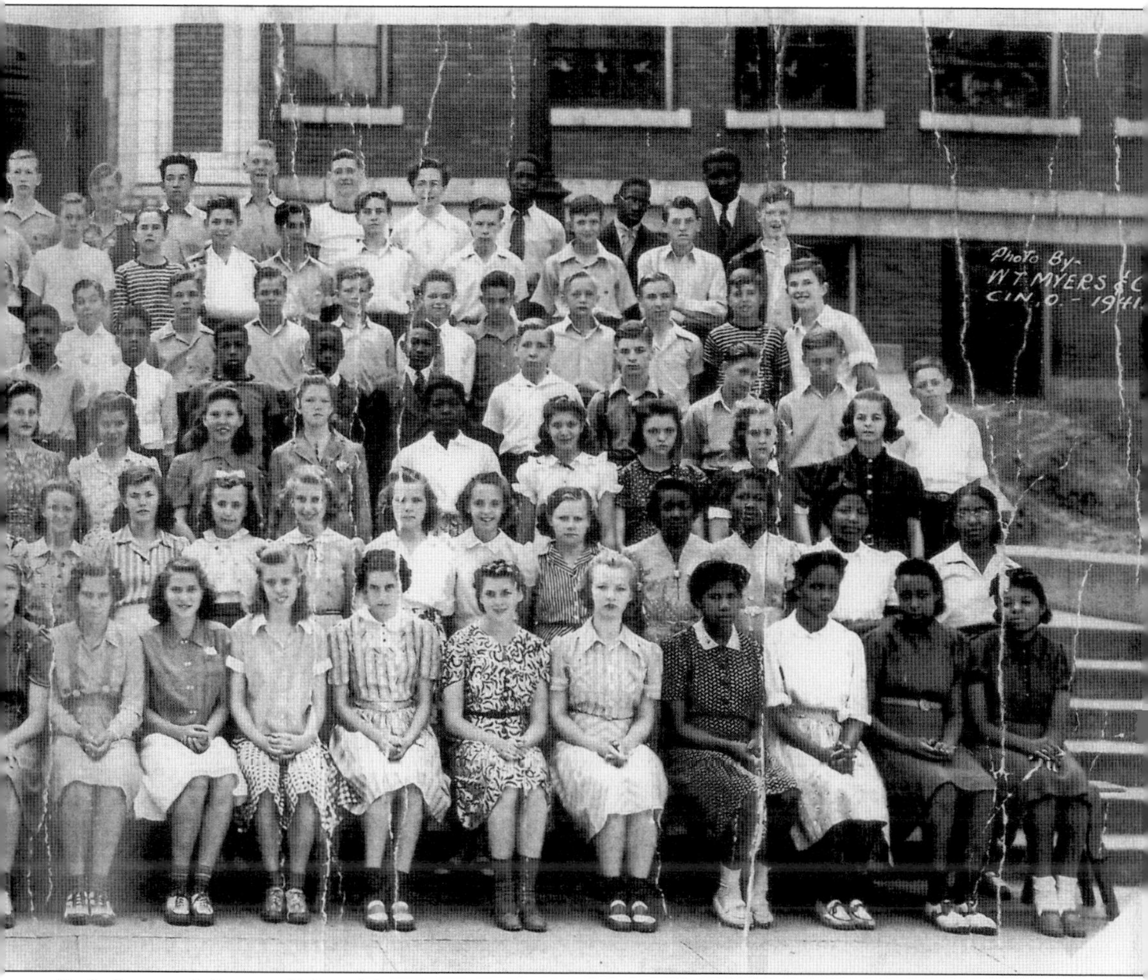

R. Lahman, J. Lewis, E. Lindsley, J. Louis, G. Lyons, T. Martin, F. Mccullough, M. McGill, W. McGray, I. McGuffey, K. McKhan, M. McKinney, A. McNeil, R. Mealy, B. Melson, W. Merker, G. Miller, R. Miller, R. Miller, J. Noel, F. Payne, B. Penn, J. Perkins, R. Phillips, A. Pohl, L. Prebble, J. Reeves, B. Reher, W. Reihs, R. Rice, R. Rosenberger, V. Rosey, E. Ross, D. Salt, H. Sanger, C. Satterfield, H. Schateman, E. Segar, F. Seymour, R. Shaw, M. Shinkle, C. Smith, E. Spaui, R. Sponsel, S. Stapp, E. Stevenson, H. Sturgeon, R. Tait, M. Thompson, W. Thompson, W. Todd, A. Tucker, C. Tucker, G. Tucker, M. Underwood, K. Vaughn, S. Vaughn, R. Vearil, W. Voris, A. Ward, M. Weils, V. Wermuth, J. White, E. Wilkening, R. Williams, J. Wilmers, F. Winningham, L. Wood, B. Zapf, and J. Zerges.

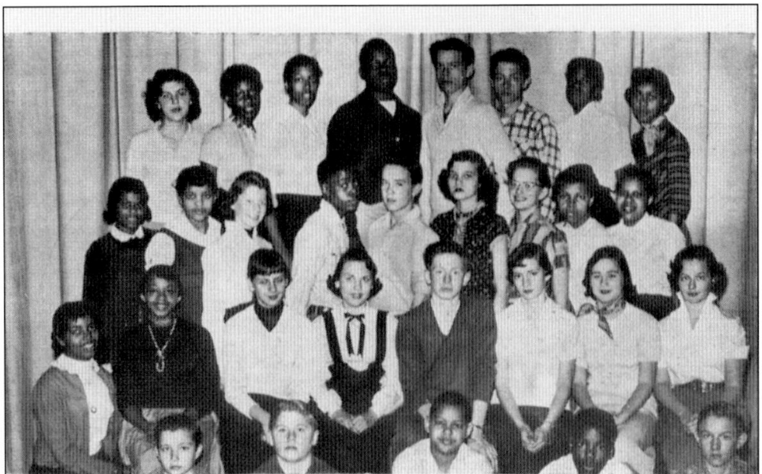

STUDENT COUNCIL

Row 1 L to R: Gerald Taylor, Roy Lowish, Rodford Berry, George Kennedy, Richard Krieger.
Row 2: Margie Evans, Jannis Jasper, Judy Hopewell, Judy Howard, Jim Wells, Phyllis Whitehead, Barbara Conway, Martha Wernsing
Row 3: Leah Burnham, Sylvia Bishop, Patty Benzing, James Blathers, Paul Wright, Loretha Smith, Ellen Fagan, Janet Moore, Joan Rogers.
Row 4: Nancy Callahan, Vera O'Neal, Phyllis Leahr, Leroy Blannon, Jerry Minton, Tom Hern, Minnie Durham, Kay Drane.

The Madisonville Lyon Junior High student council for 1955–1956 consisted of Phyllis Whitehead, president; Judy Howard, vice president; Judy Hopewell, secretary; and James Wells, treasurer.

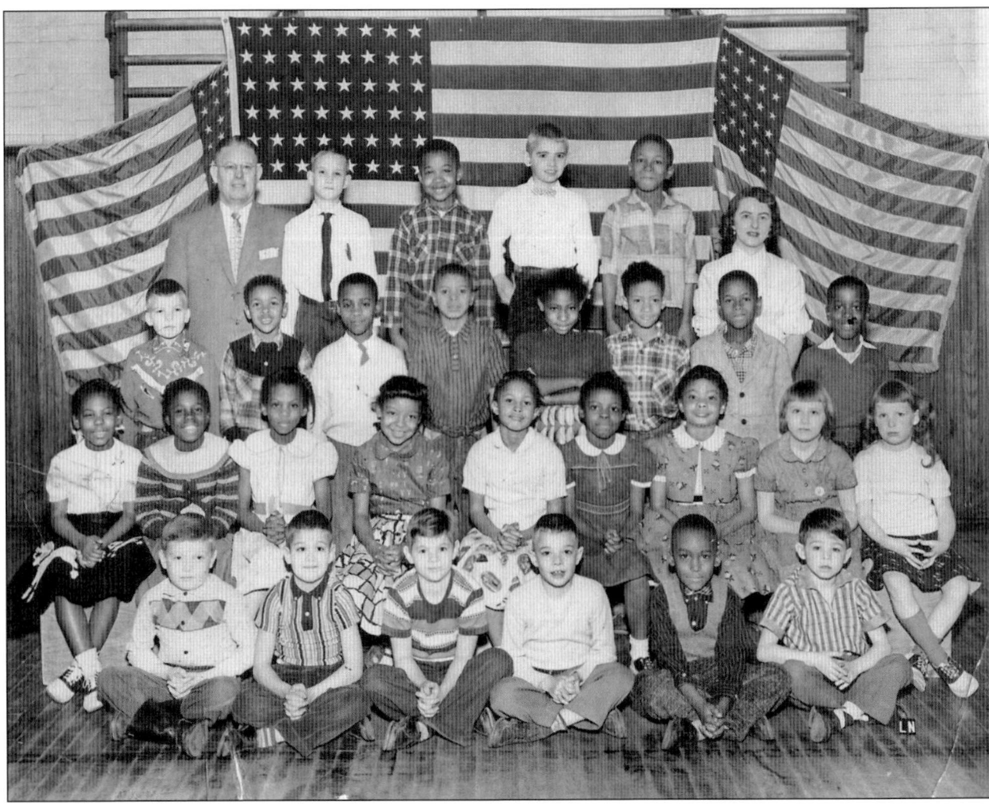

The Madisonville Elementary School second grade had its photograph taken in 1957.

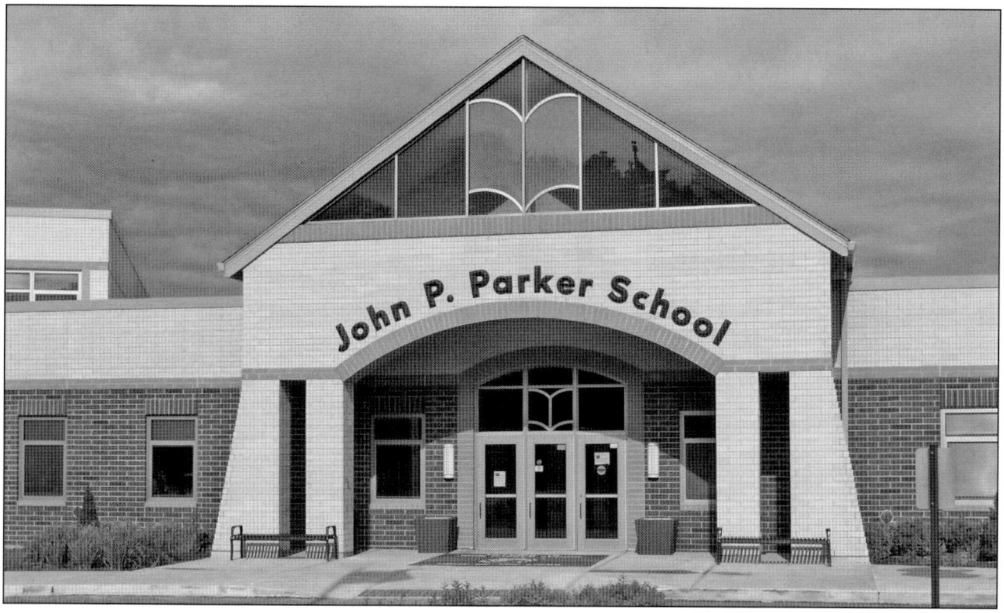

This site at Anderson Place has been used as a school since opening its doors on September 4, 1956. It was first called the Edmund D. Lyon Junior High School and opened with 750 students and 33 teachers. The school was named after Dr. Lyon, who had served as superintendent of Madisonville Schools in the early 1900s as well as principal of Woodward, Hughes, and East (later Withrow) High Schools. The name was changed to Anderson Place Elementary School in 1980, when Cincinnati Public Schools restructured the grade school system. It became John Parker Elementary School in 2005. The current school building was constructed 2006, keeping the same name.

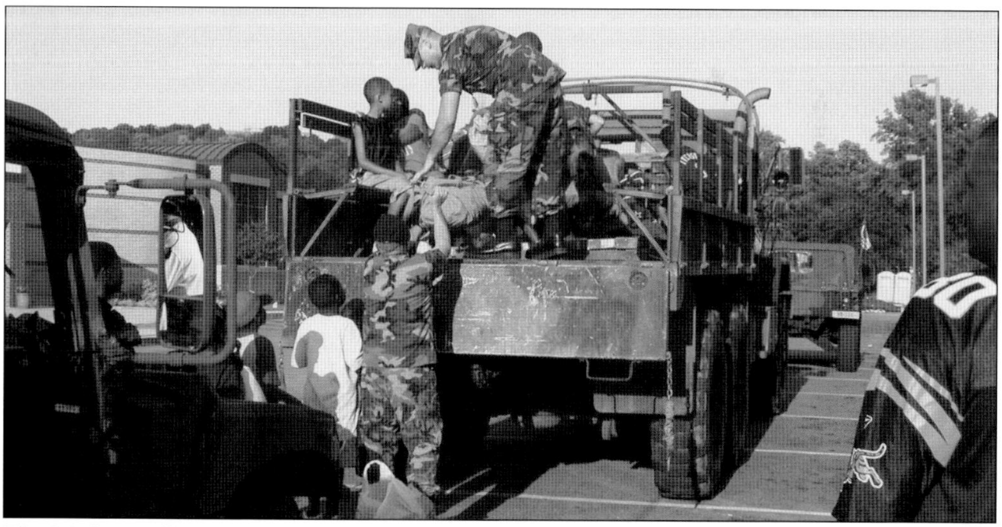

The Madisonville Weed and Seed Program partnered with National Guard and Cincinnati police to give young men from Madisonville an opportunity to not only spend a weekend camping but also to learn about life. These children come from John P. Parker Elementary School. John Parker was born a slave, and it was common not to teach slaves to read. Contrary to the social rules of the time, two young white boys of the household taught him to read anyway. At some point, he purchased his freedom, moved to Ripley, Ohio, and established a foundry there.

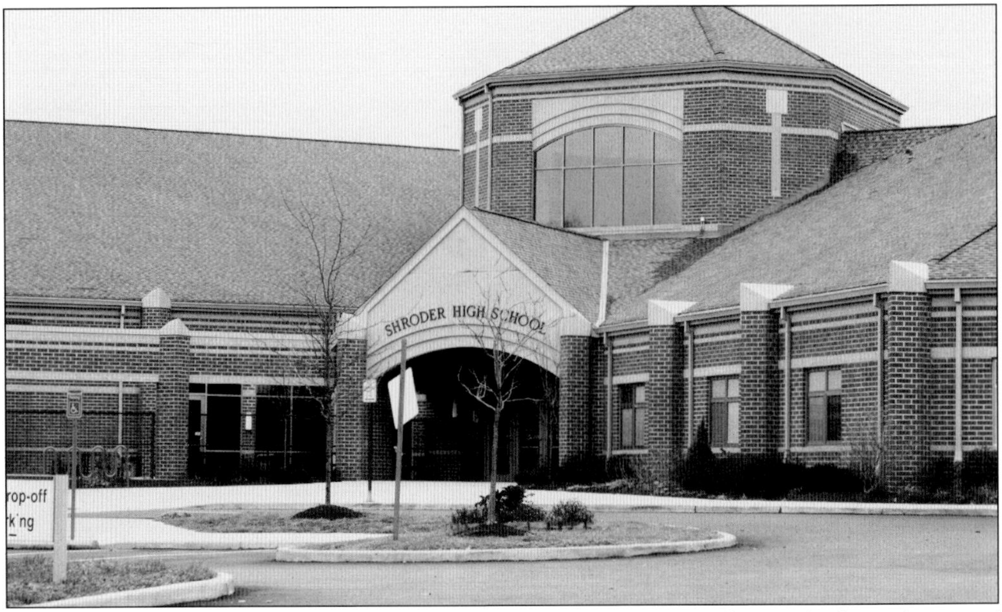

In 2007, Shroder High School, the second high school in Madisonville, was built on the site of Eastwood Elementary School, which served the 1950s-era Eastwood Village, which was created for returning veterans, until the village was demolished in 1979. After 10 years, the school was repurposed as Eastwood Paidea Elementary School, a Cincinnati magnet school that was demolished to make way for Shroder High School.

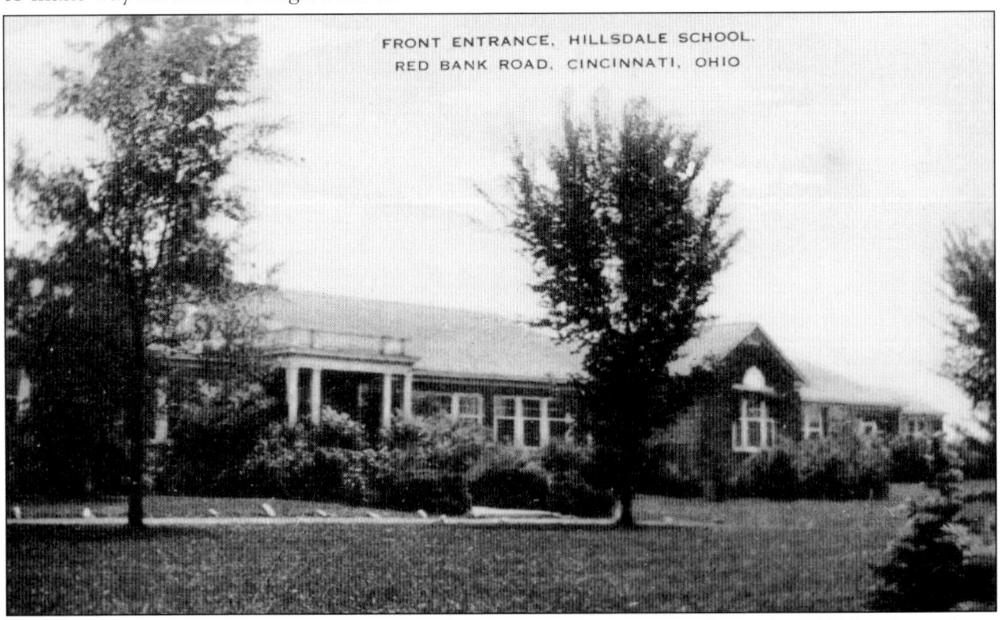

Seven Hills School, named for the seven hills of Cincinnati, was formed in 1974, when three institutions combined on the site of Hillsdale School, which was founded by Miriam Titcomb in 1928. Lotspeich School, which was founded by Helen Lotspeich in 1916, and Miss Doherty's College Preparatory School for Girls, founded by Mary Harlan Doherty in 1906, joined Hillsdale School to become Seven Hills School. The new school is a nondenominational private school and is open to children of all races and creeds.

Four

CHURCHES THAT SHAPED OUR TOWN

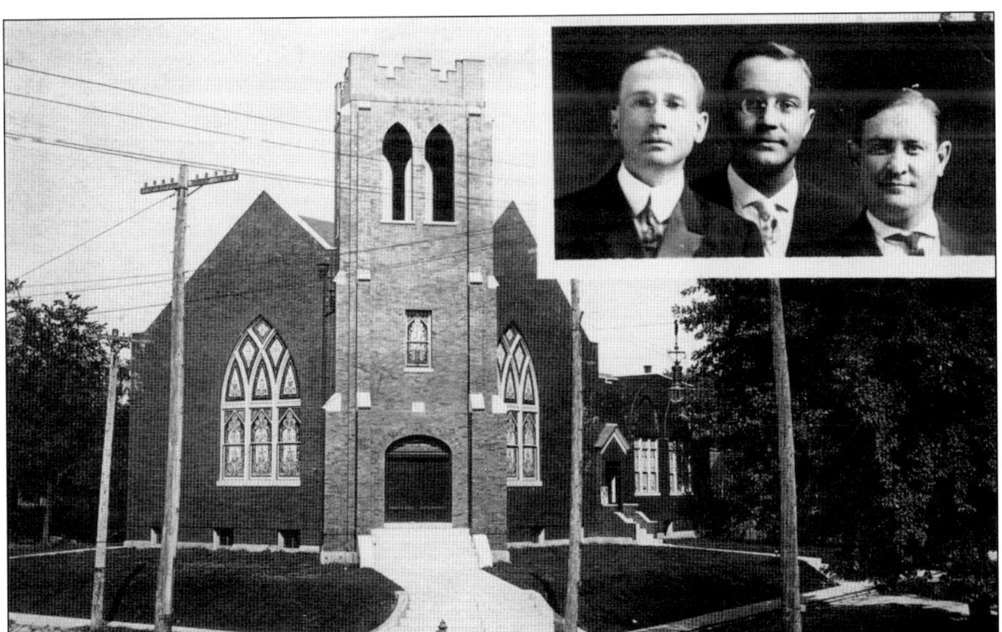

First Christian Church was located at Ward and Prentice Streets and closed in 1977 after 100 years in Madisonville. This souvenir postcard was given to all who attended its school on "Rally Day" on October 6, 1912, compliments of L.H. Lueders, a photographer on 6013 Main Street. Appearing in it are, from left to right, Roy L. Brown; Harry F. Rector, minister; and D. Emmett Snyder.

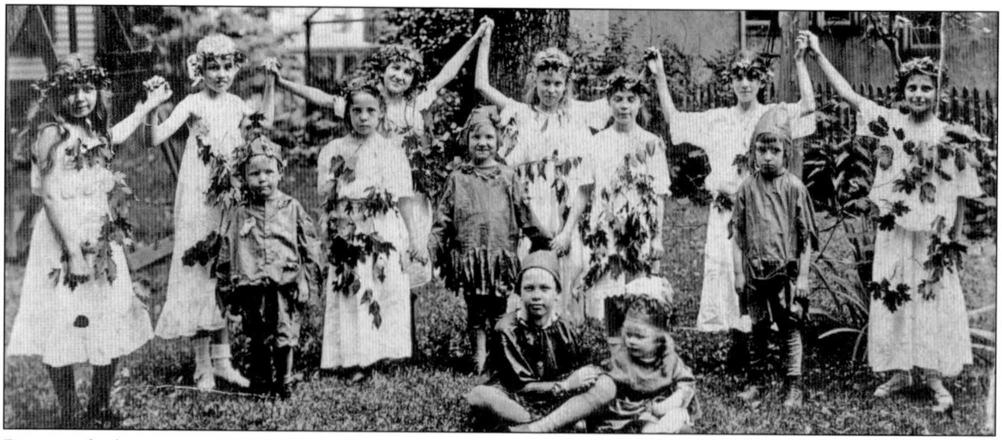

Pictured above is a 1900s May Day celebration with children playing on the Madisonville Methodist Church grounds. On May Day, the maypole was erected outside in good weather in view of the festivities. It was a pole with about 20 different colored ribbons hanging from the top. Each maypole dancer, generally a child, held the end of a ribbon and danced around the pole, weaving in and out and making a pattern with the colored ribbons down the pole. Different dances produced different patterns, and the children had to move closer and closer to the pole the more they danced, because their ribbons became shorter. When the teacher thought that the ribbons were becoming too short, the children had to dance the other way to unwind the ribbons. People often dressed up, and women and girls wore flowers in their hair.

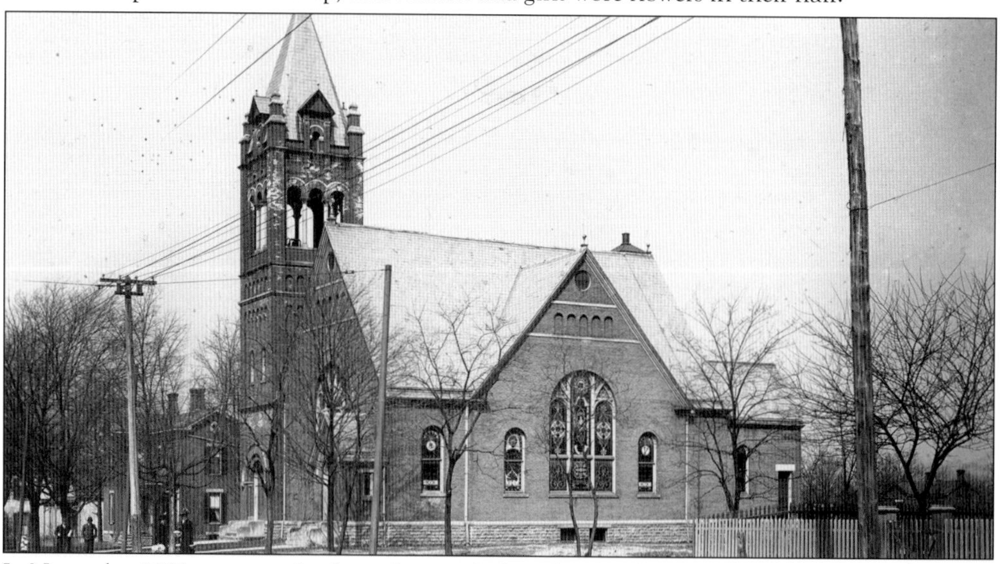

In November 1801, a group of early settlers, including the Ward, Bramble, McCollum, Muchmore, and Robinson families, organized a Methodist church for their small community. That same year, the first Methodist Episcopal Church of Madison, a log cabin, was erected on land donated by Uzziel Ward. It lasted only two years before fire destroyed it. For the next 21 years, services were held in the homes of members. In 1824, money was collected to erect a new church building on the present site, donated by Benjamin Muchmore. In 1857, a new church was built, and a new parsonage was added in 1872. The church continued to grow with the community, and by 1887, the congregation had outgrown the church building. The church was demolished and a new church built in its stead, dedicated on April 19, 1891. Additions and improvements were made in 1908 and 1913. Above is the Methodist Episcopal Church of Madisonville around 1920.

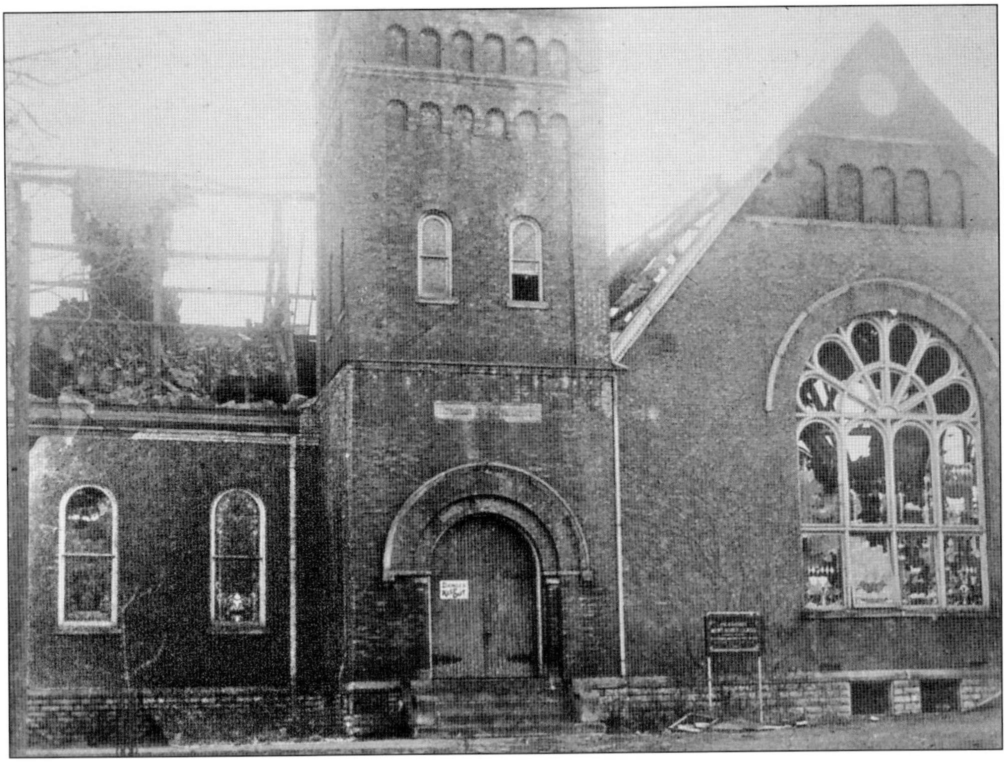

Little more than six months after the centennial celebration of the establishment of the Methodist Episcopal Church of Madisonville, disaster occurred. Clara Maphet, then living in the family home next to the parsonage, recounted for Madisonville's sesquicentennial: "Early in the morning January 6, 1925, I was awakened by something. It was a fireman trying to awaken the pastor. Looking out the front window, I saw what I first thought to be fog. Then I discovered it was smoke, and rushed to the back door. The whole neighborhood was a brilliant red, and the front of our church was vanishing in terrible flames." A heavy firewall prevented the fire from spreading to the Sunday school section, built in 1913, but the church was destroyed. However, even as the fire was being extinguished, church members were planning the construction of a new, larger church to suit their growing congregation.

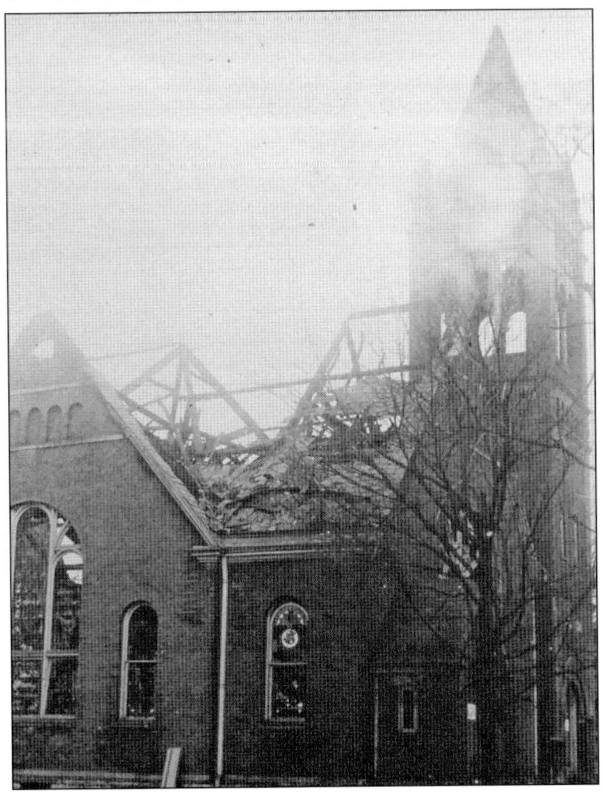

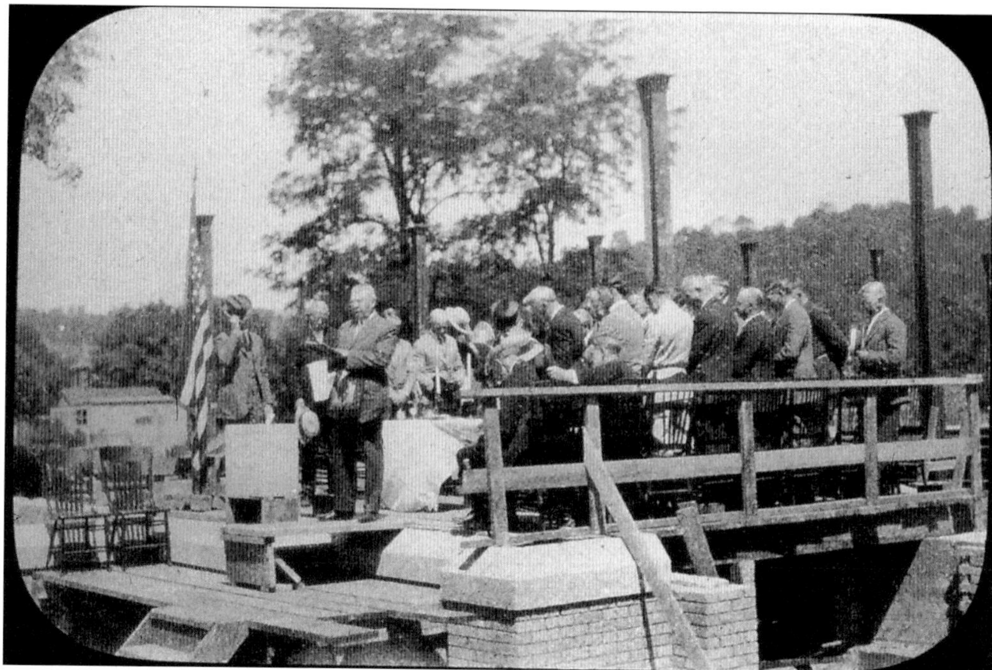

On March 11, 1926, the building committee recommended to the board of trustees that the contract to rebuild the church be awarded to the firm of Weber and Bell. The new church was dedicated in May 1927, and a week of special services marked the occasion.

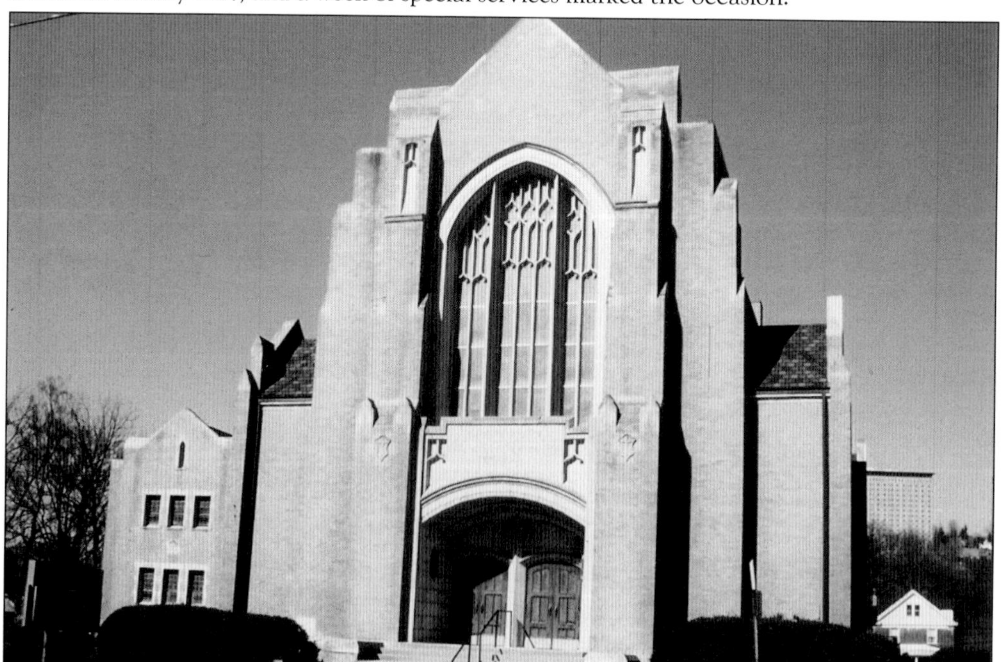

In 1939, the Methodist Episcopal Church of Madisonville became the Madisonville Methodist Church. During the 150th anniversary of the church, celebrated on December 9, 1951, a descendant of Uzziel Ward was baptized at the church. Today, it is the Korean-Madisonville United Methodist Church.

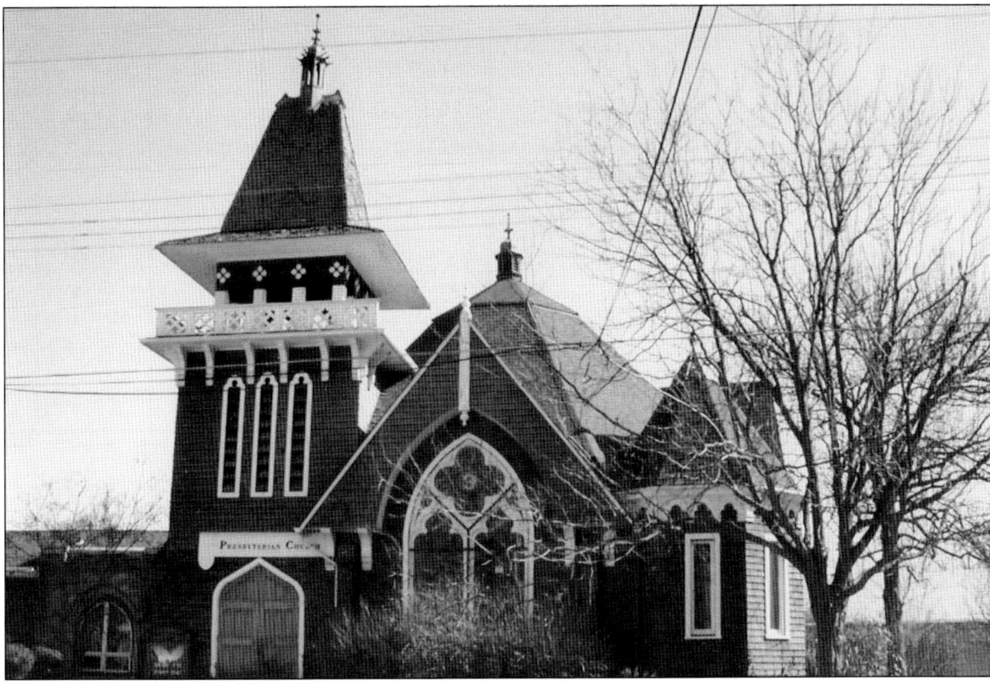

Eastminster Presbyterian Church members began holding services in Madisonville in 1867. In February 1880, the trustees purchased the lot at 4606 Erie Avenue and built the first church for $2,500 under Pastor Clarence Hills. On December 10, 1899, the present church was dedicated on the same frontage after the old building was moved to the rear of the property. The name Eastminster was adopted on May 6, 1932, under Pastor Henry Chace. In October 1937, the new brick Sunday school building was completed. The church thrived under Rev. Roland Skeel, who took over in 1952, and later under Rev. William Weckerly, who began in 1972. A tornado struck on October 1, 1977, and a tree almost five feet in diameter and over 100 years old fell across the front of the building. Branches caused weakening of the front stained glass window, loss of the tower, and extensive damage to inside plastered walls of the sanctuary, but all was rebuilt to its past glory.

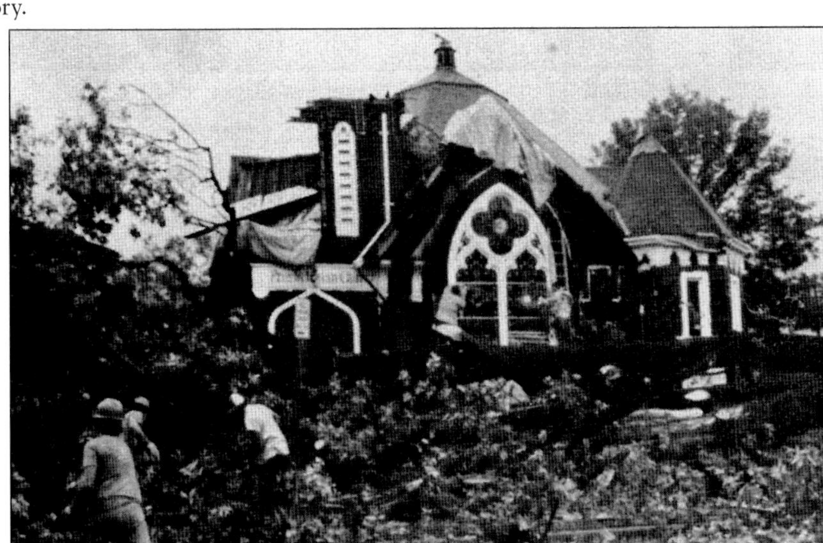

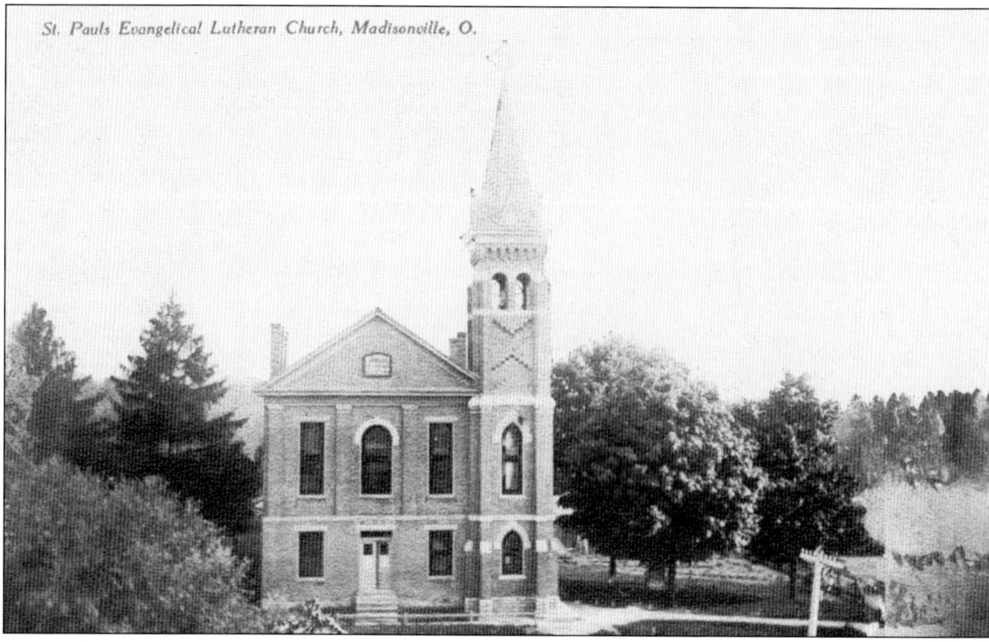

St. Paul Evangelical Lutheran Church was organized on February 16, 1868, and held its first services in Madisonville School. That March, a permanent site was purchased from Benjamin Stuart for $600, less a small donation of $50 by Stuart. Construction commenced immediately at 5433 Madison Road and concluded in December 1868, when the redbrick edifice was dedicated. Until the interior tower steps were built in 1884, the congregation climbed outside stairs to the upper-floor worshipping area; the pastor and his family lived on the first floor. All services were originally held in German, but in 1908, bimonthly English services were offered. In 1920, the church started offering German and English services every Sunday, and German services ceased in 1954. The parochial day school served 68 students after it opened in 1906.

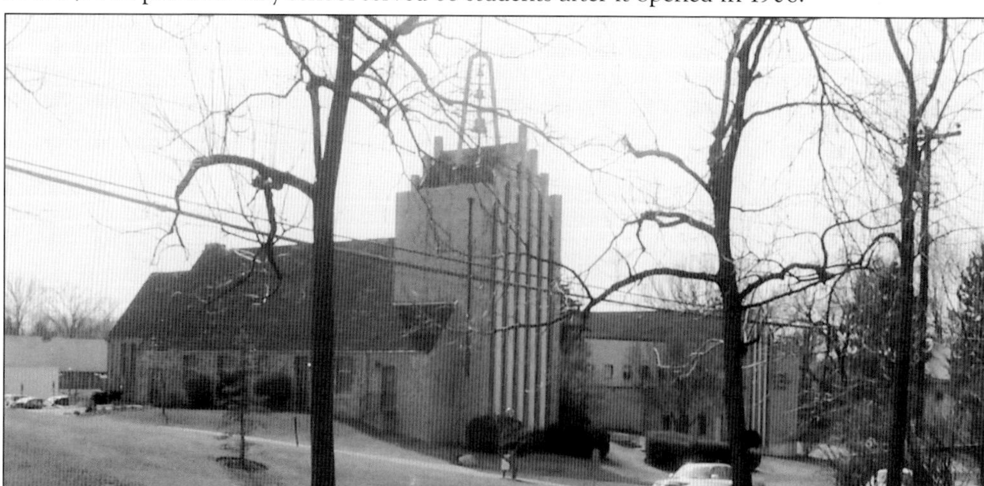

The St. Paul Evangelical Lutheran Church is seen here around 1958. In 1928, a fund was established to build a new church edifice, but it was not until January 17, 1943, that Edward J. Schulte was commissioned to draw up plans. Work started in 1951 on the site after tearing down the old church, and the new structure was dedicated in June 1952. By 1959, the congregation was looking forward to constructing a new school building and church tower.

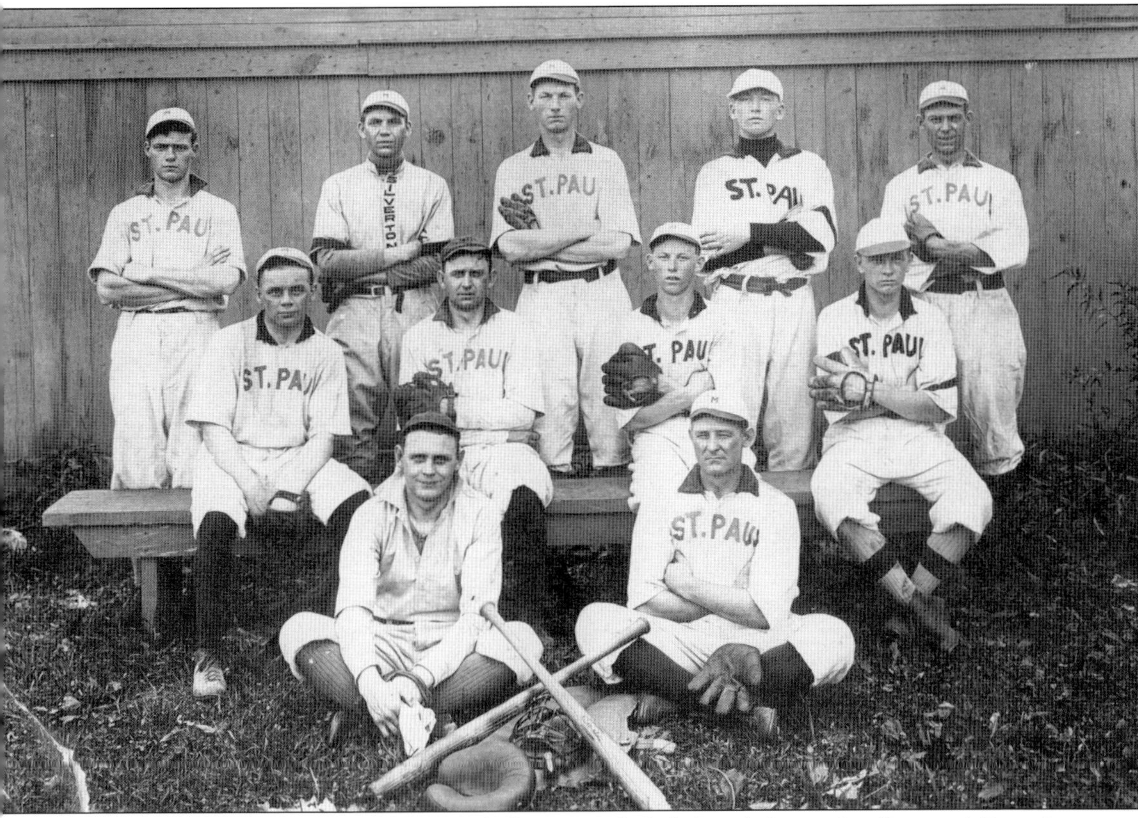

The 1912 St. Paul Lutheran Church baseball team included, from left to right, (first row) Ernie ? and Bill Kolthoff; (second row) Ernie Mwinzen, unidentified, Ed Ward Kroeger, and Fred Kolodzik; (third row) Al Kripeger, Otto Seilkop, Fred Kroeger, Bill Aker, and Ed Kolthoff. The beloved E.J. Ollmann (January 30, 1882–March 1, 1935) served the church for 28 years as a teacher at St. Paul Lutheran School, as well as organist, choir director, and secretary of St. Paul's Church. He would have taught these younger baseball players in school as well as the older players' children. Ollmann lived at 5421 Madison Road and his interment was held in the Laurel Cemetery.

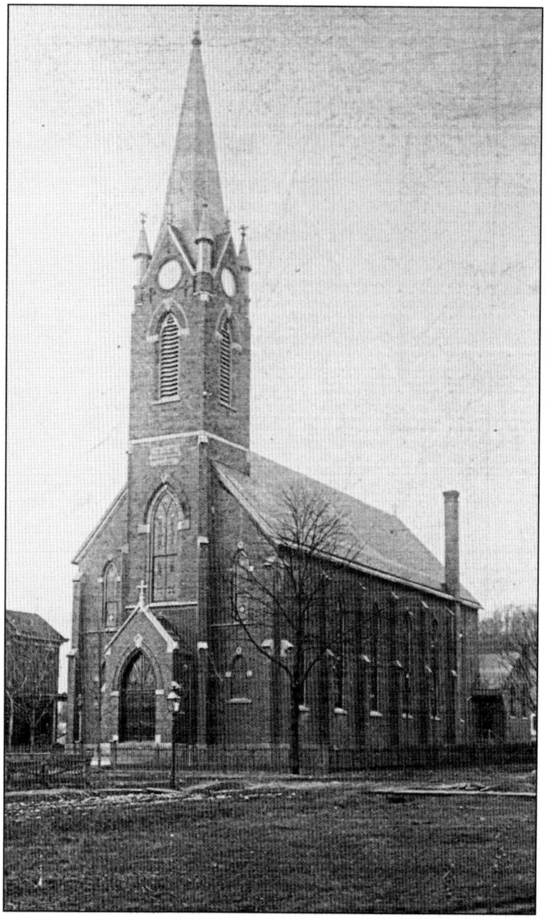

St. Anthony Church, seen here, was the first Catholic church in Madisonville and was considered the mother parish of the southeastern section of Cincinnati. In 1859, a small wooden church was dedicated by Archbishop John Purcell as St. Michael Church. Years later, Fr. Anthony Walburg saw the need for a larger building and a better location and donated a tract of land to build a brick church and school, dedicated in honor of St. Anthony in 1874.

The students of St. Anthony School gathered for this photograph in 1890. George V. Hack, "Manny" Hack's father, is fifth from left in the fourth row. The current four-story brick school, the third in parish history, was built in 1924. The St. Anthony School closed in 1977. The school building is now home to the Lighthouse Community School.

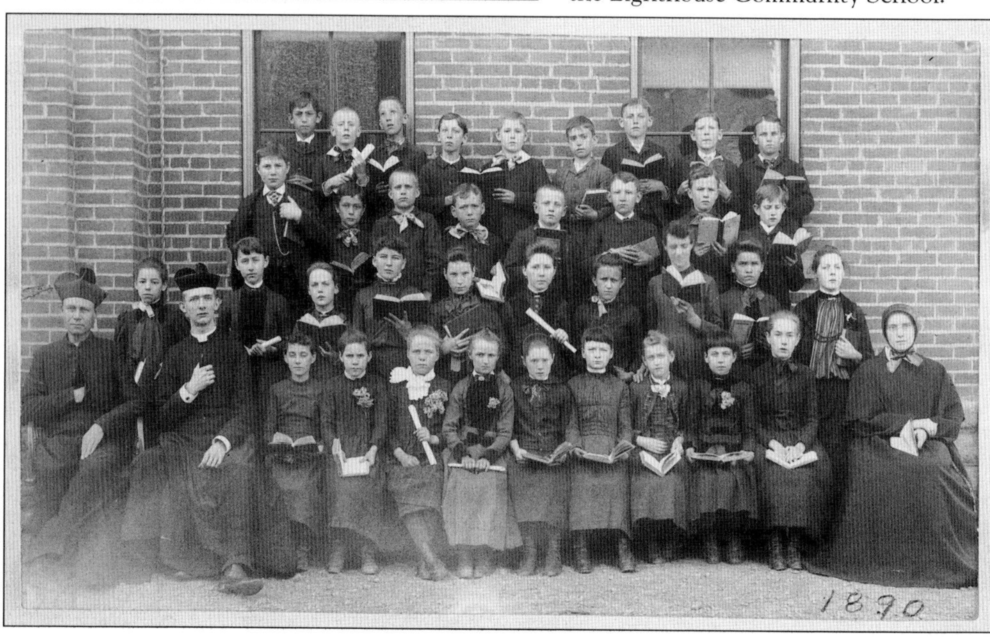

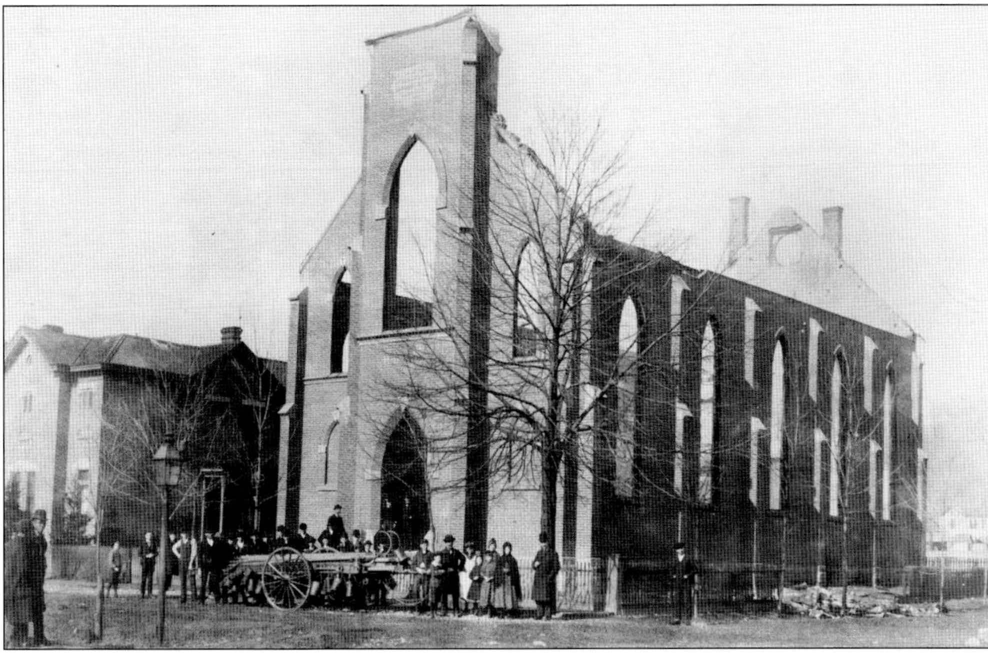

St. Anthony Church was destroyed by fire on January 25, 1891. The three altars and all the furnishings were destroyed within 30 minutes. In May of that same year, the cornerstone for the new St. Anthony Church was laid by Father Walburg and the pastor at the time, Father Hahne. The new church was dedicated in October 1891 in a ceremony officiated by Archbishop William Elder. A new bell, which was the gift of all the citizens of Madisonville regardless of creed or color, was dedicated that afternoon at a second ceremony.

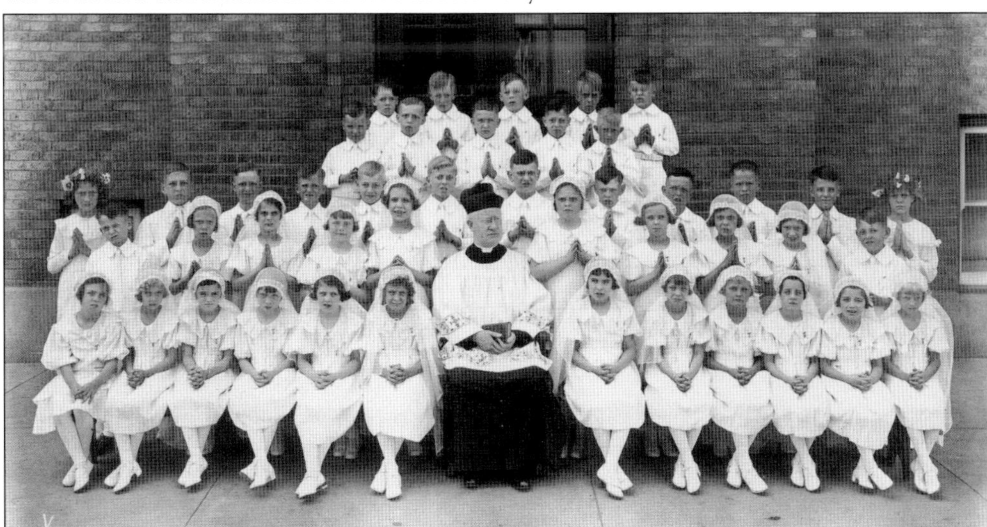

A First Communion class from the 1920s is pictured at St. Anthony's Church. First Communion is an important festive occasion for Roman Catholic families. Traditions surrounding First Communion usually include large family gatherings and parties to celebrate the event, and special clothing is worn. The clothing is often white to symbolize purity. Girls wear fancy white dresses and a veil attached to a wreath of flowers or a hair ornament. These were commonly passed down to them from sisters or their mother.

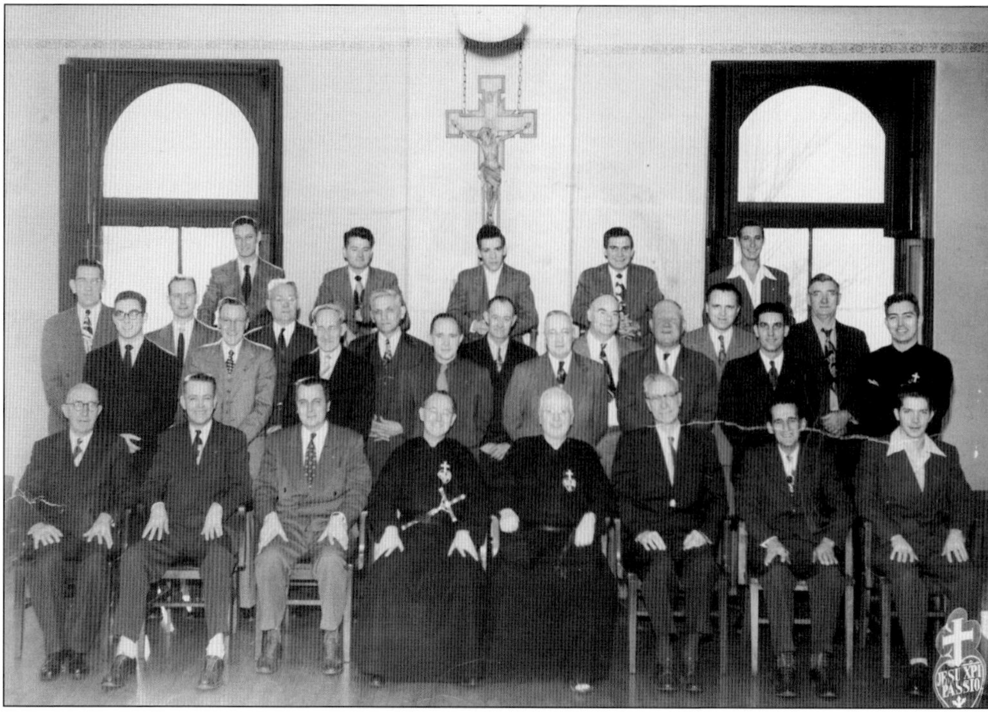

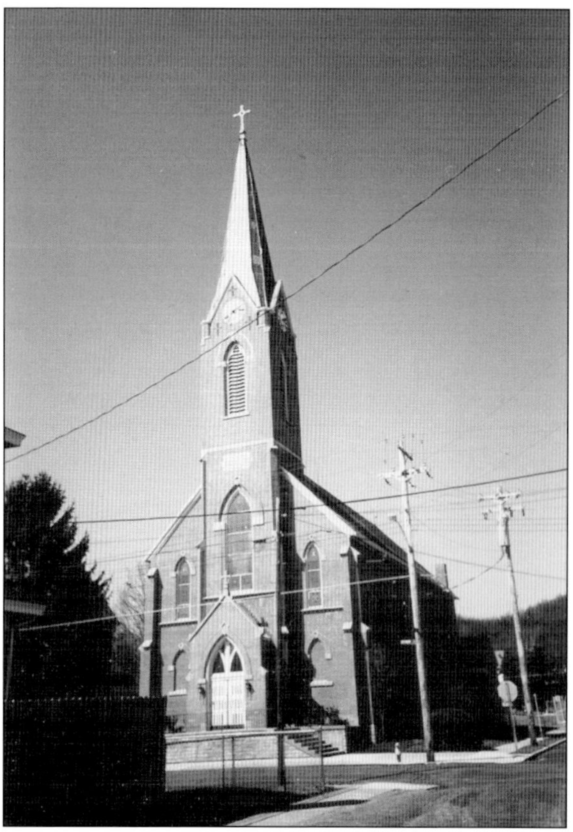

This group gathered for a photograph at the St. Anthony Madisonville Retreat on December 8–10, 1950, with pastor Rev. Henry A. Westleman presiding.

On July 1, 1902, the congregation of St. Anthony Church received a clock for the church tower from the residents of Madisonville. The clock was valued at $625 and was the only public clock tower in Madisonville. There were several expansions and modernizations of the church, rectory, and school. In 1909, the church celebrated its golden jubilee with Archbishop Henry Moeller presiding, and Archbishop John McNicholas presided at its diamond jubilee in 1934. St. Anthony Church is now over 150 years old.

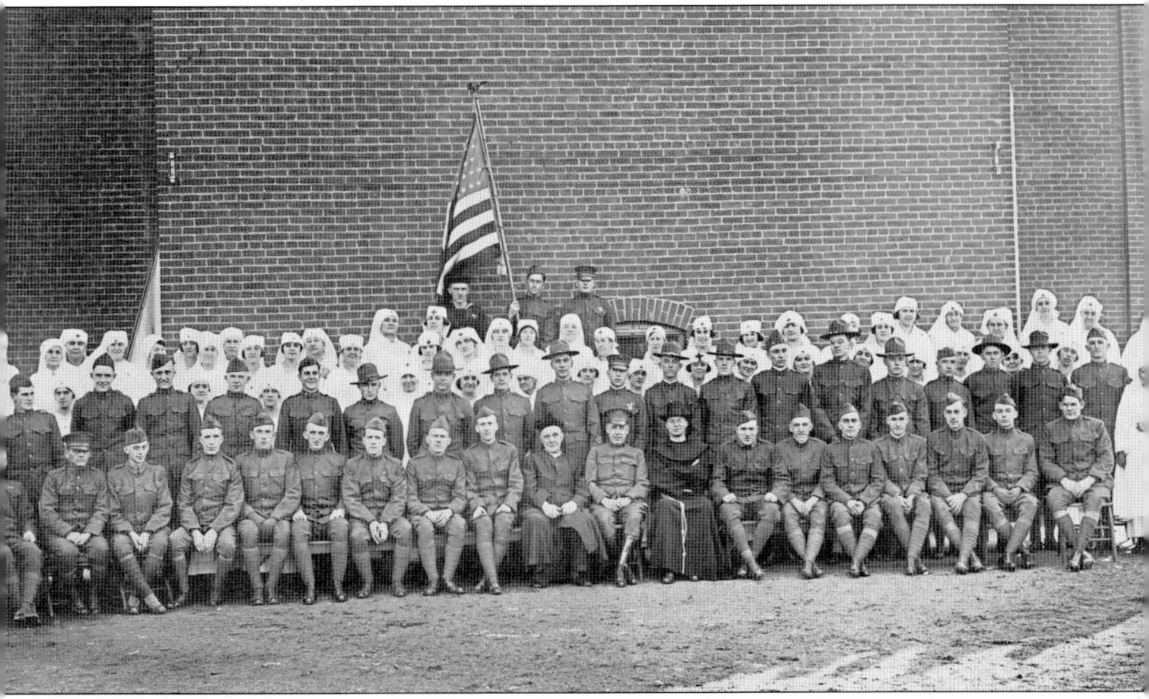

This is a souvenir photograph of the "Blessing of the Bronze Tablet" on November 30, 1919. The tablet was erected in St. Anthony Church to perpetuate the patriotic deeds of the soldiers and Red Cross members of the congregation from 1917 to 1919.

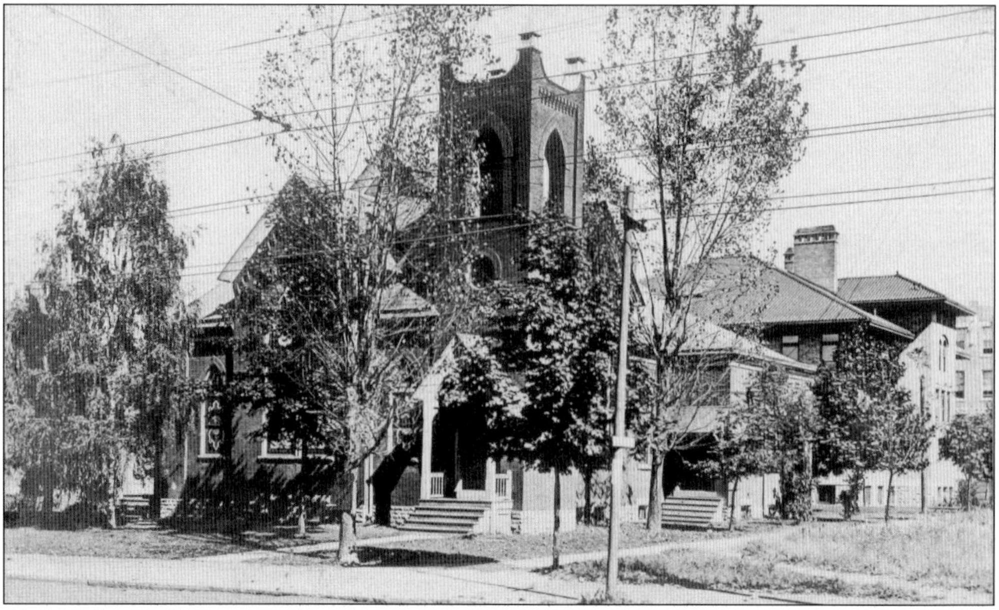

The Madisonville Baptist Church at 4814 Whetsel Avenue was dedicated on July 6, 1876, by Pastor H.L. King but was destroyed by fire on February 24, 1889. The church was rebuilt at a cost of $5,666.86 on the same site and was rededicated on September 18, 1889, by committee members W.H. Settle, J.F. Bramble, and L.G. Joynes. Unfortunately, this church building was short-lived, also being destroyed by fire on May 7, 1892. The third and present building was built at a cost of $6,898.38 and dedicated on December 19, 1892, by committee members W.H. Settle, W.A. Hunt, and R.W. Lowther. In 1899, electric lights were installed, and in 1909, steam heating was installed, along with new floor covering and frescoed walls. In 1921, the church school was built at a cost of $16,000, and in 1925, the pipe organ was installed for $4,000.

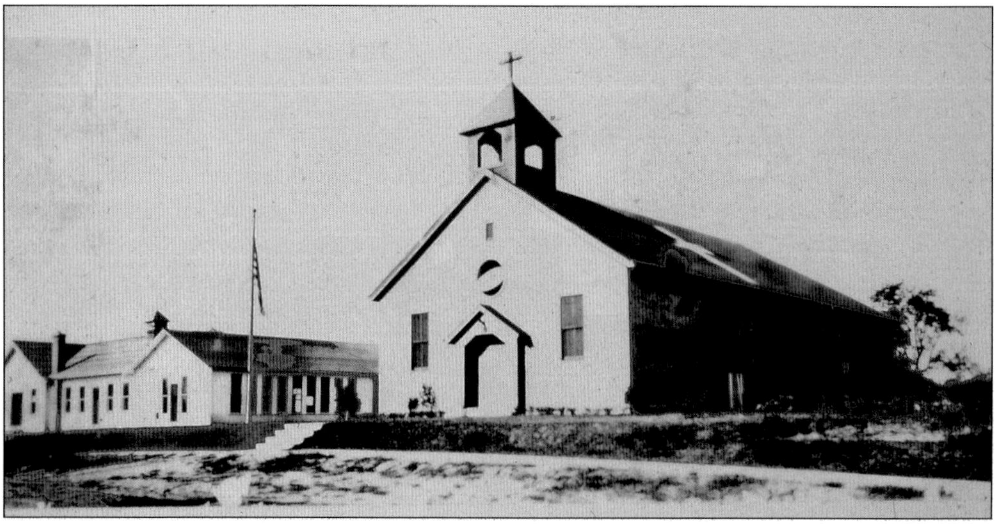

St. Margaret of Cortona Church was created by ardent Catholics in the south Madisonville-Fairfax area who found traveling to St. Anthony Church a hardship. Archbishop Moeller met them with enthusiastic approval to build a parish to serve the area. The church was built on a field of mud on the corner of Islington Avenue and Watterson Avenue in 1920. The original church building is now Cortona Hall.

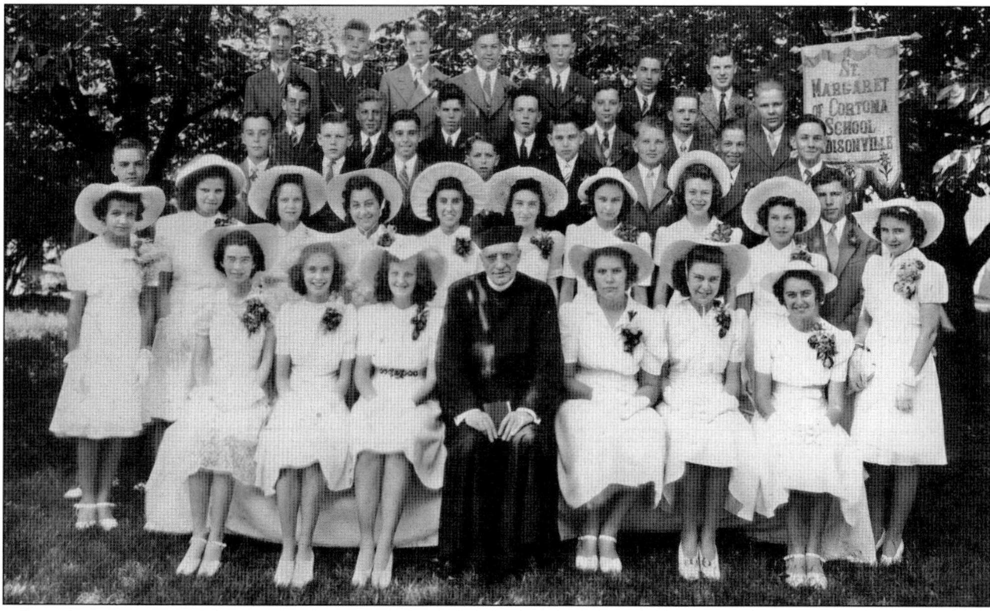

This photograph of the eighth-grade graduating class of 1941 from St. Margaret of Cortona School shows, from left to right, (first row) M. Coffey, J. Aubrey, L. Roelker, Fr. Eugene Gerlach, A. Belser, R. Bruemmer, and M. Kollman; (second row) J. Louden, E. Maue, M. Verdon, Ruth Ann Busald, D. Oswald, H. Poland, M. Edmonds, H. Cook, A. Reidy, and J. Bath; (third row) E. Meyer, J. Wilmers, R. Schultz, D. Stricker, B. Murphy, B. Ruggerio, B. Granger, B. Roma, W. Nieman, and J. Mulvaney; (fourth row) B. Wieland, A. Heller, B. Kelly, F. Flemming, T. Hunneman, B. Welsch, and C. Rape; (fifth row) W. Flammers, H. Buetke, A. Fischer, B. McMahon, W. Sterman, T. Yaegel, and E. Cornelius.

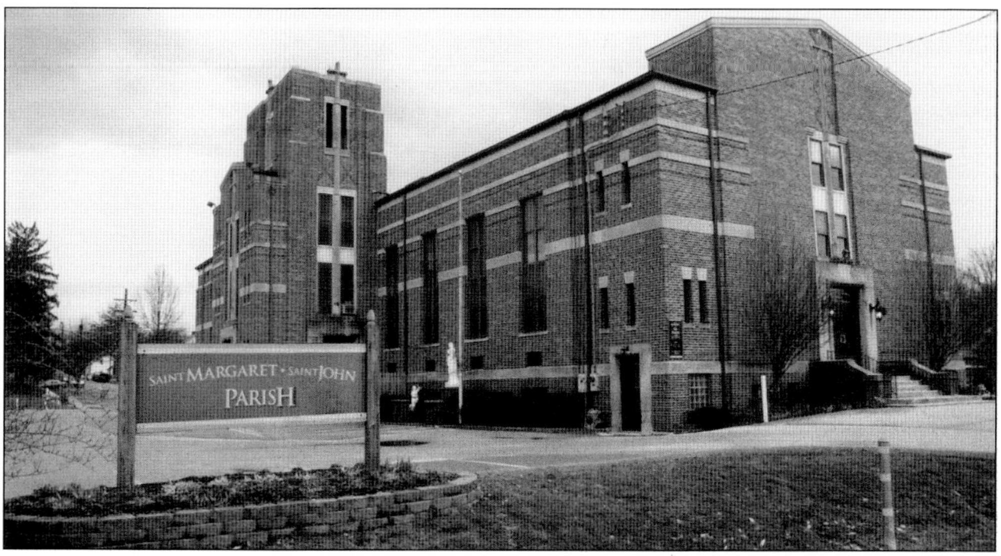

The first section of the current St. Margaret of Cortona School was dedicated in an October 1927 mass. The first midnight mass was held in the current church building on December 25, 1950. The current school and church building was dedicated in a mass by Archbishop Karl Alter in June 1951. St. Margaret's and St. John's congregations have since combined. The school has been renamed Prince of Peace Catholic School.

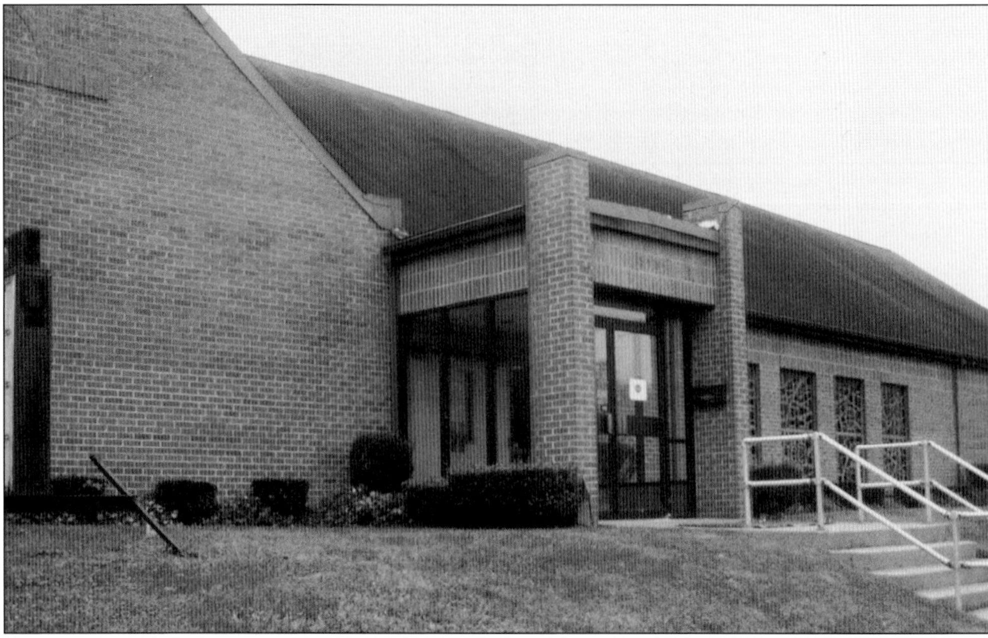

The Gaines United Methodist Church came from humble beginnings in 1873, holding services in a building at the corner of Roanoke Street and Madison Road. By 1884, a small frame building (below) was moved from Red Bank Road to Desmond Street and became the congregation's first church. The congregation moved to another location before 1980, when the present church was dedicated. Planning for the present church began in 1978 and ground was broken in September 1979 on this third building of the Gaines United Methodist Church at 5707 Madison Road. Two houses were demolished to make way for this church and grounds, which sit on two acres. Services began in November 1980.

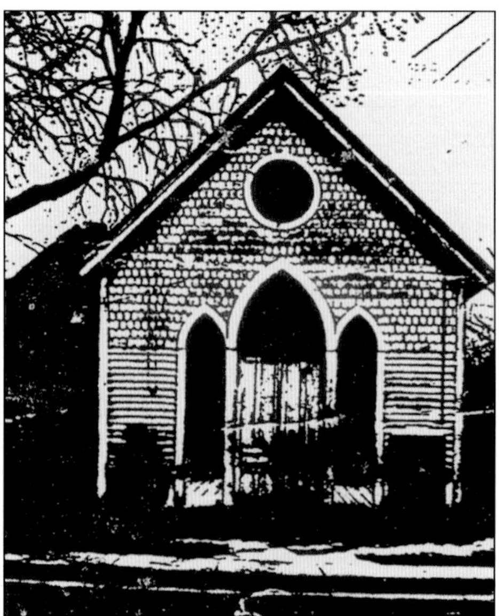

First Building of the Gaines United Methodist Church was located on Desmond St.

The Dunbar area, between Old Red Bank Road and Red Bank Expressway, was settled by African Americans in the early 1800s. This church was built in the Dunbar area in 1907 by the New Mission Missionary Baptist Church and was occupied until 1963, when a new church was built on Ravenna Street. This little church continued to be used, most recently as the Macedonia Primitive Baptist Church, but it was demolished in 1995 when the area was redeveloped.

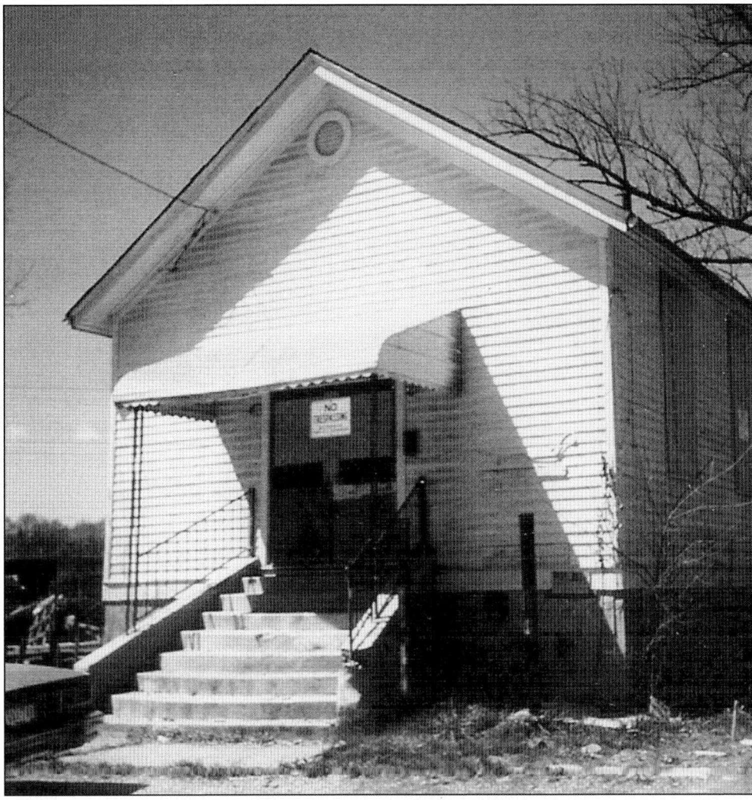

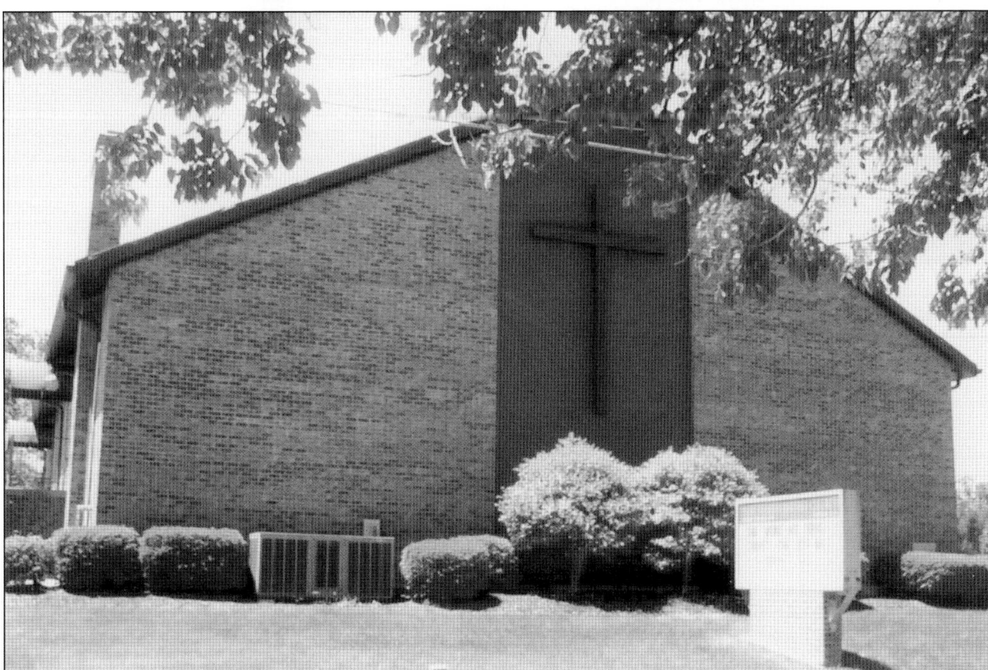

After moving in 1963 to Ravenna Street, the New Mission Missionary Baptist Church thrived, soon outgrowing the new church. In the 1980s, a new church was constructed.

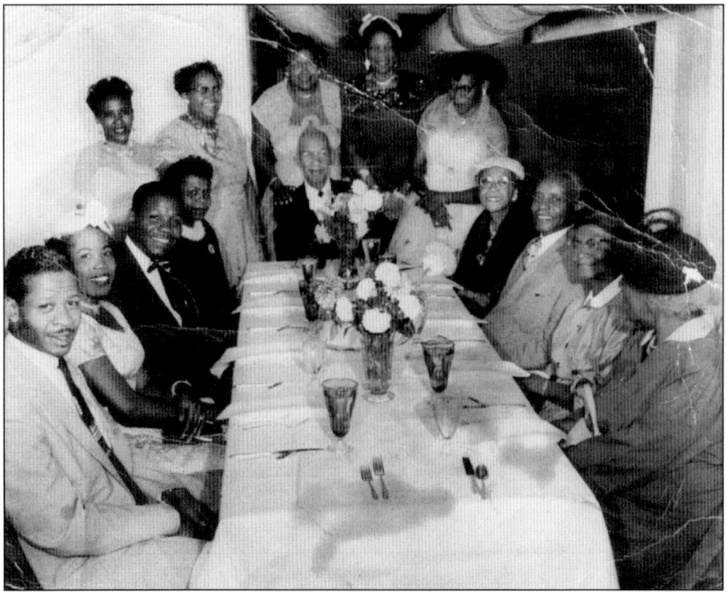

This 1950s dinner reception was held in the basement of the New Mission Missionary Baptist Church in Dunbar and included, from left to right, (sitting on left side) Rev. G. Brown, A. Brown, Reverend Williams, and M. Williams; (standing) M. Harshaw, F. Henley, B. Thomas, L. Williams, and B. Green; (sitting on right side) G. Sullivan, M. Sullivan, Reverend Dunlap, ? Dunlap, and unidentified.

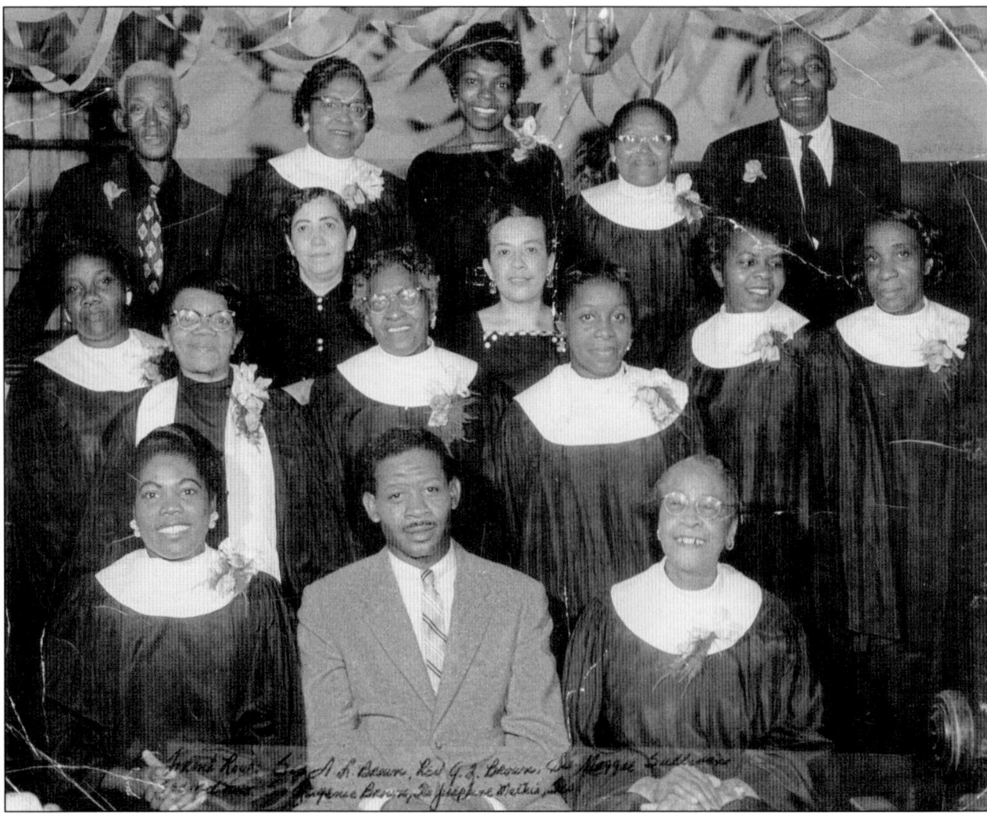

The Baptist choir at the little New Mission Missionary Baptist Church in Dunbar included A. Brown, Rev. C. Brown, M. Sullivan, L. Brown, J. Mathis, J. Hamilton, Papa Rice, and three King sisters.

Five

Postwar Heydays

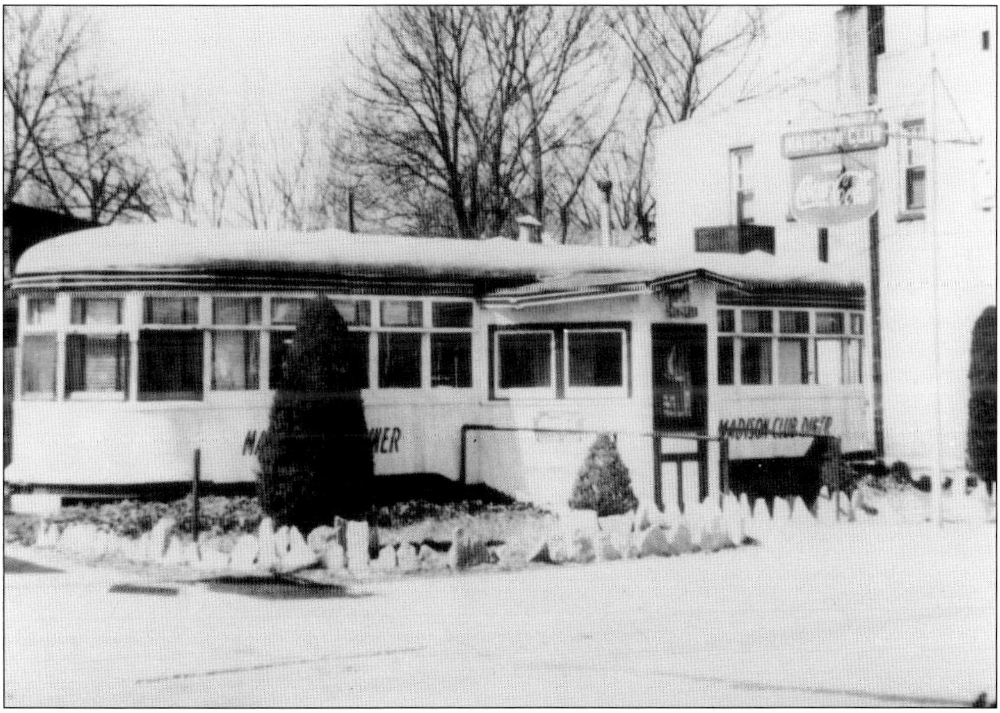

The Madison Club Diner on Plainville was a 1940s classic. Before the regional shopping centers, most Cincinnati neighborhoods had their own shopping districts. One of the most inclusive and largest centers was in Madisonville, clustered mainly along Madison Road and Whetsel Avenue. From the 1930s to 1960s, with the expansion of businesses along these corridors, Madisonville became the commercial center for eastern Cincinnati. Shoppers attracted from the surrounding towns, villages, and unincorporated areas could find just about anything they needed in the complex of available stores and shops. A short inventory of those stores includes: 12 food stores, 8 clothing and shoe stores, 10 eating places, 4 pharmacies, 10 service stations, 7 banks and financial institutions, 10 furniture stores, 3 bakeries, 5 beauty salons, 2 jewelers, 3 small gift shops, a 5&10¢ store, 3 auto dealers, 2 record shops, 2 dry cleaners, 2 flower shops, a camera store, a bicycle shop, 2 barbers, and stores for electrical and automotive supplies, paint and hardware, and coal and building materials.

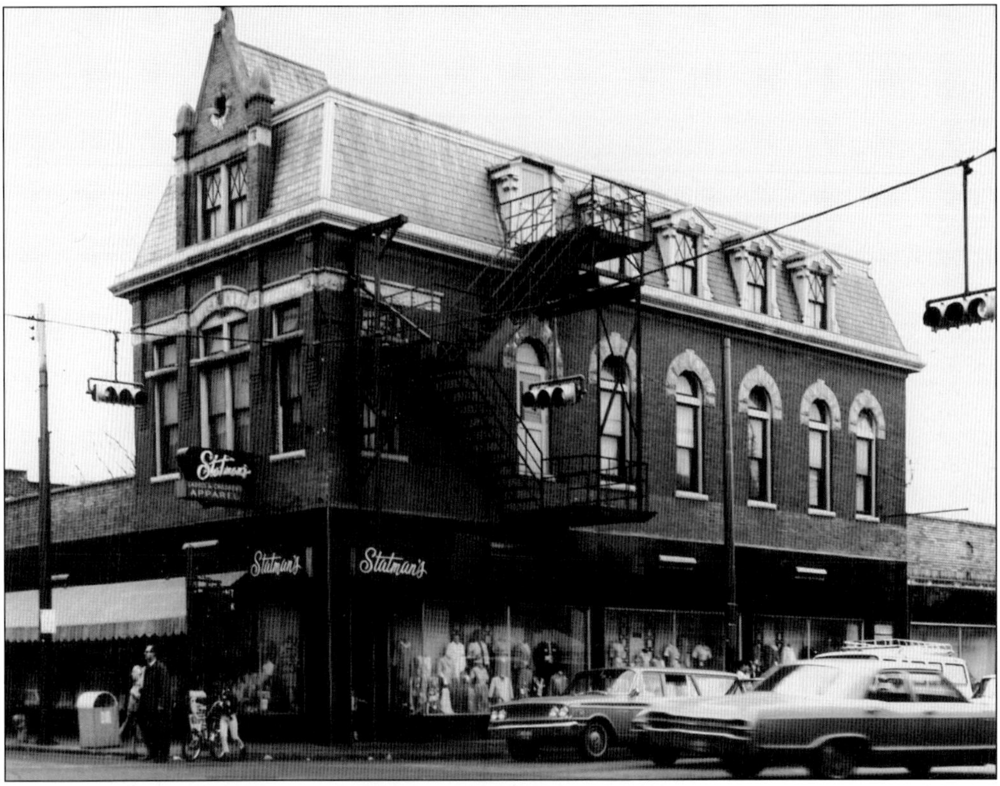

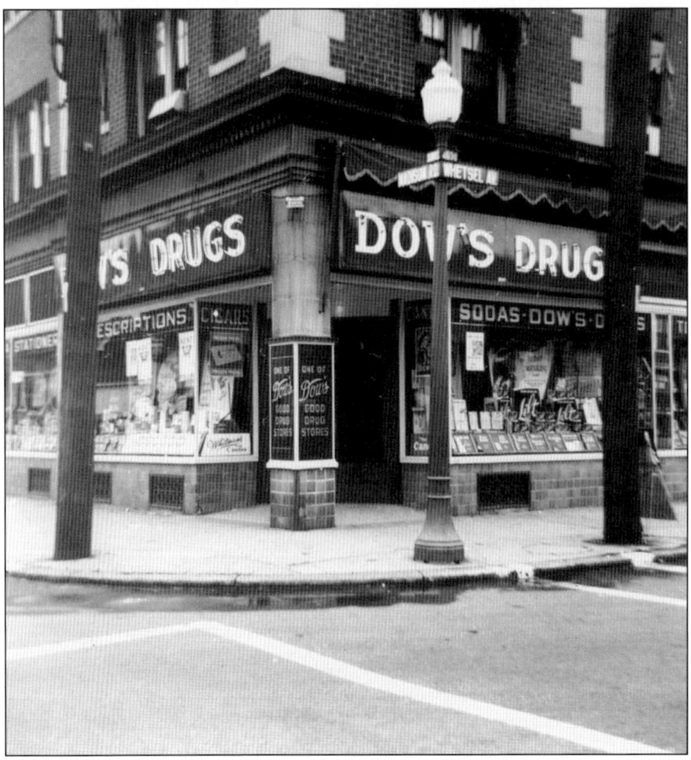

Since 1896, this building on the southwest corner of Madison Road and Whetsel Avenue has welcomed generations of Madisonville residents and others to the square. During the heyday of the business district, it housed Stein's Ready to Wear and, later, Statman's Department Store. The building became vacant in 1985 and fell victim to the wrecking ball in 2003.

One of the main stores in the Madison Building, constructed in 1925, was Dow's Drugs, seen here in the 1950s.

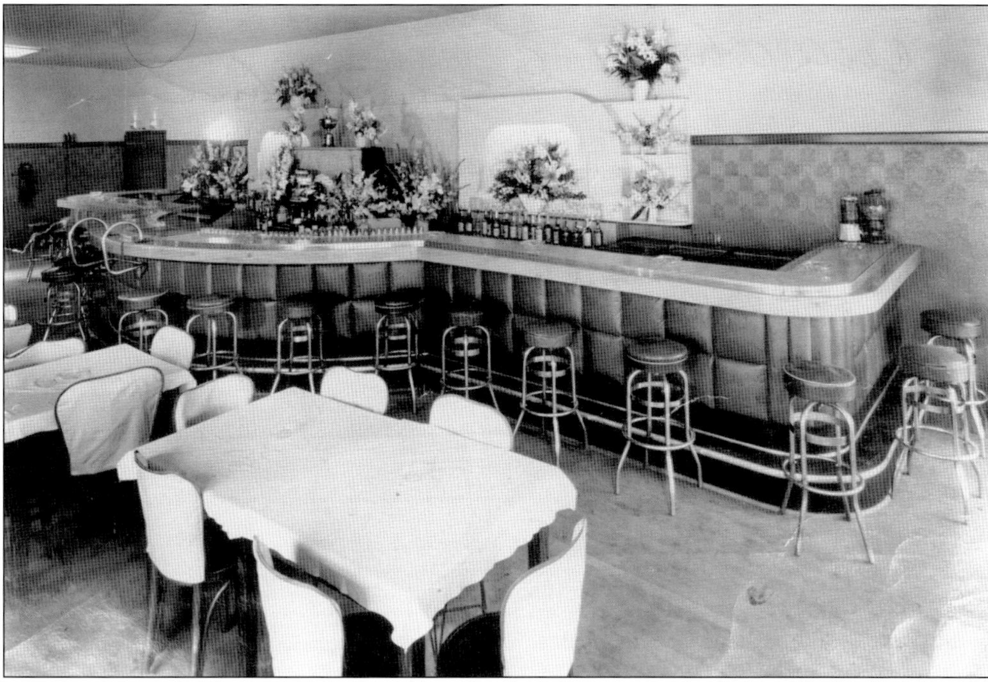

Built in the 1930s, George Hahnel's Piano Bar, seen here in 1948, was at the corner of Bramble Avenue and Plainville Road. It is a longtime gathering place where everybody knows your name and it is currently known as the Bramble Patch and owned by Paul Schweppe, a longtime Madisonville resident. This local establishment has changed hands several times, but the interior looks similar to the way it did long ago.

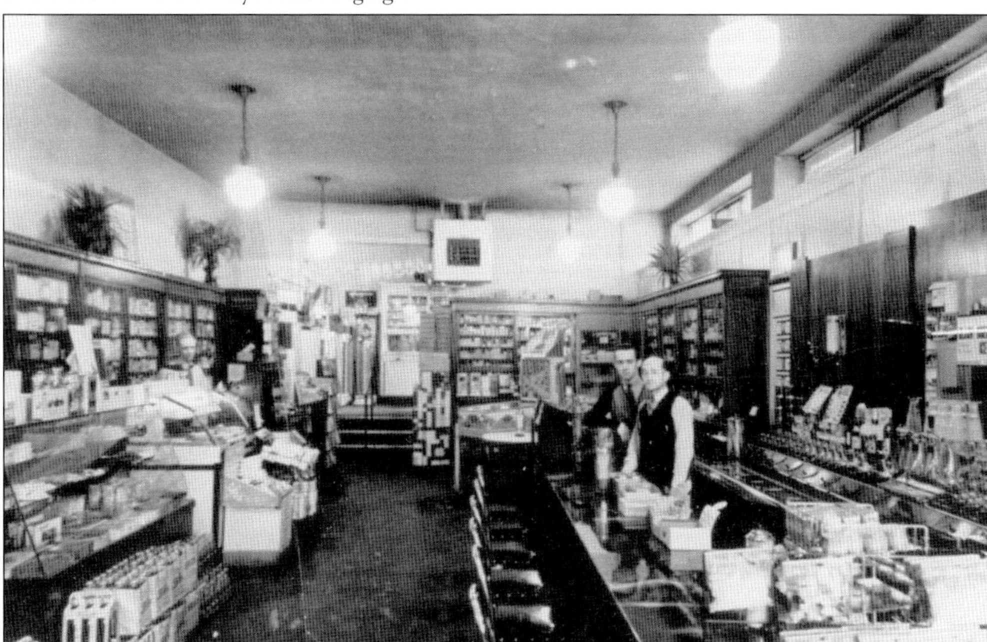

Albert Koehler (nearest) stands behind the counter at Koehler Pharmacy, on the corner of Bramble and Whetsel Avenues, in the 1940s.

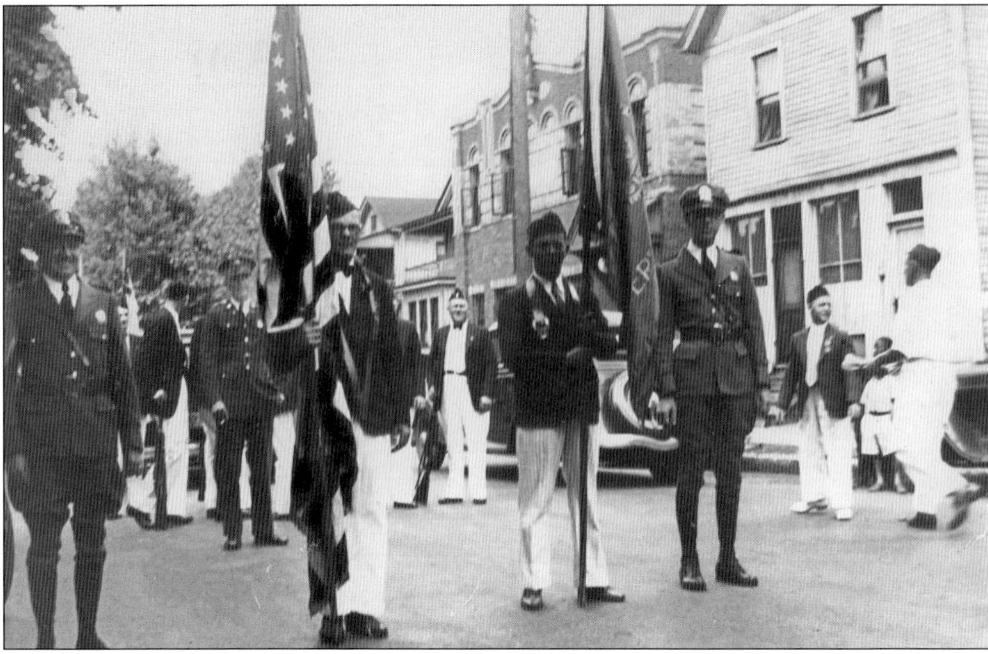

The Memorial Day Parade in 1935 moves from upper Whetsel Avenue past the old police substation. The front four men are, from left to right, Edward Penny, Warren Hunt, Oscar Buxton, and Martin Wehr.

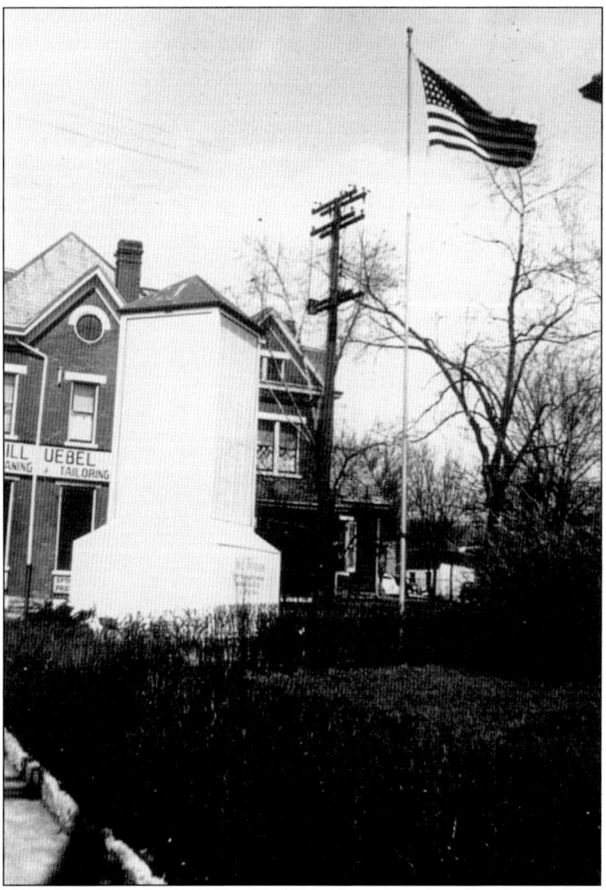

The Memorial to Armed Forces of World War II was located on the corner of library property at Whetsel Avenue and Prentice Street. As young men left to enter the armed services, their names were painted on this wooden monument. This structure stood for years until it was replaced in 1950 by a permanent memorial.

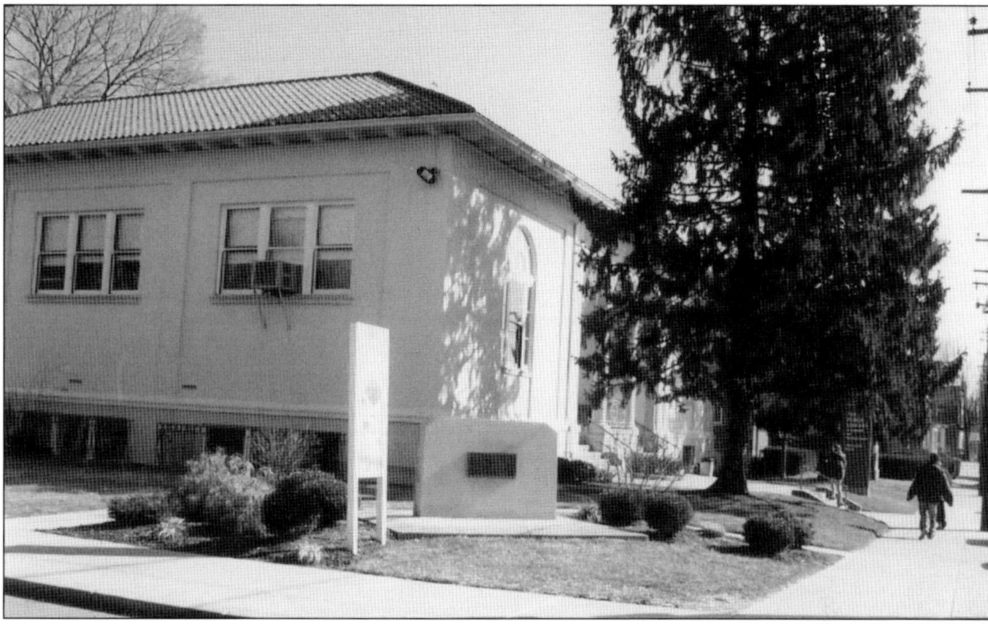

The Madisonville Library Memorial Corner was dedicated in November 1950 with a granite monument in honor of the war dead of the community. Erected by the Edward C. Gehlert Post, American Legion, the memorial was accepted on behalf of the citizens of Madisonville by Fred G. Ward, whose great-great-grandfather reportedly settled in the area in 1795. A permanent record of the names on the honor roll was maintained during World War II.

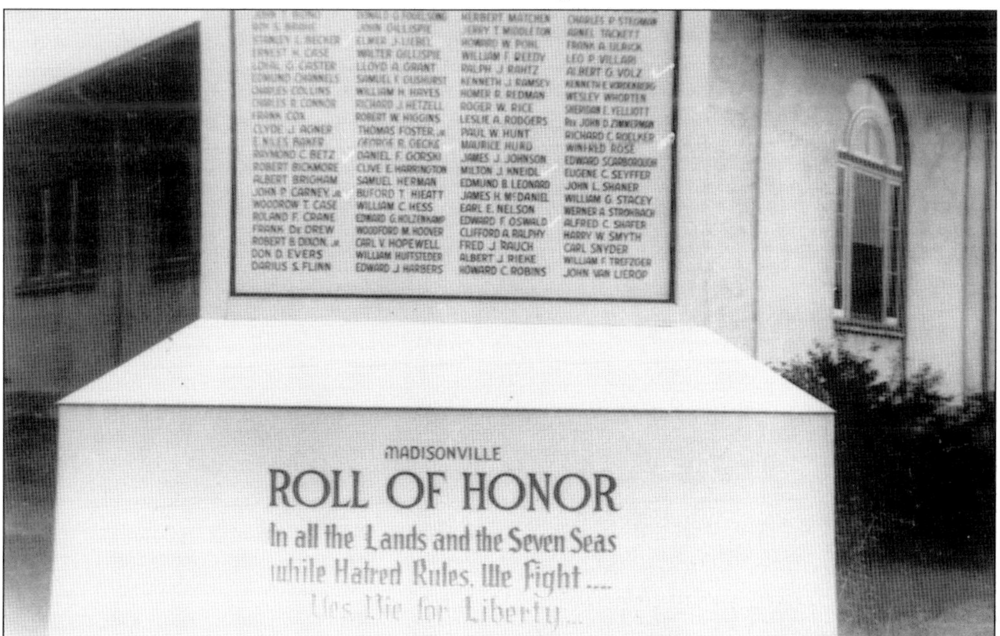

Armed forces members included in one section of the Roll of Honor are V. Mannino, P. Mannino, T. Ford, P. Steuter, B. Losh, P. Busam, J. Meckstroth, S. Lanam, J. Downs, E. Frank, L. Frank, B. Kisser, J. Carrol, W. Wolf, J. Sniering, W. Dunn, B. Martin, J. Kneipp, C. Kneipp, L. Bicket, J. Riehle, W. Schmidt, R. Bicket , ? Frankenberg, B. Shay, A. Kiefer, D. Busald, E. Ross, and C. Werley.

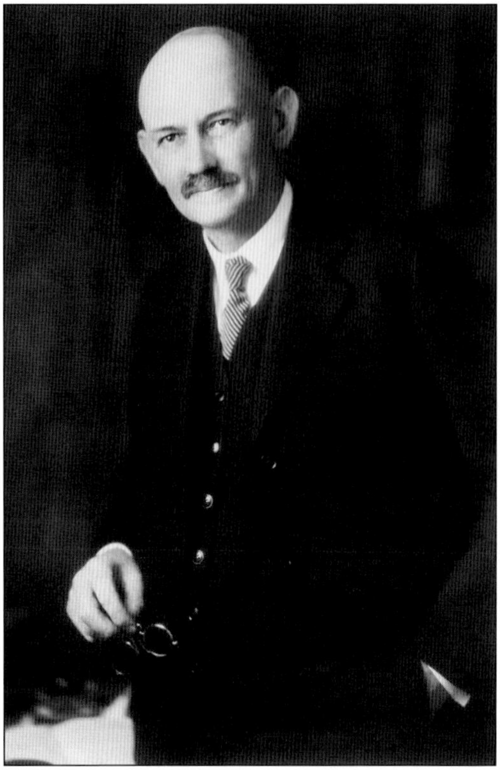

Dr. Arthur L. Knight practiced medicine on Erie Avenue in Madisonville for 46 years after graduating from Miami Medical College in Cincinnati in 1880. Dr. Knight served as the chief of staff at Good Samaritan Hospital from 1925 to 1929 and was a member of the American Medical Association, American College of Physicians, and Academy of Medicine. He was also a founding member of the Madisonville Round Table. He died in his home in Madisonville in 1936 at the age of 70.

Dr. Paul Grove was another prominent physician in Madisonville who lived at 4907 Stewart Avenue in the Madison-Stewart National Register District. His former house was demolished in 1980 to make way for the St. Paul Lutheran Village housing expansion.

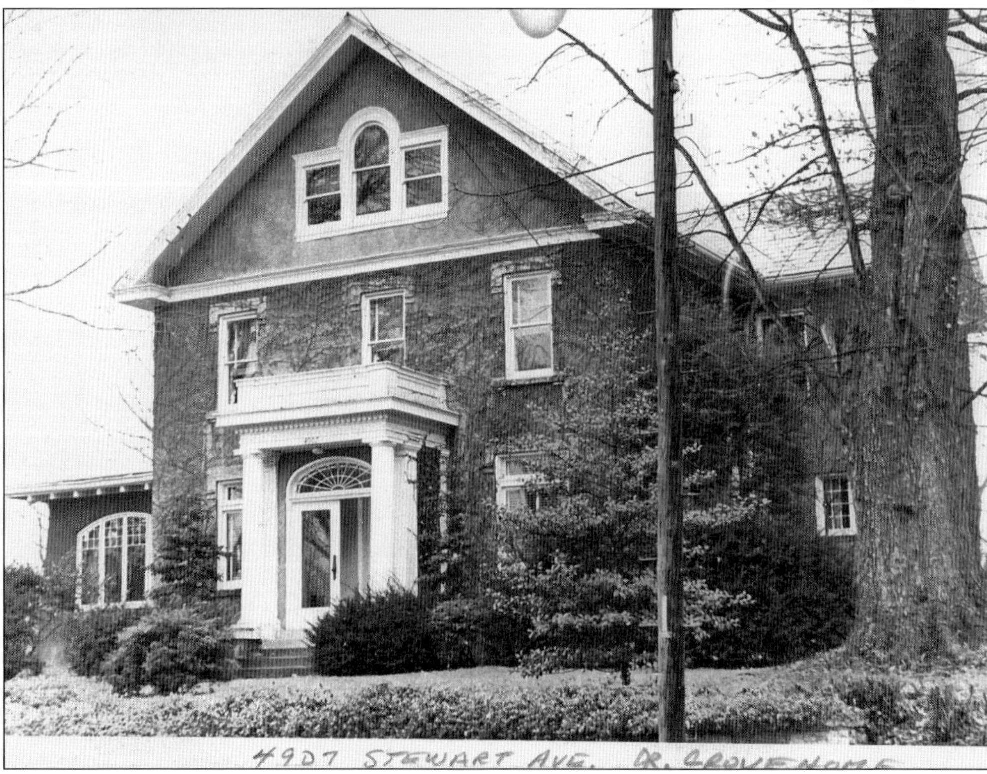

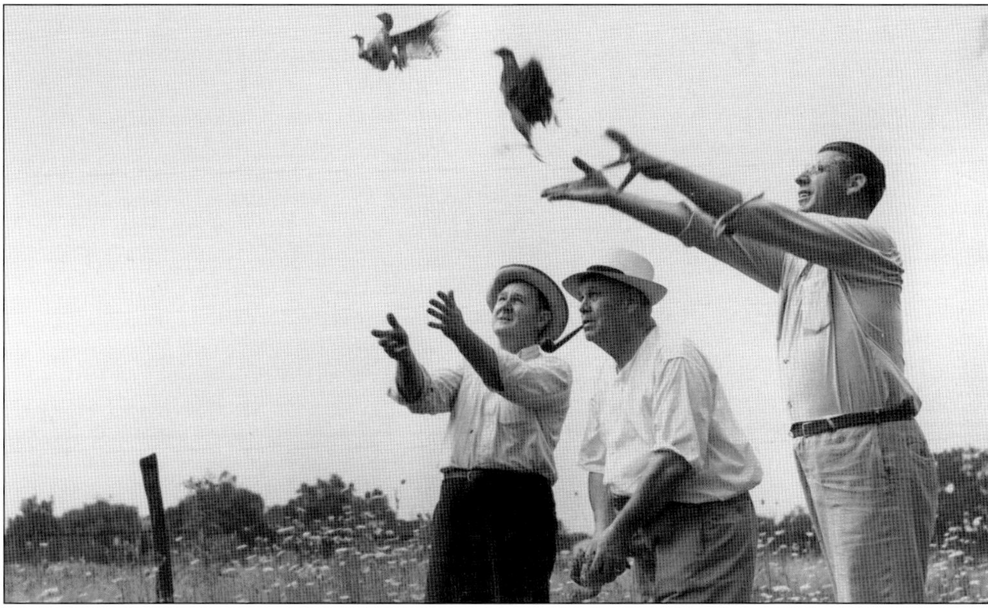

Madisonville resident George V. Hack and his son, Emmanuel George "Manny" Hack, of 6225 Madison Road, placed third in a homing pigeon race from Warrensburgh, Missouri, to Cincinnati in July 1933. His birds covered the 507 miles in 11 hours and 28 minutes. Here, Manny Hack (left) and his friends release guinea hens for a race in 1948, by which time passenger pigeons were extinct.

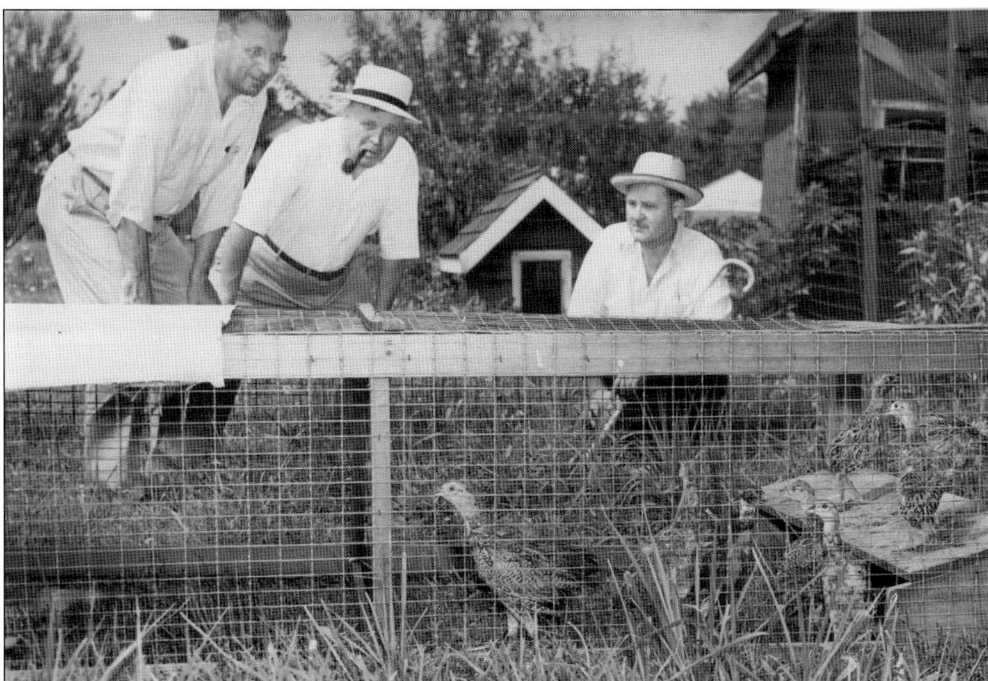

Manny Hack (right) raised several varieties of birds as well as other animals. After being stationed in Mexico during his military service, he brought home some animals for the Cincinnati Zoo. He was well known in Madisonville for his love of animals.

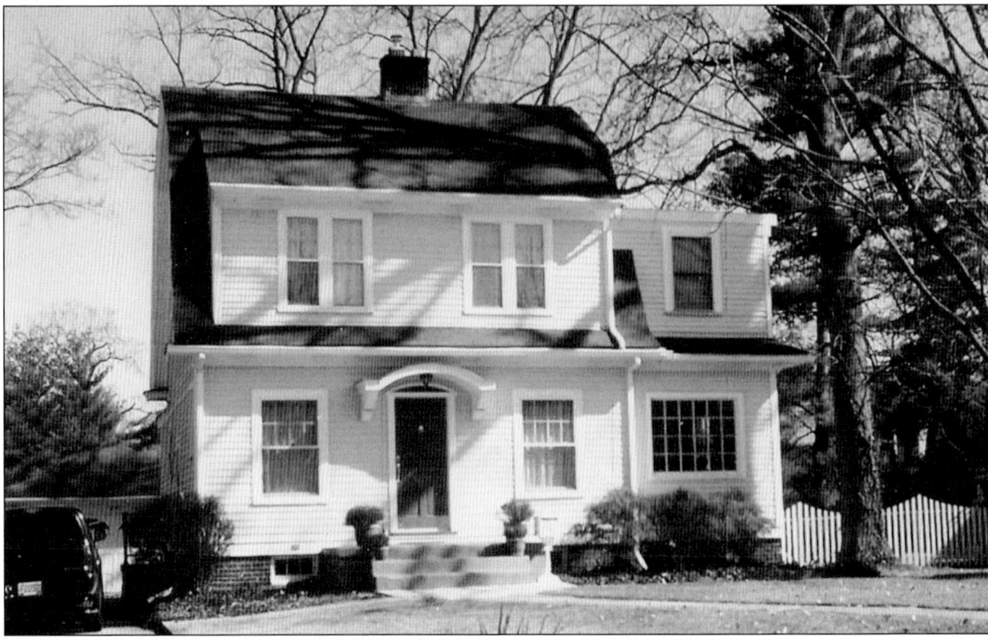

This 1932 Sears house is on Eastwood Circle in the Eastwood Historic District, which is listed in the National Register. The house is the Puritan model, a two-story Dutch Colonial house with hooded front entrance, wood siding, gambrel roof, and original latticed porte cochere over the driveway. These Sears catalog homes were sold to customers pre-packaged to be delivered on-site, containing all material down to the kitchen sink.

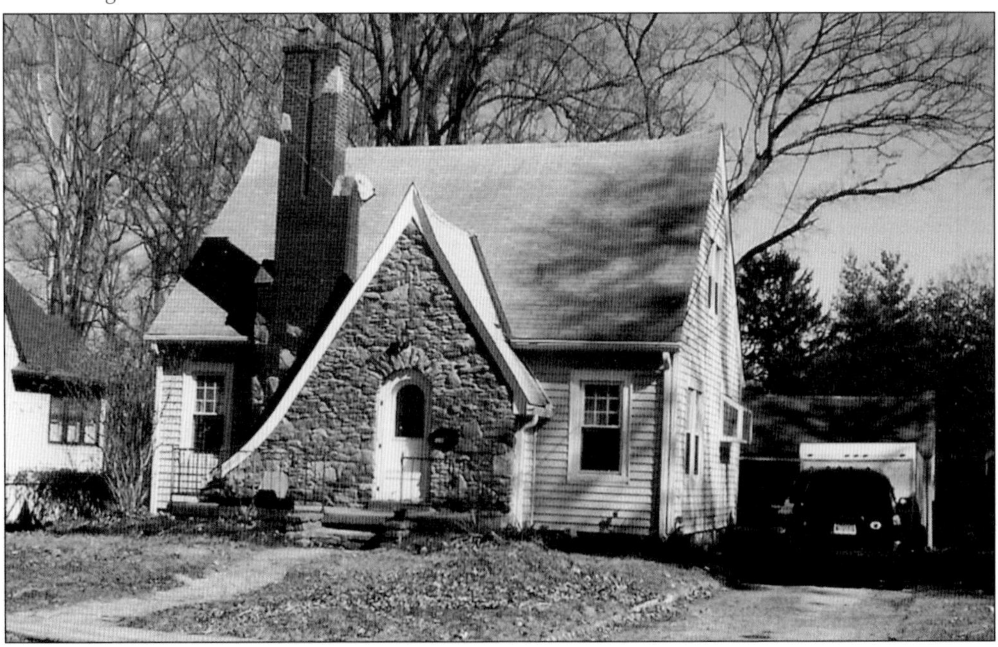

Another Sears house kit, this small one, called the Maplewood, has a matching detached double-garage. It features a prominent brick and stone chimney next to the front-facing gable with one flared side sweeping closer to the ground than the other. "S" is stamped on the basement stonework, indicating a Sears house.

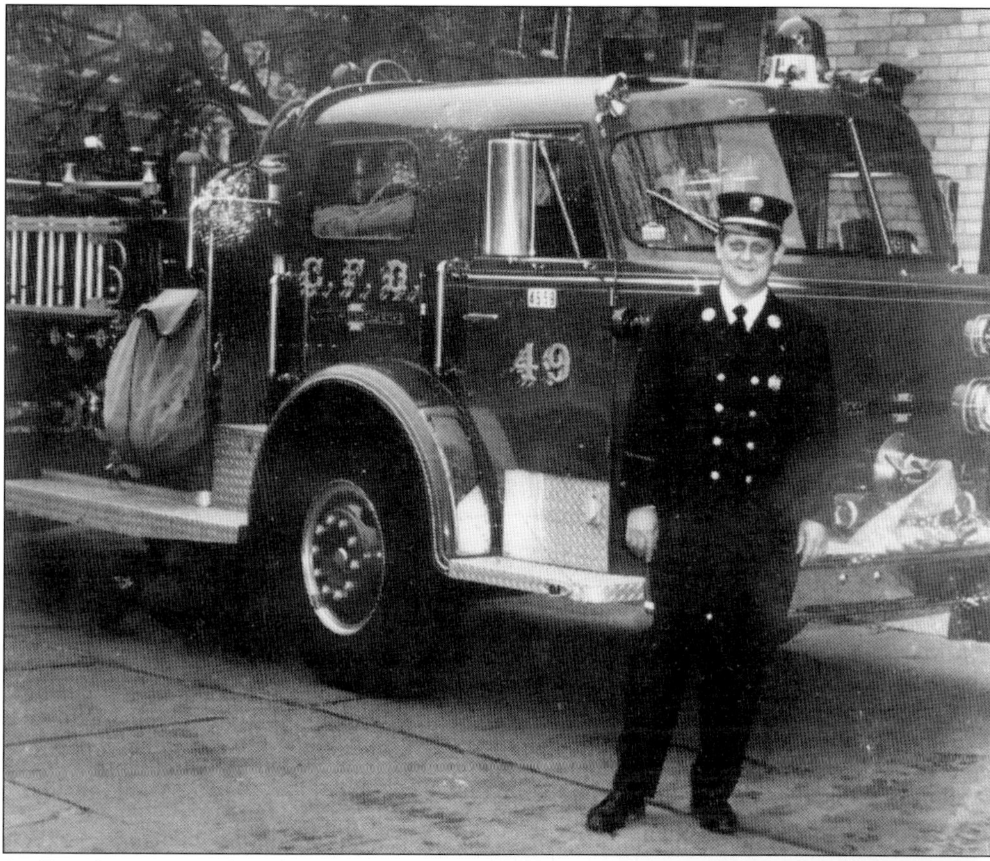

Lt. Don Stange served at the Madisonville firehouse in the 1940s, as did his great-uncle, Albert Hack, who was a volunteer with the company in 1910, when the present firehouse was built.

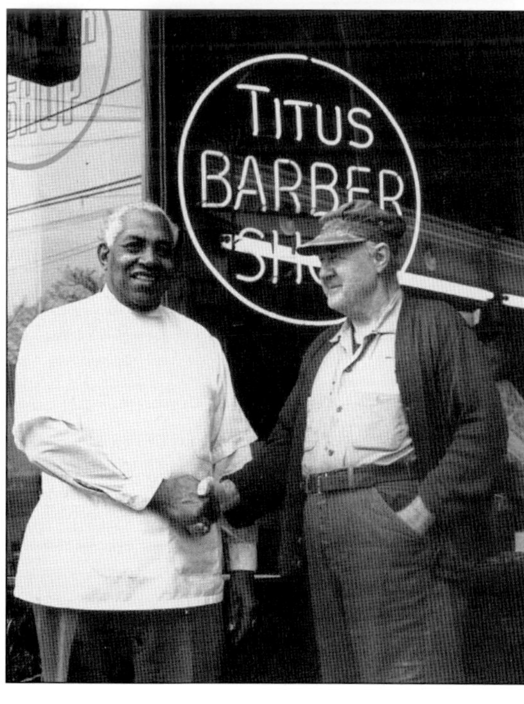

Alfred Titus (left) stands in front of his barbershop with Manny Hack. Titus and his friend David Benne learned their trade as young men from master barber Eli Gifford in the early 1900s. Both apprentices established shops in Madisonville; Benne stayed active into his 80s.

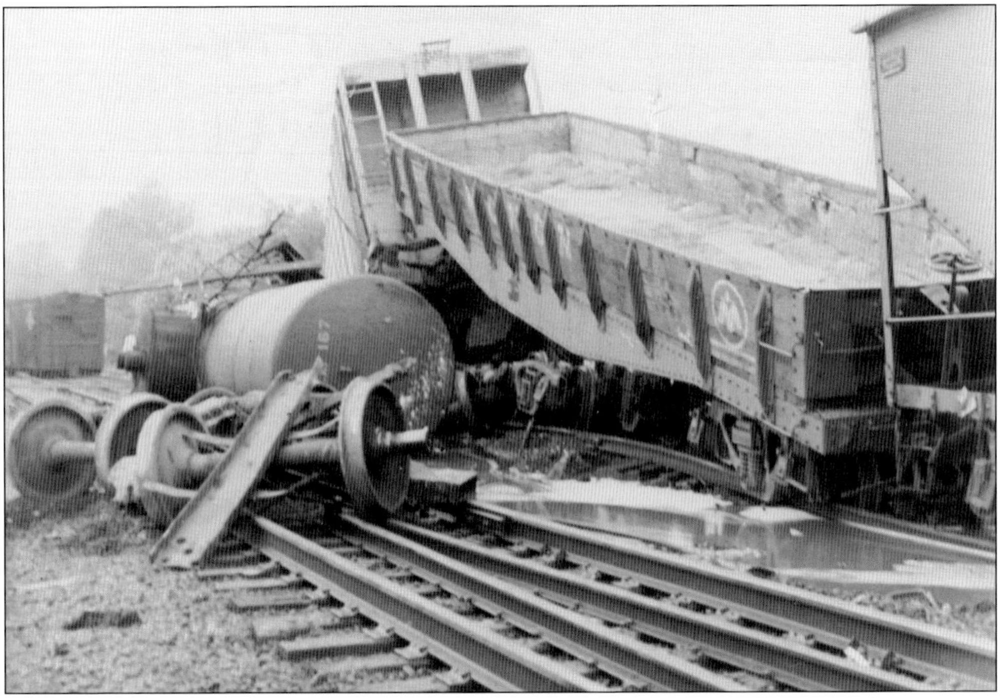

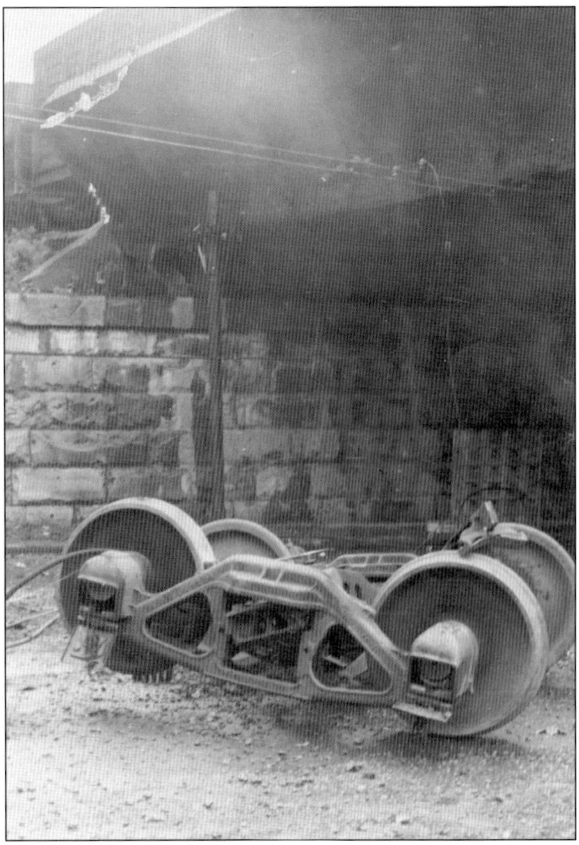

On June 9, 1950, a second train wreck occurred in Madisonville at the Whetsel Avenue overpass, 40 years after the first wreck at the same location. The 1950 wreck was described as much more spectacular, though thankfully there were no injuries, and the intersection took on a carnival atmosphere, with onlookers from all over Cincinnati. B&O train no. 97, coming from Parkersburg, West Virginia, to Cincinnati carrying 72 cars, derailed when a piece of metal from the train landed on the track, causing an empty car to jump track.

There was a massive pileup, and six of the cars tumbled down and were described as "a twisted pile of metal" by the *Eastern Hills Journal*. Debris from the train lies in the middle of Whetsel Avenue in this photograph of the scene. It took 30 hours to remove the wreckage.

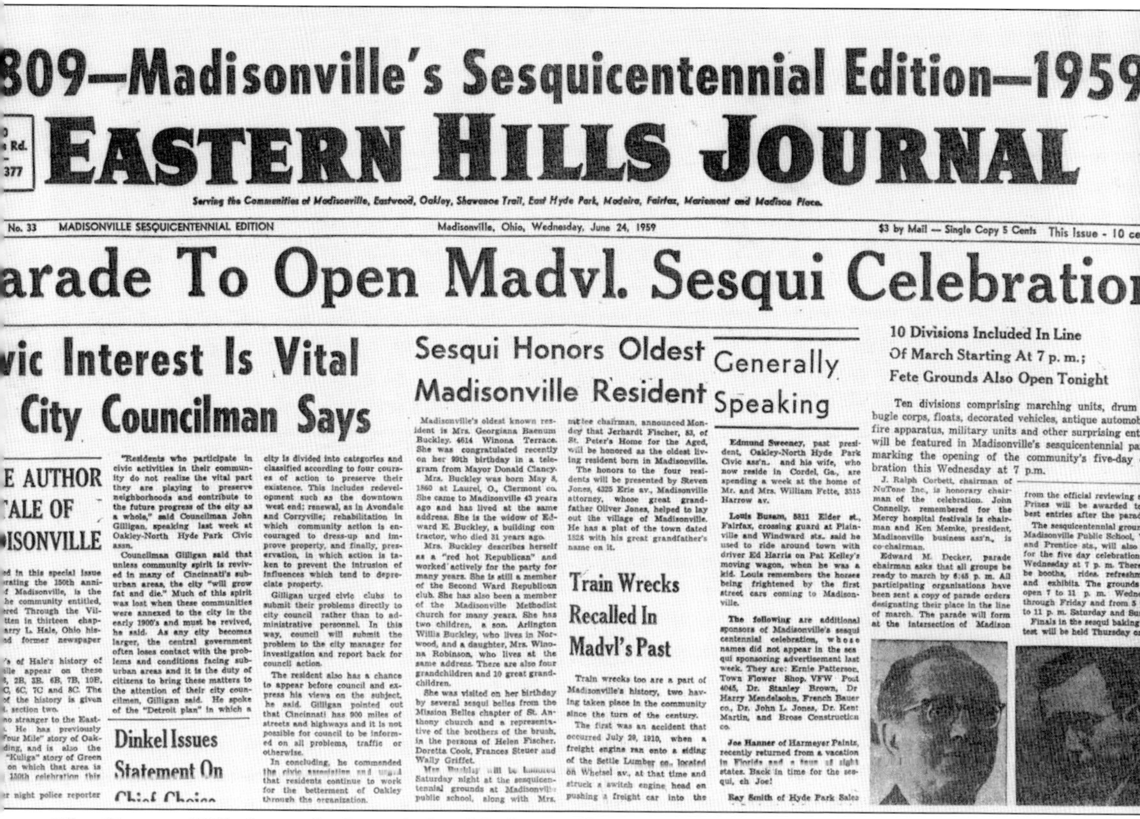

809—Madisonville's Sesquicentennial Edition—1959

EASTERN HILLS JOURNAL

Serving the Communities of Madisonville, Eastwood, Oakley, Shawnee Trail, East Hyde Park, Madeira, Fairfax, Mariemont and Madison Place.

No. 33 MADISONVILLE SESQUICENTENNIAL EDITION | Madisonville, Ohio, Wednesday, June 24, 1959 | $3 by Mail — Single Copy 5 Cents This Issue - 10 ce

arade To Open Madvl. Sesqui Celebratio

vic Interest Is Vital City Councilman Says

"Residents who participate in civic activities in their community do not realize the vital part they are playing to preserve neighborhoods and contribute to the future progress of the city as a whole," said Councilman John Gilligan, speaking last week at Oakley-North Hyde Park Civic assn.

Councilman Gilligan said that unless community spirit is revived in many of Cincinnati's suburban areas, the city "will grow fat and die." Much of this spirit was lost when these communities were annexed to the city in the early 1900's and must be revived, he said. As any city becomes larger, the central government often loses contact with the problems and conditions facing suburban areas and it is the duty of citizens to bring these matters to the attention of their city councilmen, Gilligan said. He spoke of the "Detroit plan" in which a city is divided into categories and classified according to four courses of action to preserve their existence. This includes redevelopment such as the downtown west end; renewal, as in Avondale and Corryville; rehabilitation in which community action is encouraged to dress-up and improve property, and finally, preservation, in which action is taken to prevent the intrusion of influences which tend to depreciate property.

Gilligan urged civic clubs to submit their problems directly to city council rather than to administrative personnel. In this way, council will submit the problem to the city manager for investigation and report back for council action.

The resident also has a chance to appear before council and express his views on the subject, he said. Gilligan pointed out that Cincinnati has 900 miles of streets and highways and it is not possible for council to be informed on all problems, traffic or otherwise.

In concluding, he commended the civic association and urged that residents continue to work for the betterment of Oakley through the organization.

E AUTHOR ALE OF ISONVILLE

ed in this special issue rating the 150th anni- f Madisonville, is the he community entitled, ered Through the Vil- tten in thirteen chap- arry L. Hale, Ohio his- d former newspaper

's of Hale's history of ille appear on these , 2B, 3B, 6B, 7B, 10B, C, 6C, 7C and 8C. The of the history is given . section two.

no stranger to the East- . He has previously Four Mile" story of Oak- ding, and is also the "Kuliga" story of Green on which that area is 150th celebration this

r night police reporter

Dinkel Issues Statement On Chief Choice

Sesqui Honors Oldest Madisonville Resident

Madisonville's oldest known resident is Mrs. Georgiana Baenum Buckley, 4614 Winona Terrace. She was congratulated recently on her 99th birthday in a telegram from Mayor Donald Clancy.

Mrs. Buckley was born May 8, 1860 at Laurel, O., Clermont co. She came to Madisonville 43 years ago and has lived at the same address. She is the widow of Edward E. Buckley, a building contractor, who died 31 years ago.

Mrs. Buckley describes herself as a "red hot Republican" and worked actively for the party for many years. She is still a member of the Second Ward Republican club. She has also been a member of the Madisonville Methodist church for many years. She has two children, a son, Arlington Willis Buckley, who lives in Norwood, and a daughter, Mrs. Winona Robinson, who lives at the same address. There are also four grandchildren and 10 great grandchildren.

She was visited on her birthday by several sesqui belles from the Mission Belles chapter of St. Anthony church and a representative of the brothers of the brush, in the persons of Helen Fischer, Doretta Cook, Frances Steuer and Wally Griffet.

Mrs. Buckley will be honored Saturday night at the sesquicentennial grounds at Madisonville public school, along with Mrs. mittee chairman, announced Monday that Jerhardt Fischer, 83, of St. Peter's Home for the Aged, will be honored as the oldest living resident born in Madisonville.

The honors to the four residents will be presented by Steven Jones, 4325 Erie av., Madisonville attorney, whose great grandfather Oliver Jones, helped to lay out the village of Madisonville. He has a plat of the town dated 1828 with his great grandfather's name on it.

Train Wrecks Recalled In Madvl's Past

Train wrecks too are a part of Madisonville's history, two having taken place in the community since the turn of the century.

The first was an accident that occurred July 29, 1910, when a freight engine ran onto a siding of the Settle Lumber co., located on Whetsel av., at that time and struck a switch engine head on pushing a freight car into the

Generally Speaking

Edmund Sweeney, past president, Oakley-North Hyde Park Civic ass'n., and his wife, who now reside in Cordel, Ga., are spending a week at the home of Mr. and Mrs. William Fette, 3515 Harrow av.

Louis Busam, 5811 Elder st., Fairfax, crossing guard at Plainville and Windward sts., said he used to ride around town with driver Ed Harris on Pat Kelley's moving wagon, when he was a kid. Louis remembers the horses being frightened by the first street cars coming to Madisonville.

The following are additional sponsors of Madisonville's sesqui centennial celebration, whose names did not appear in the sesqui sponsoring advertisement last week. They are: Ernie Patterson, Town Flower Shop, VFW Post 4045, Dr. Stanley Brown, Dr Harry Mendelsohn, French Bauer co., Dr. John L. Jones, Dr. Kent Martin, and Brose Construction co.

Joe Hanner of Harmeyer Paints, recently returned from a vacation in Florida and a tour of eight states. Back in time for the sesqui, eh Joe!

Ray Smith of Hyde Park Sales

10 Divisions Included In Line Of March Starting At 7 p. m.; Fete Grounds Also Open Tonight

Ten divisions comprising marching units, drum bugle corps, floats, decorated vehicles, antique automob fire apparatus, military units and other surprising ents will be featured in Madisonville's sesquicentennial par marking the opening of the community's five-day c bration this Wednesday at 7 p.m.

J. Ralph Corbett, chairman of NuTone Inc., is honorary chairman of the celebration. John Connelly, remembered for the Mercy hospital festivals is chairman and Ken Memke, president, Madisonville business ass'n., is co-chairman.

Edward M. Decker, parade chairman asks that all groups be ready to march by 6:45 p. m. All participating organizations have been sent a copy of parade orders designating their place in the line of march. The parade will form at the intersection of Madison

from the official reviewing st Prizes will be awarded to best entries after the parade

The sesquicentennial groun Madisonville Public School, W and Prentice sts., will also for the five day celebration Wednesday at 7 p. m. There be booths, rides, refreshm and exhibits. The grounds open 7 to 11 p. m. Wedne through Friday and from 5 p to 11 p. m. Saturday and Sun

Finals in the sesqui baking test will be held Thursday on

The *Eastern Hills Journal* released this Madisonville Sesquicentennial Edition on Wednesday, June 24, 1959.

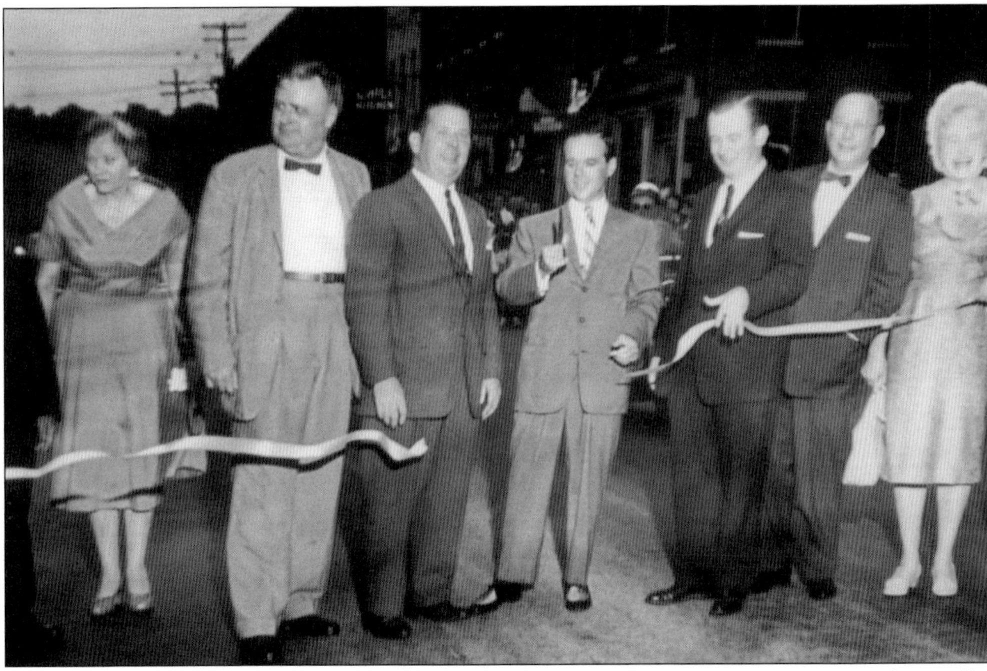

On June 24, 1959, a ribbon-cutting ceremony was held to kick off the festivities for Madisonville's sesquicentennial—a five-day period of celebration beginning with a glorious parade of 10 divisions. The participants in the ribbon cutting are, from left to right, J. Dinkel; Cincinnati officials G. Rich, and J. Decourcy; Cincinnati mayor Donald Clancy, center-stage holding the scissors; William Kelly; Walton Bachrack; and Dorothy Dolbey.

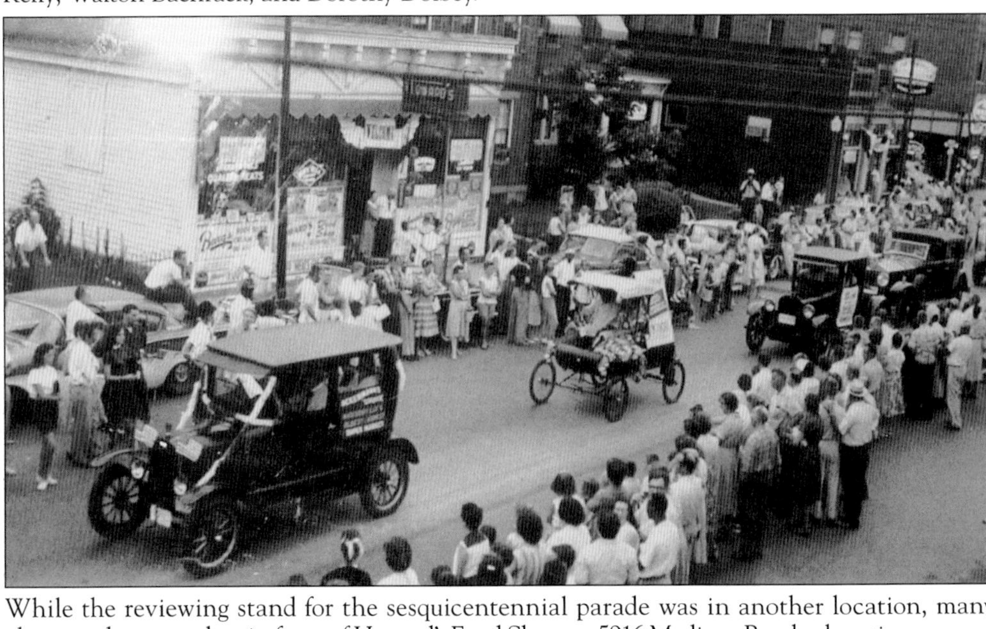

While the reviewing stand for the sesquicentennial parade was in another location, many photographs were taken in front of Howard's Food Shop on 5916 Madison Road, a longtime grocery in Madisonville. Crowds in front of this market were treated to old-model cars passing in review. The cars took their place in line in Division VI, with this Chevrolet driven by Earl Vordenberg, proprietor of a Chevrolet dealership, medaled first-place winner in the category.

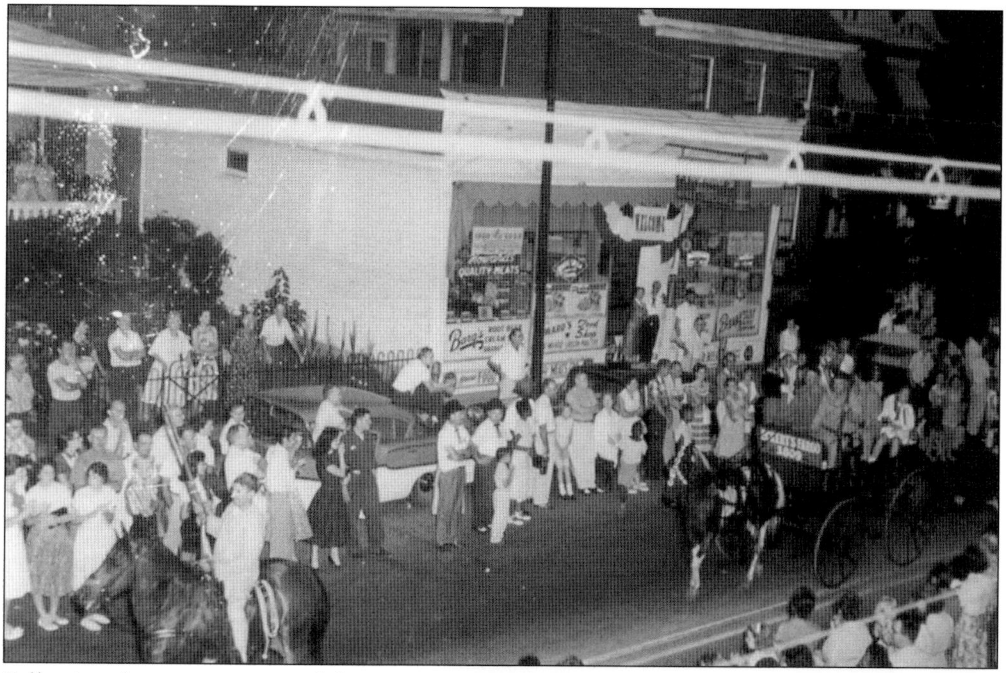

Following the vintage automobiles in the sesquicentennial parade were the vintage trucks. Passing in review before Howard's Food Shop, the only vintage truck visible in the picture is the type once used to deliver products to homes or businesses. The one pictured was used by Eckert's Meat Market. In 1959, Mr. Eckert's business was located at 6105 Madison Road.

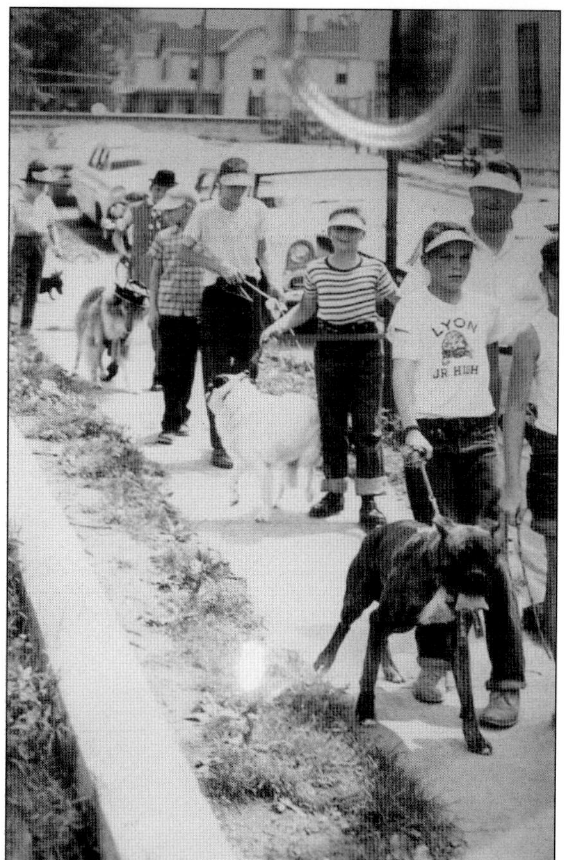

The pet parade, a feature of the sesquicentennial led by Mac McGohen, enters the judging area on the Madisonville Public School grounds. Over 50 youngsters entered the pet contest. Ribbons, baseballs, and an assortment of other gifts were given as prizes. Although no girls are pictured, the first place winner was Debbie Flynn.

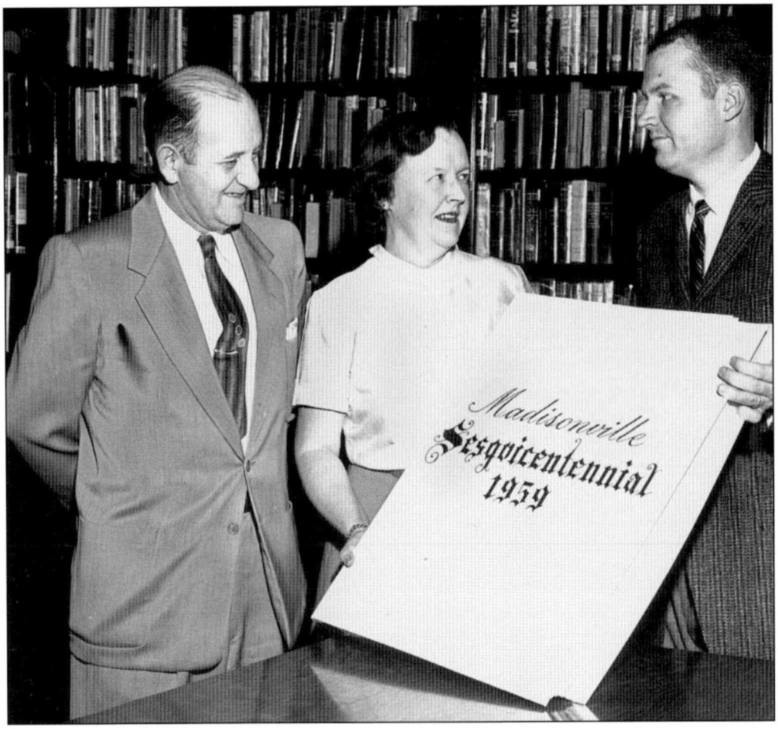

Ken Mompers, president of the Madisonville Business Association, along with Gene Ackermann, the owner of Ackermann's Super Market, presented the gift of the sesquicentennial scrapbook to the Madisonville Branch Library to be on display for all residents of Madisonville.

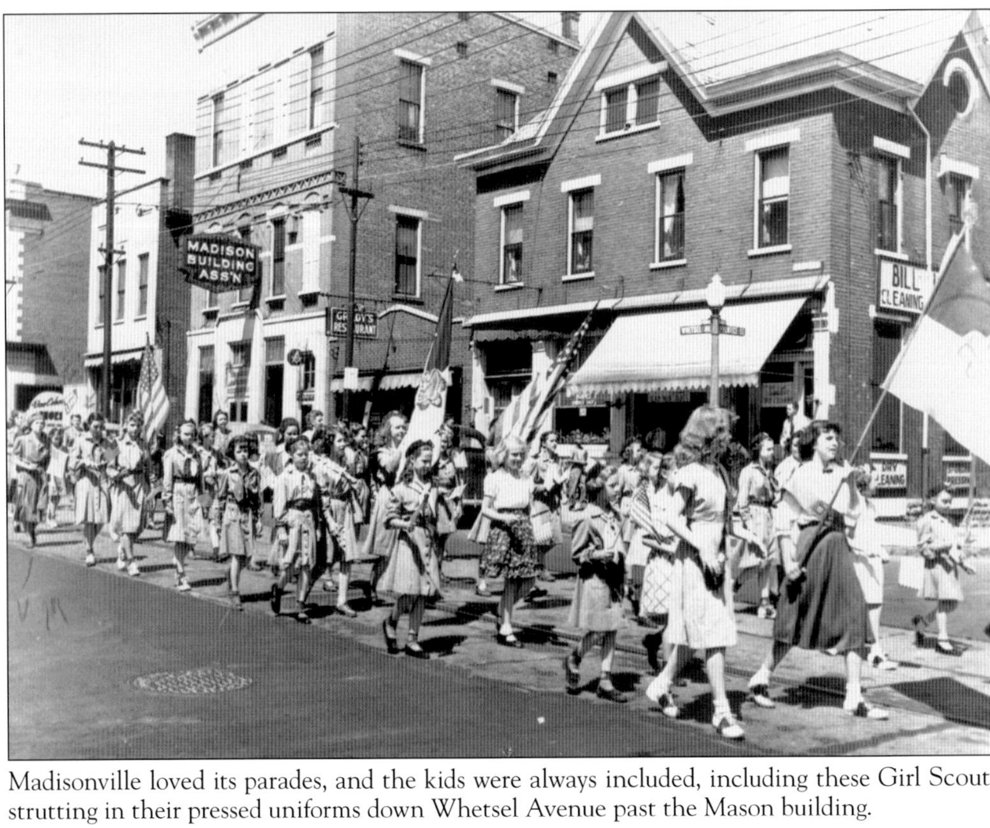

Madisonville loved its parades, and the kids were always included, including these Girl Scouts strutting in their pressed uniforms down Whetsel Avenue past the Mason building.

Six

Modern Rebirth

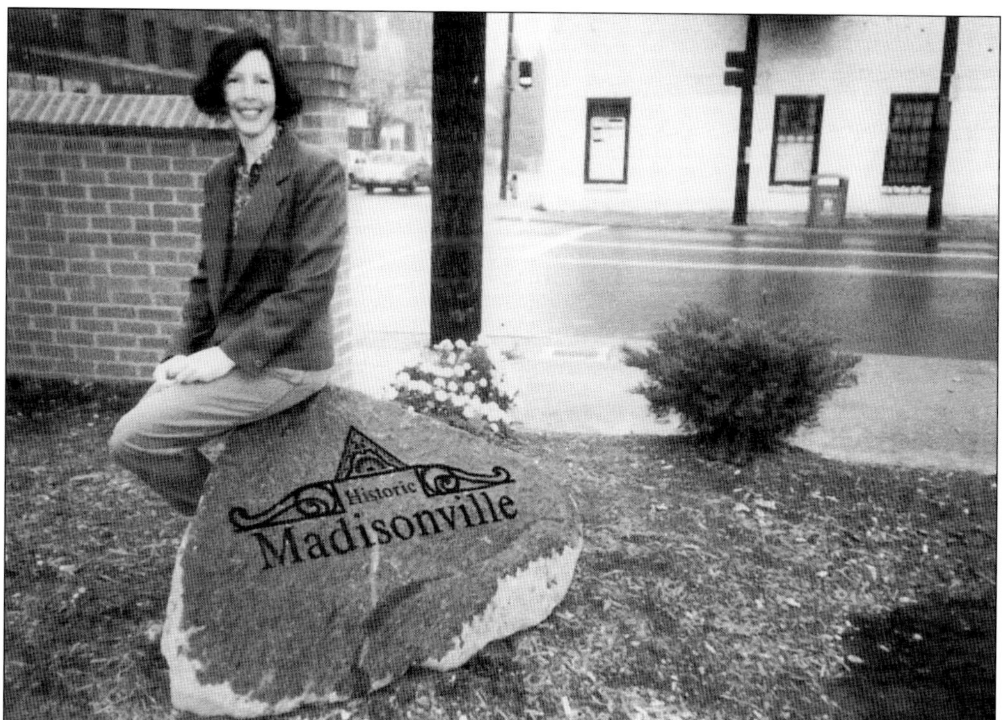

The Madisonville logo campaign of 1991 was started by the Madisonville History Committee to define Madisonville as historic because of its handsome eclectic housing stock, great location in relation to the expressways, quick access to Downtown Cincinnati, and cohesive, integrated neighborhood. The logo was designed by local businessman Jim Slaughter of Slaughter Design on Erie Avenue, with funds raised by Janet Blank—sitting on the granite stone donated by the Stone Center at 4820 Stafford Street—and Bob Brown under the leadership of Ruth Ann Busald.

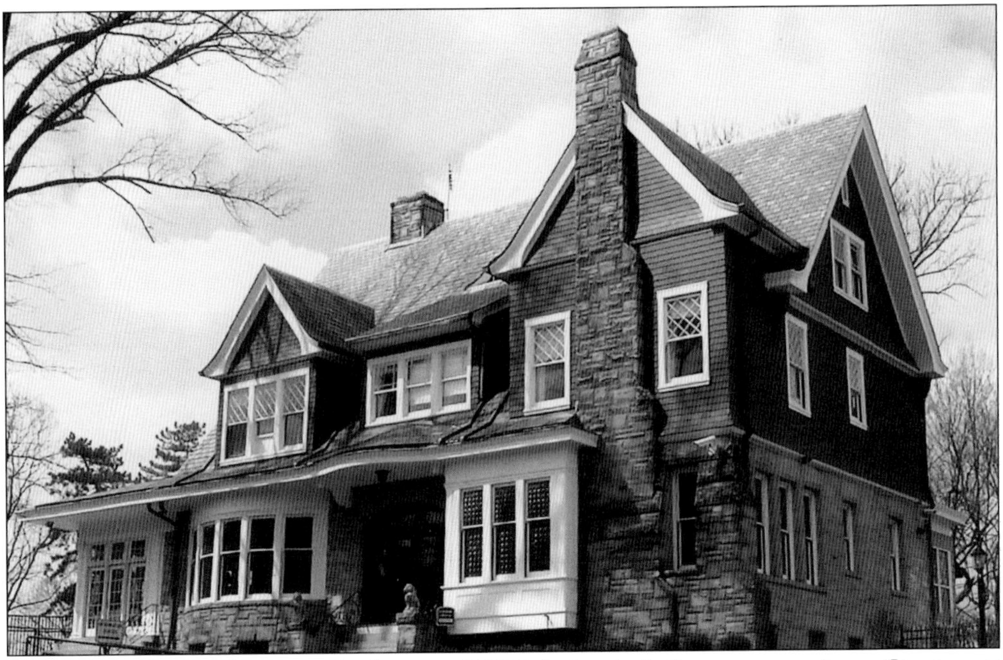

The Iretons' country home was built around 1900 for Louis A. Ireton, a prominent Cincinnati attorney. He was an avid gardener with a large greenhouse on his property and was a contributor to the *Market Growers Journal* in 1910. His son, Louis M. Ireton, graduated from East High School and, in 1928, was certified to practice law. Three generations of Iretons lived in this house before it was sold to make way for the Centennial Station apartments, but this beautiful house has been incorporated as the clubhouse for the apartment complex.

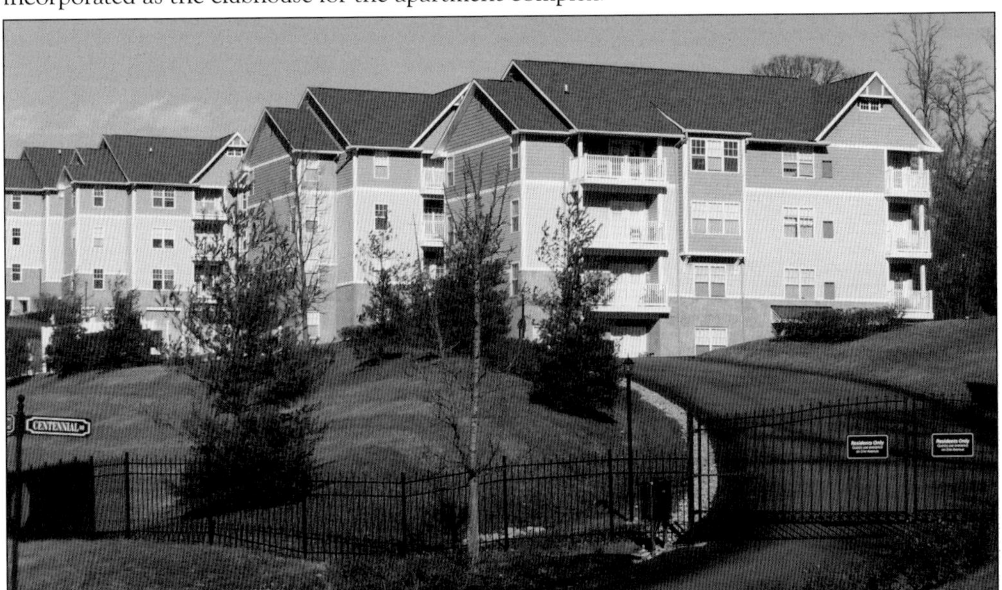

The Centennial Station upscale apartments are located on the hillside of the original 17 acres of the Ireton estate. The ground-breaking for the 300-plus apartments occurred in May 2002. This lovely gated community has many amenities to keep renters satisfied. The name came from the Red Bank station that protected the pioneers against hostile forces.

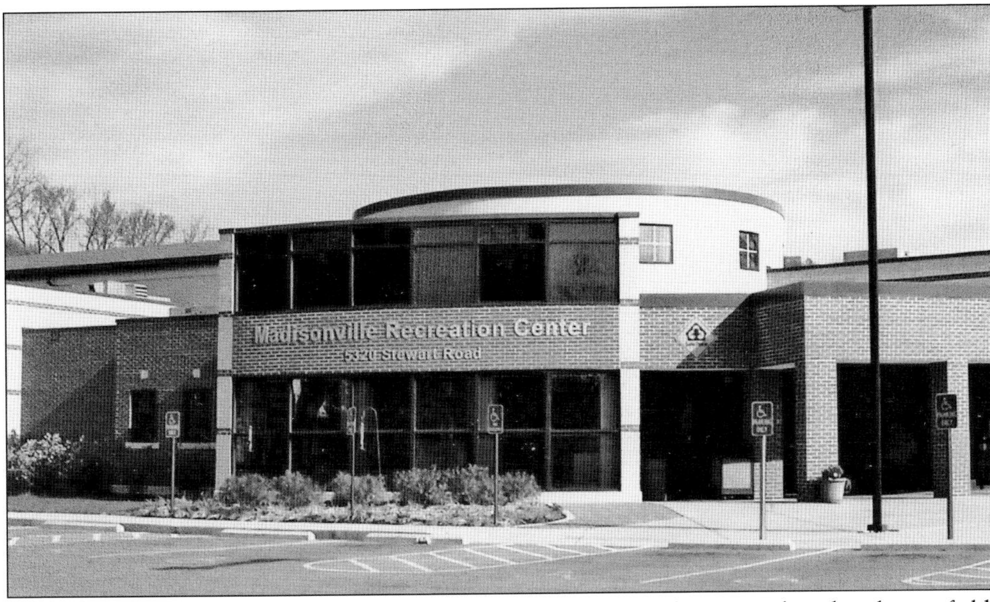

Madisonville Recreation Center, in Stewart Park, was dedicated in 2002, but the playing fields have been in use since the early 1900s. Stewart Park playgrounds were established and a pool was constructed in 1930, but it was closed in 1935, not to reopen until after repairs in 1952. The tennis courts were hard-surfaced in 1958.

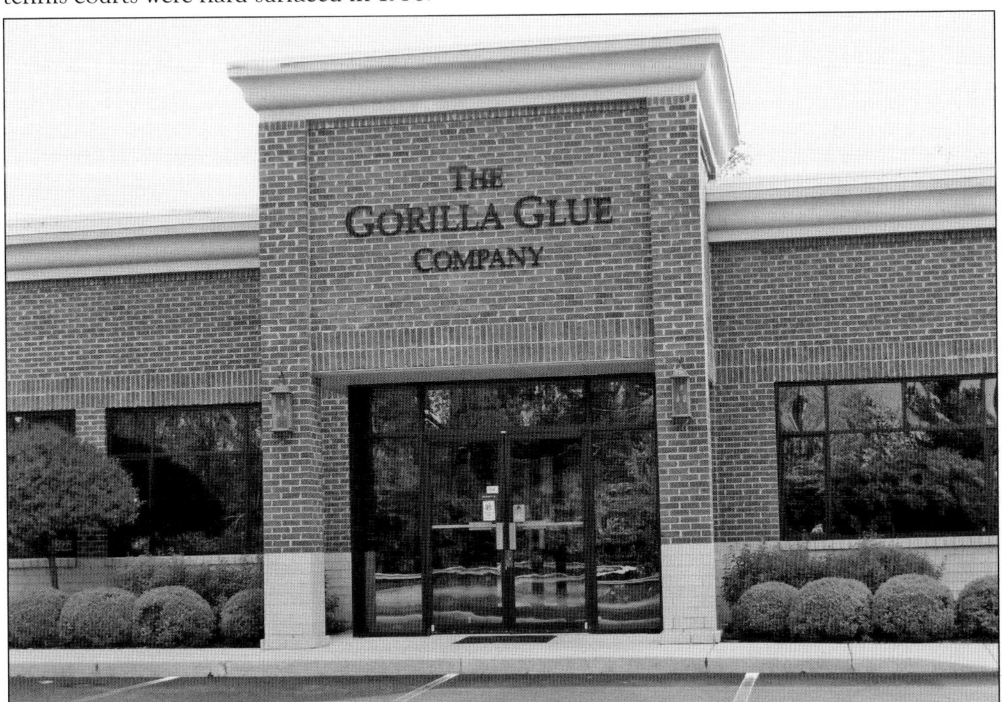

In November 2002, a ground-breaking ceremony was held in an area known as Corsica Hollow along Red Bank Expressway. One of the first structures to be completed, in 2003, was the building that now houses the Gorilla Glue Company. Formerly called the Lutz Tool Company, the company was so successful with the production of Gorilla Glue that it is now the company's name.

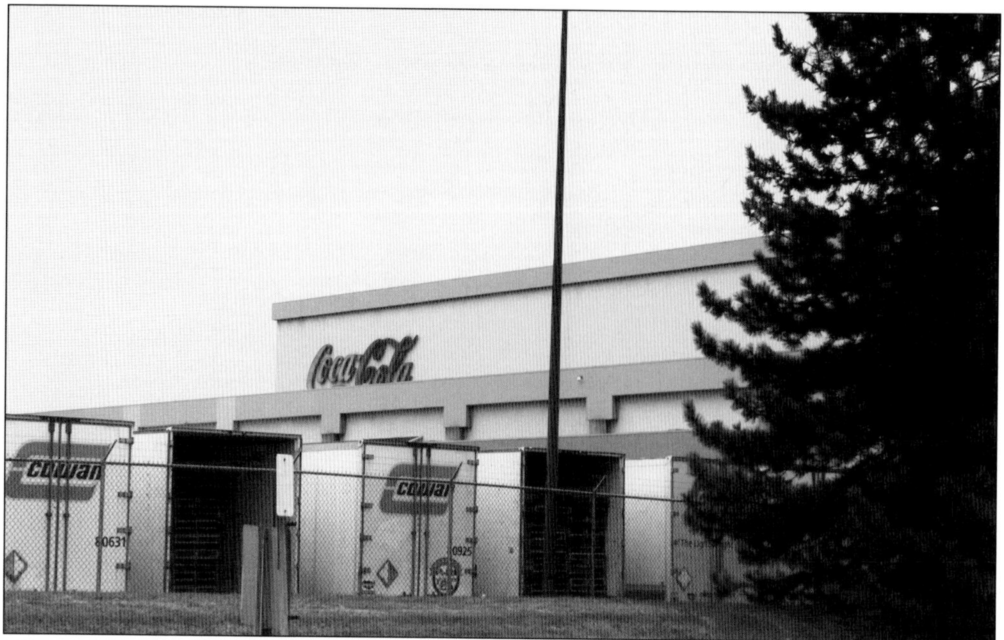

The post–World War II Eastwood housing development, built for veterans in 1948 on over 80 acres, was demolished in the 1970s to make way for the Eastwood commercial center. The Coca-Cola distribution plant was one of two anchors of the commercial development, which was completed in the 1980s. In partnership with the City of Cincinnati, the Madisonville Community Urban Redevelopment Corporation (MCURC) was a major factor in developing the site.

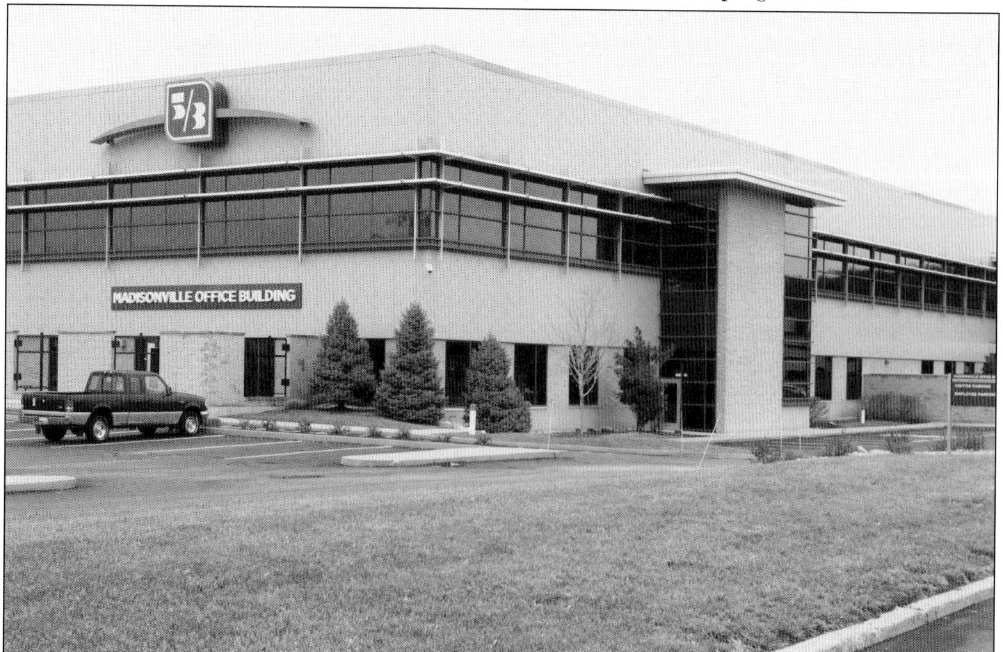

The Fifth-Third office complex started in 2000 with the renovation of the US Shoe Company—the other anchor to the Eastwood development. The US Shoe open house was held at the same time as a ground-breaking ceremony for the next facility in the complex.

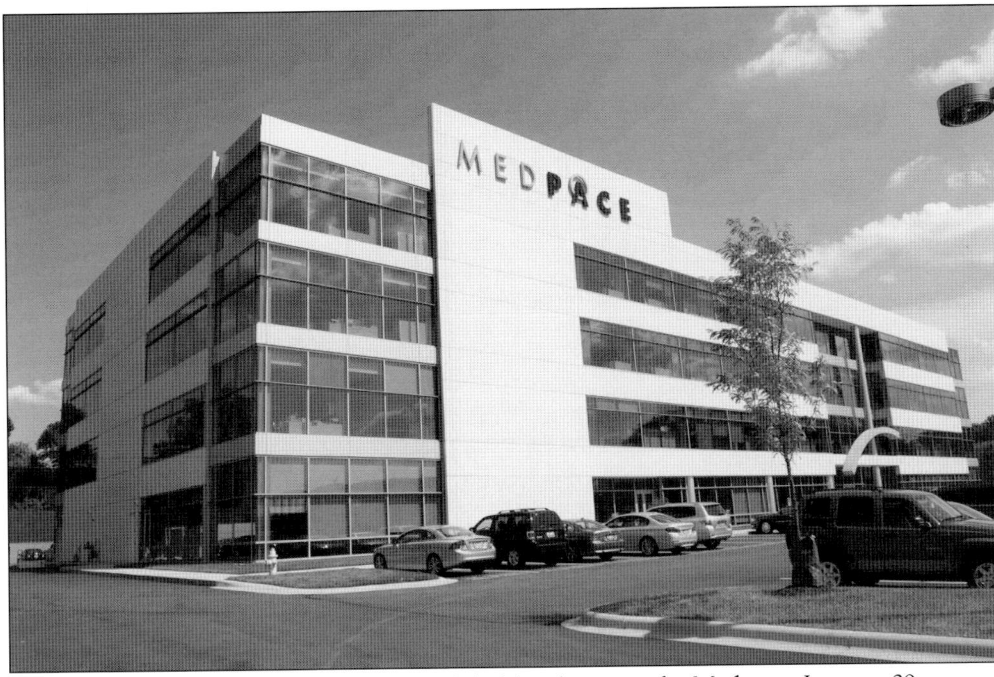

Ground was broken in 2010 for the new global headquarters for Medpace, Inc., on 29 acres at Red Bank Road and Madison Road, the site of the old NuTone plant. Medpace is a leader in clinical pharmaceutical research and development. This is the first in what will be a complex of buildings.

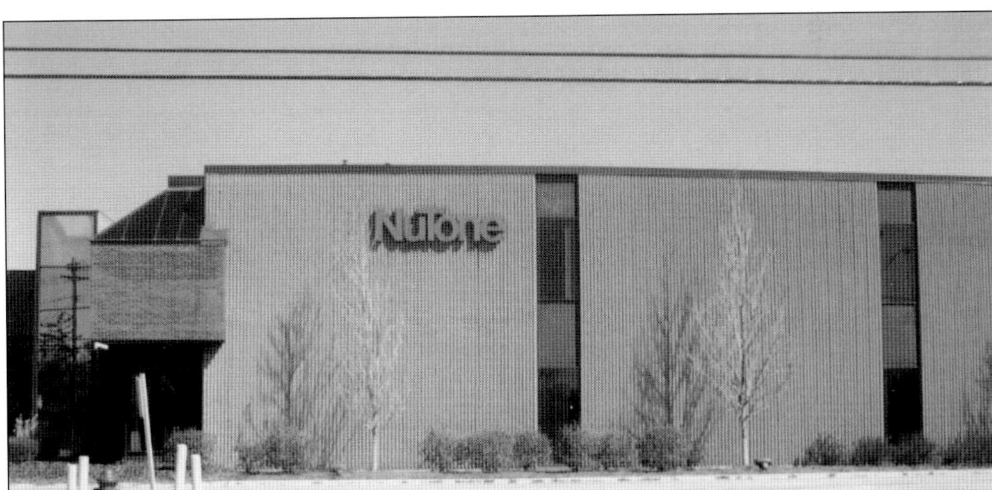

NuTone was founded in 1936 as a door chime company by Ralph and Patricia Corbett. The company relocated to Madisonville in 1949 from Downtown Cincinnati, expanding into manufacturing of bathroom accessories, kitchen ventilating systems, and much more.

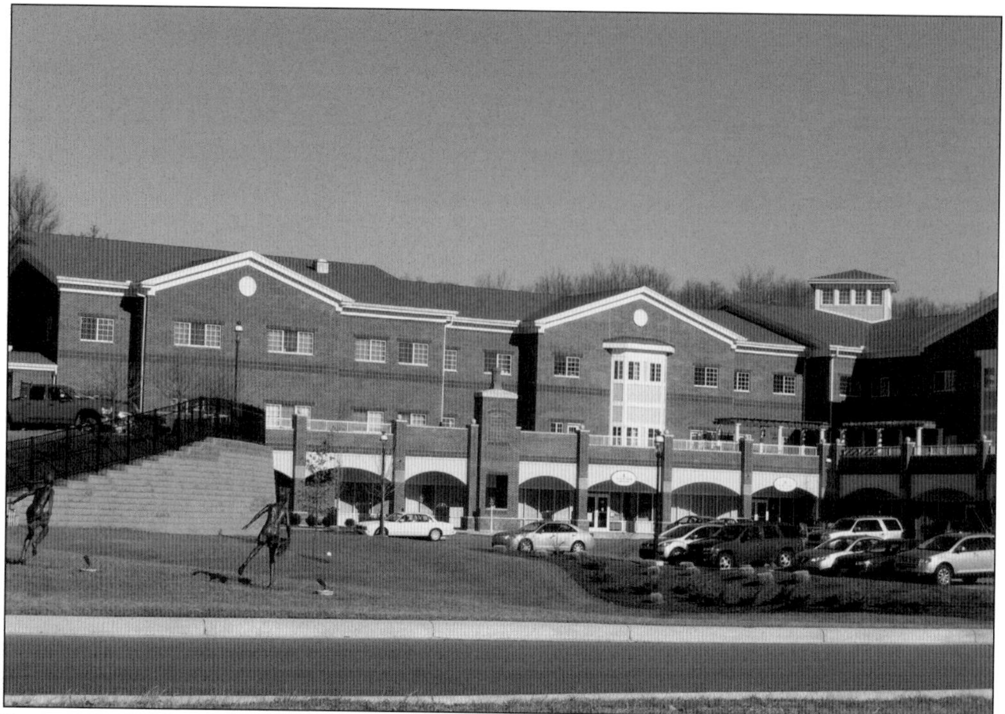

Part of the Madison Circle development is on the site of the old Oakley Drive-In Theater and the Southwestern Publishing Company. Southwestern Publishing began in Cincinnati in 1903 and moved in 1954 to Madisonville, where it remained a community business anchor until 2002, when it moved to Mason, Ohio.

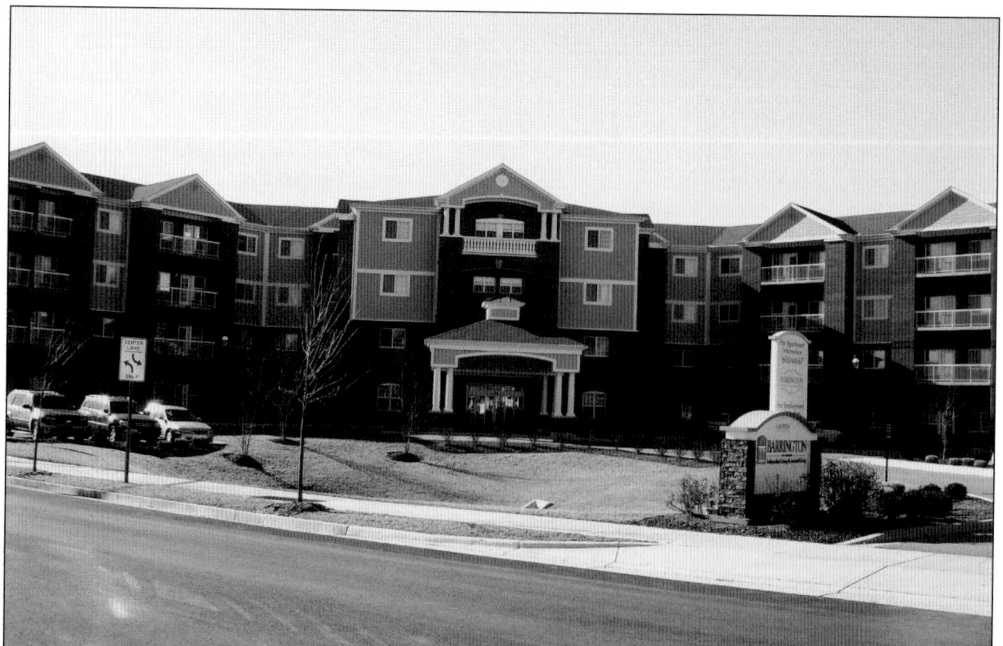

Barrington–Care Spring independent living and assisted living space is in the Madison Circle development, which has become a prime development area for the Madisonville community.

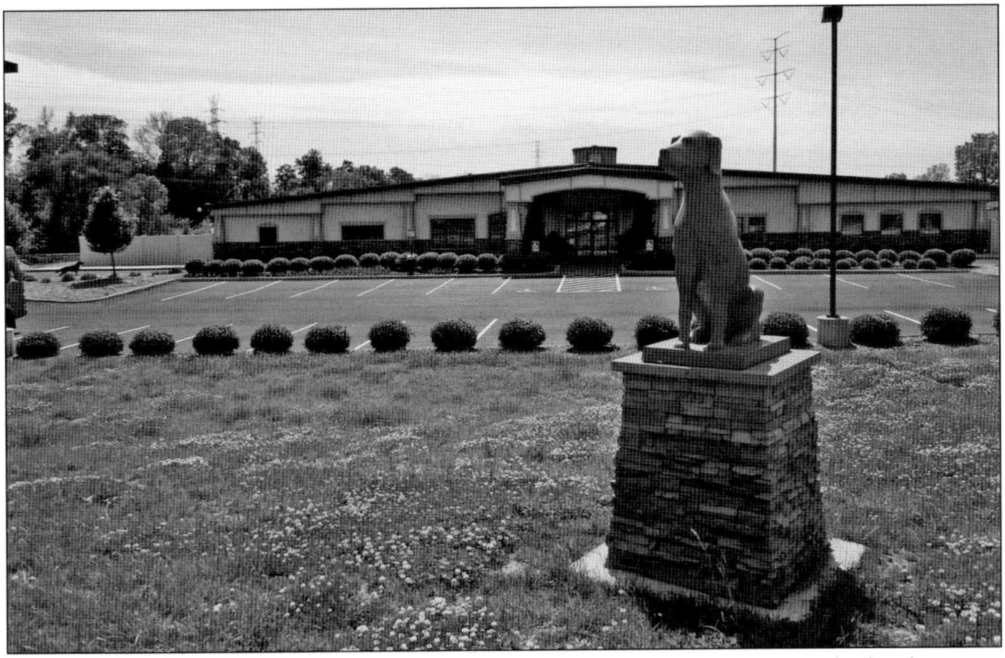

The Red Dog Daycare, Boarding, Pet Resort & Spa is another Madison Circle development. Cincinnati's first purpose-built facility specifically designed for four-legged family members was the first building in Madison Circle to be completed. The complex also sports an indoor aquatic center and dog park. Look for the Red Dog statue.

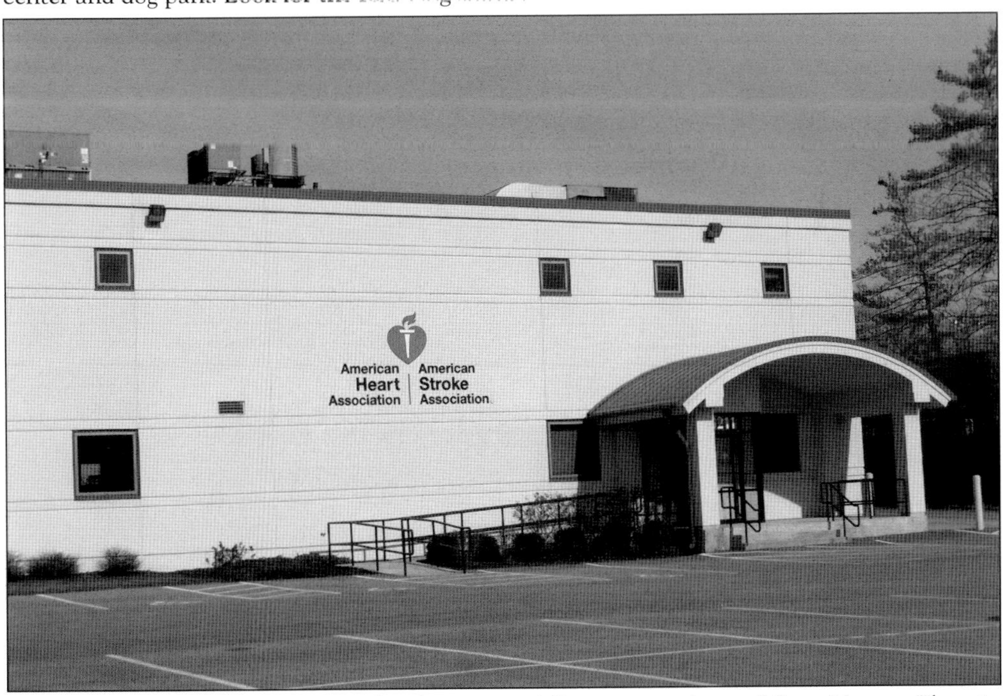

The American Heart Association headquarters of Cincinnati relocated from Vernon Place in 2007 to 5211 Madison Road on the site of the old Southwestern Publishing Company. It is a welcome asset to the community.

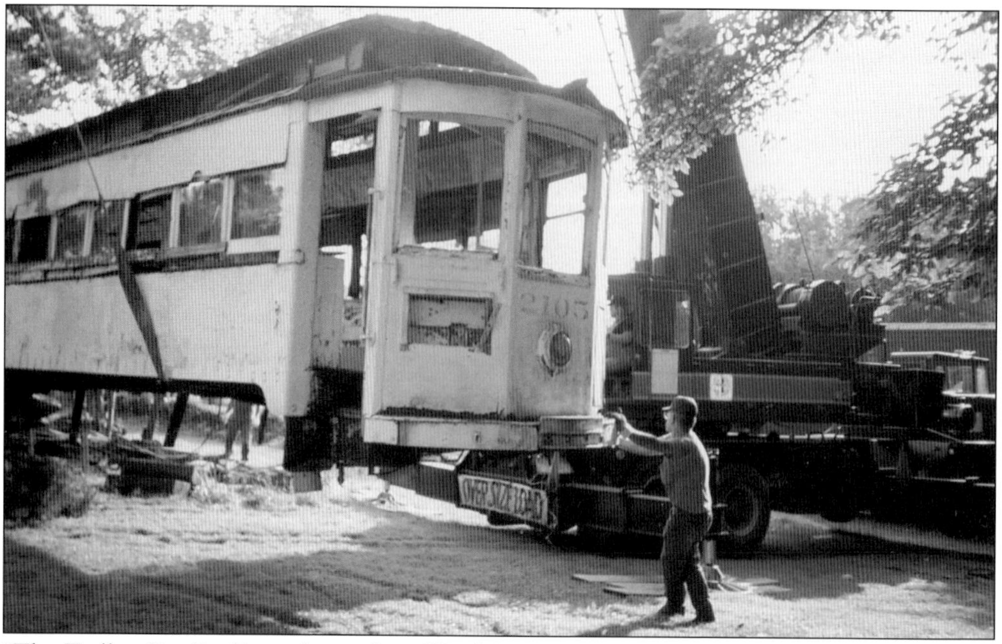

"The Trolley Car Find" was located on Wind Street near the top of Whetsel Avenue. Owner Amy Chambers hated to see her five-ton lawn ornament go but was happy it found a good home at the Seashore Trolley Museum in Kennebunkport, Maine. The trolley was built in 1917 by the Cincinnati Car Company on Spring Grove Avenue, one of the country's largest manufacturers of trolley cars. A moving crew lifted the trolley by crane onto a flatbed truck at a cost of $4,000 to the museum.

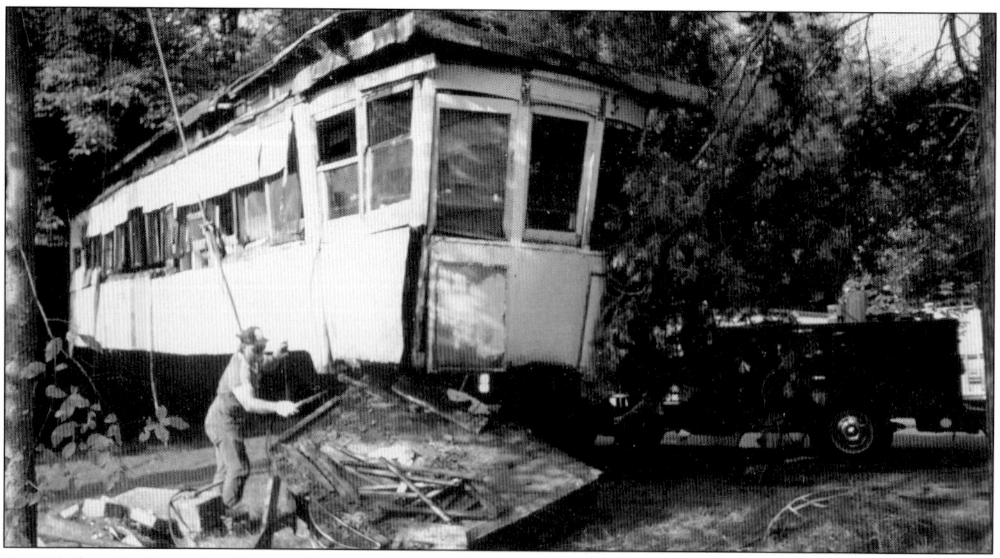

At 44 feet in length, the peeling, sagging white trolley had only one torn seat and a few torn flowery-blue window shades remaining. Many of the windows were in good shape, but the wooden frames supporting them were rotting, much like the rest of the body after years of neglect. It was sent to the Seashore Trolley Museum on September 1, 1993, for restoration costing $100,000, but it was still a gem and a special acquisition for the museum, which is eagerly awaiting the arrival of Car No. 2105. It will take several years to restore the trolley for display.

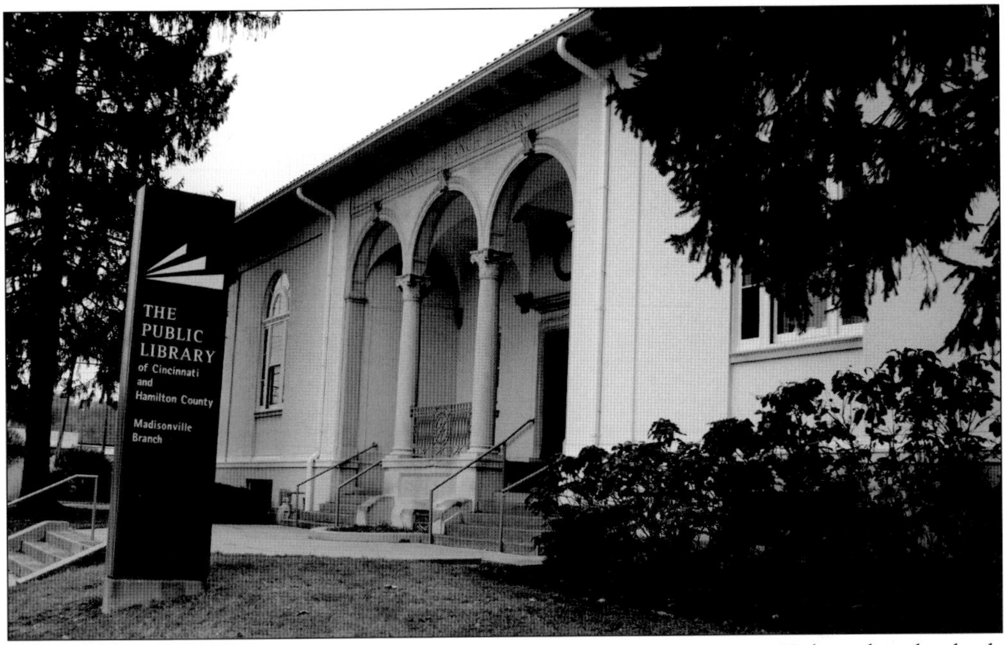

The Madisonville Public Library was built in 1925 by architect Henry Hake, who also built Madisonville High School. This Mediterranean-style building contains copies of Italian sculptures and a Rookwood tablet in honor of Dr. Arthur Knight's contribution to literacy in Madisonville. Hidden initials from the architect are inscribed behind one of the pillars.

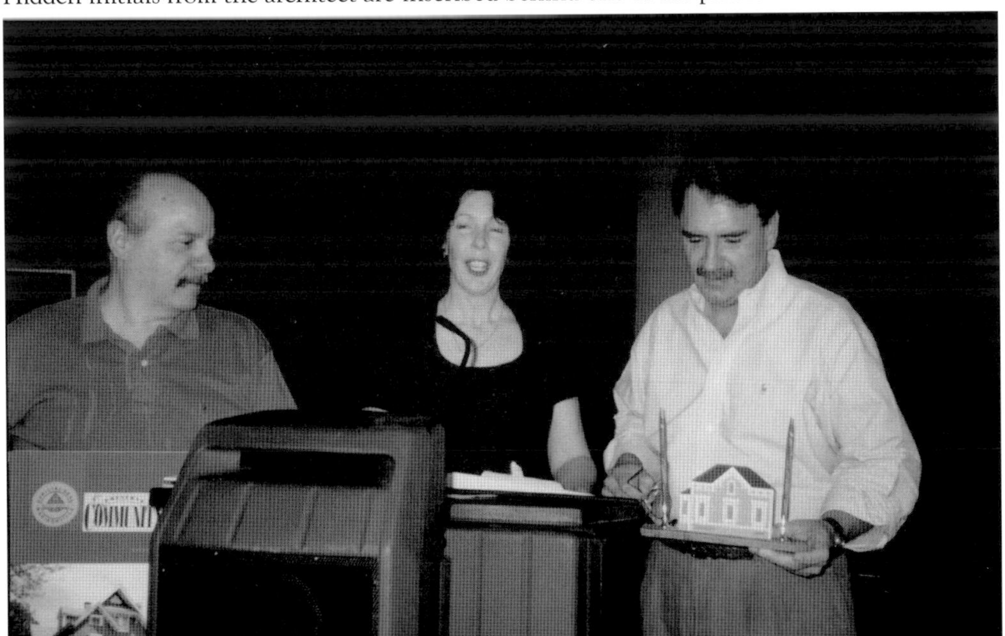

Bob Brown was the first recipient of the Madisonville History Committee Historic Housing Preservation Award. The May is celebrated nationally as Preservation Month, with Madisonville focusing on housing stock. Brown's house was the historic Peabody House on Erie Avenue.

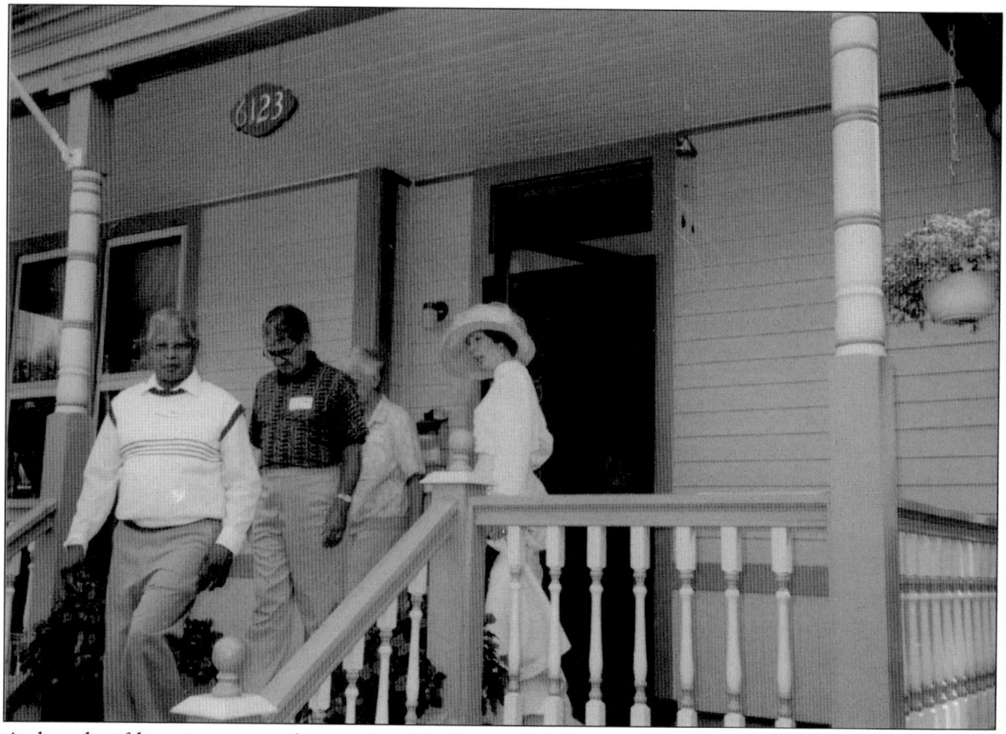

A decade of housing tours showcasing Madisonville's historic houses at many sections of town were orchestrated by the Madisonville Business Association in cooperation with the Madisonville Historical Society. These tours were elaborately staged, with horse-drawn carriages taking participants around the dedicated tour, ending in a large garden party under a tent on the grounds of the Stewart estate.

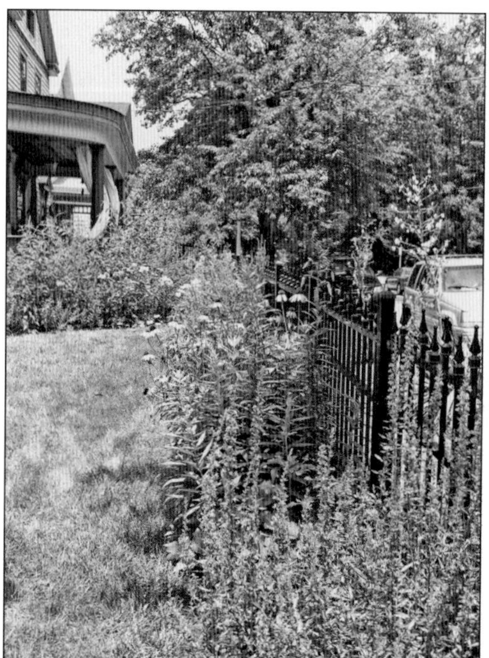

Annual garden tours showcase Madisonville yards and show off local gardeners' landscapes, fruit trees, vegetable gardens, and flowers. The garden club has been run for years by Marcia Richardson and Janice Sheatzley. This historic Ward Street house was built by the father of Charles Sawyer, who was born in this house in 1887 and taught for decades in area schools.

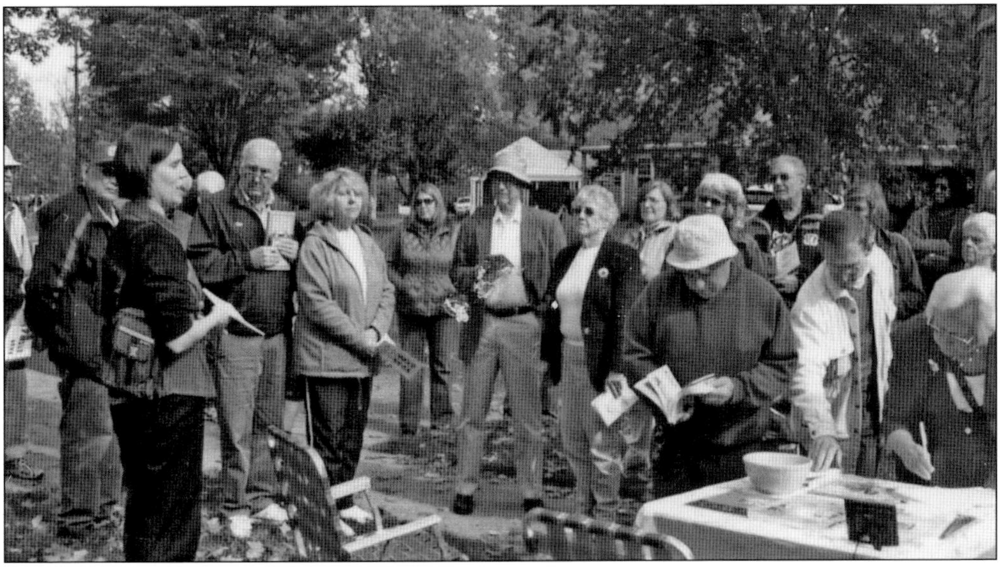

The Eastwood neighborhood of Madisonville joined the National Register of Historic Places because it has the most concentrated collection of Sears homes in Cincinnati. Credit goes to Anne Vanoy for compiling the data needed to get the area listed. This area encompasses a 15-acre tract containing about 86 homes developed in the 1920s and 1930s. Vanoy planned and conducted a walking tour after contacting several owners, who opened their doors for review. The Madisonville Historic Society partnered with Vanoy for an extremely successful event that drew people from all areas of Cincinnati.

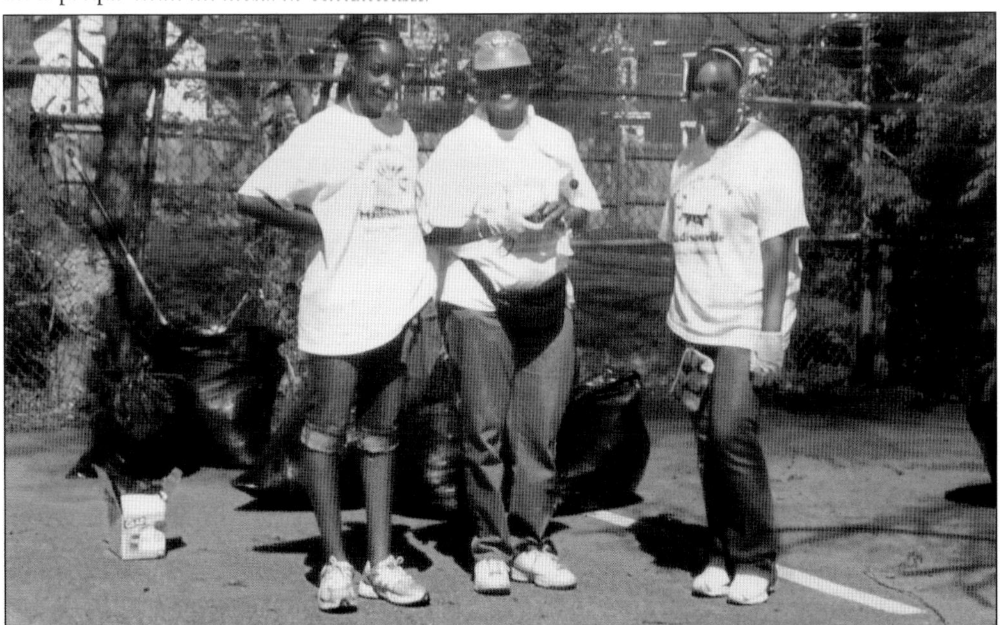

This annual "Super Saturday" clean-up and citywide beautification project, where groups of volunteers target Madisonville's public areas, has been spearheaded by the beautification committee for more than 30 years. Good people and volunteers have come and gone, but younger people take their place and contribute their talents.

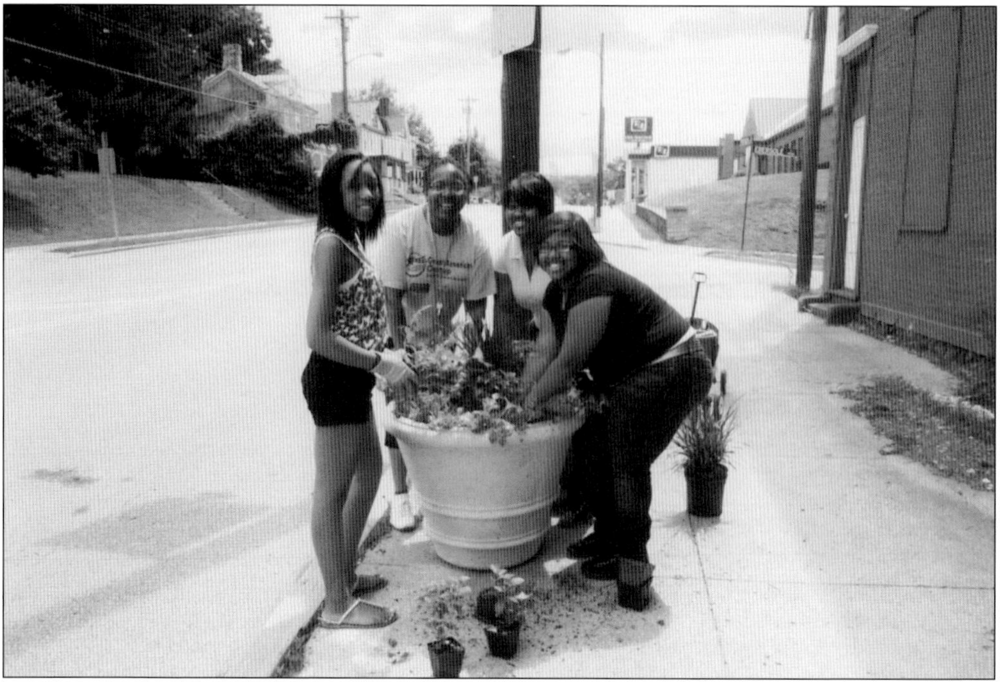

Four participants plant flowers in one of the large planters situated on each corner of Madison Road and Whetsel Avenue as part of the beautification committee's ongoing project, headed by Carolyn Winstead.

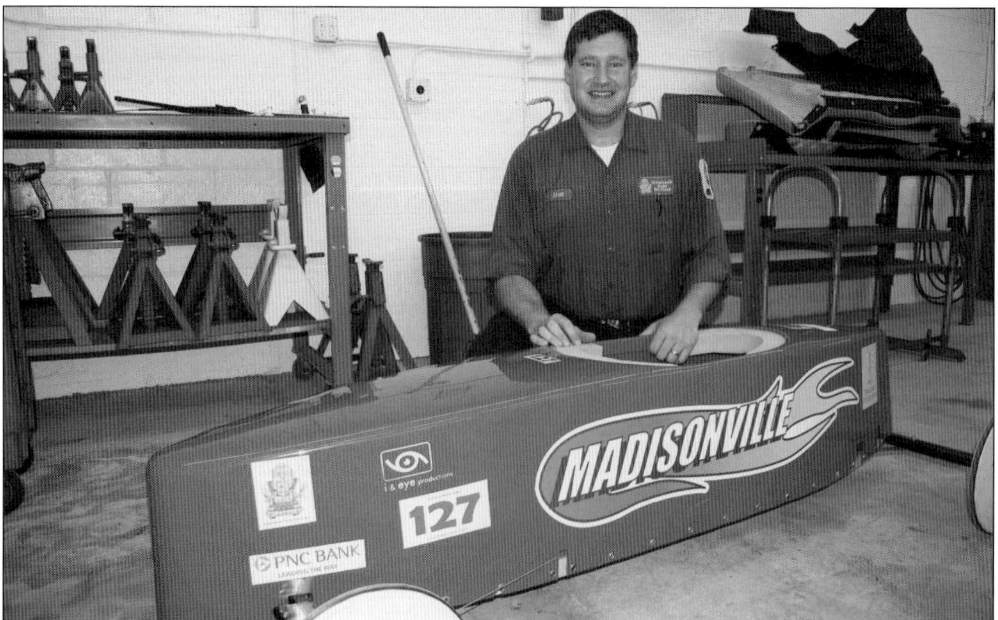

The Madisonville Soap Box Derby race coordinator, Matt Overbeck of Overbeck Auto on Madison Road, poses with one of the cars built in his shop for the event, held every August at Bramble Park. In the Mayor's Cup race, a citywide event, the top three positions were taken by Madisonville youngsters. (Courtesy of the *Community Press.*)

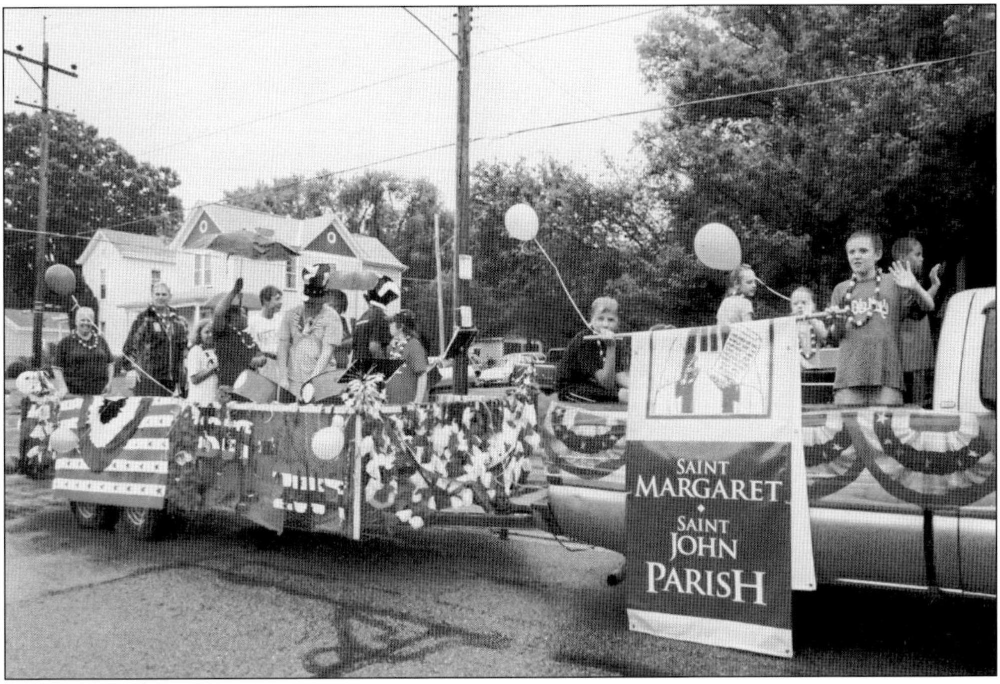

The St. Margaret–St. John Parish float, one of many participating in the Madisonville bicentennial Fourth of July parade, comes down Whetsel Avenue, which is lined with spectators. The parade ran about a mile, culminating at Bramble Park, where the festival was held.

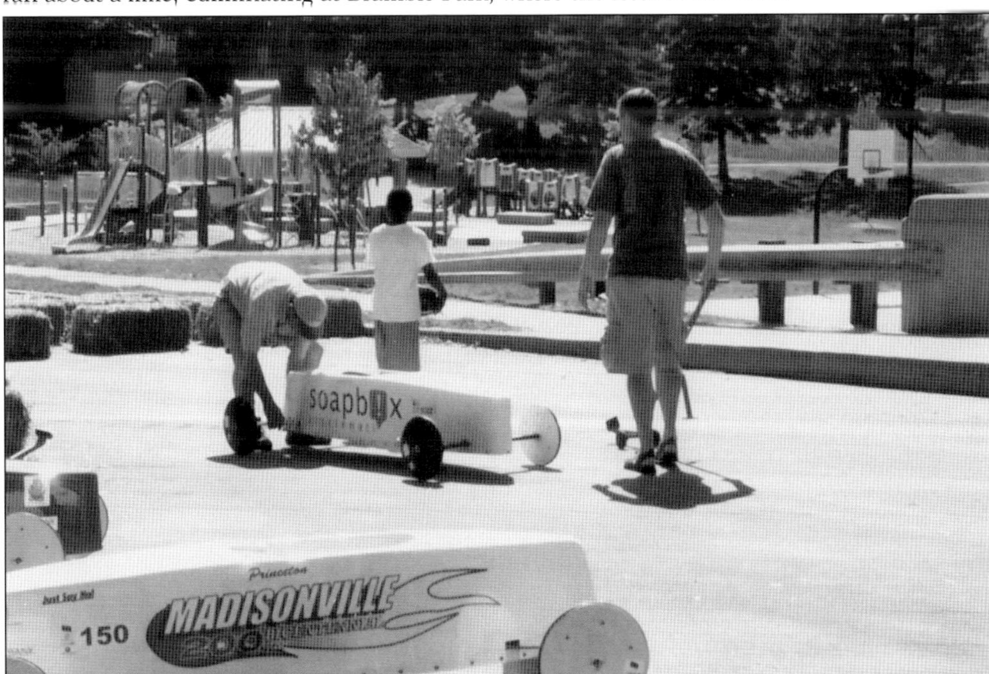

The soapbox derby is an annual event on the Bramble Avenue hill next to Bramble Park, with time trials held in the spring and the main event in the summer. The Madisonville bicentennial's main event was a large festival held at Bramble Park with hundreds of neighbors attending.

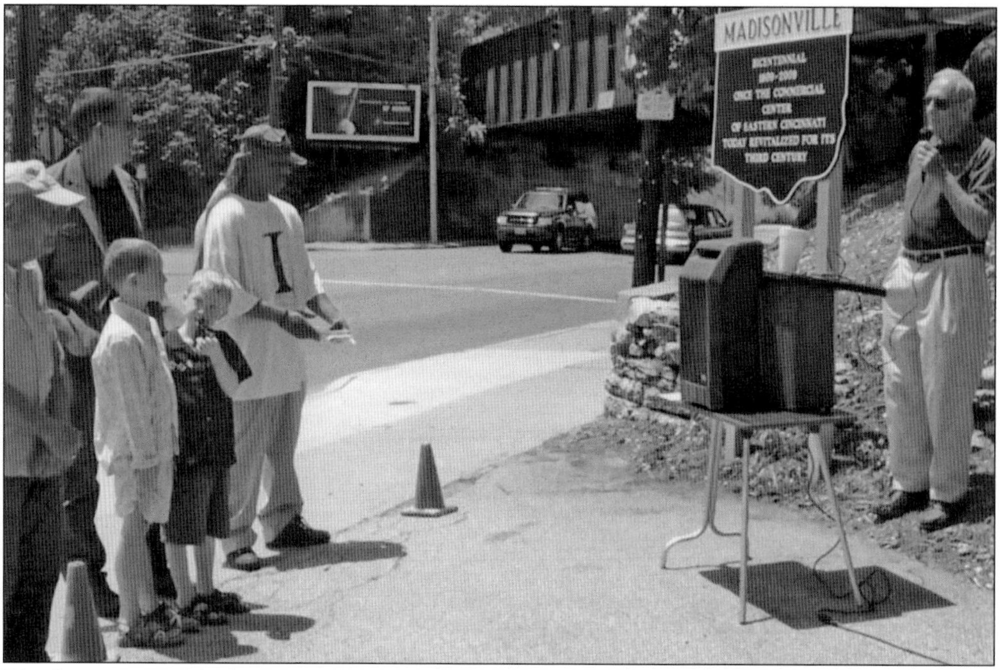

The bicentennial highway marker was placed along Madison Road near Madisonville's east entrance. The sign reads: "Bicentennial 1809–2009. Once the commercial center of eastern Cincinnati, today revitalized for its third century." Madisonville community council president Bob Igoe served as the master of ceremonies during the event.

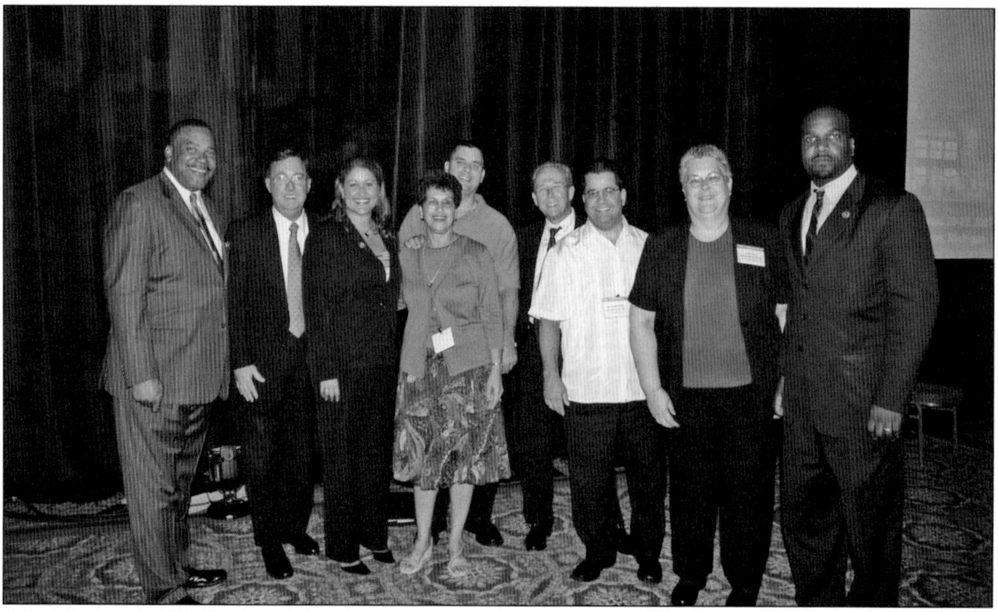

The Madisonville Weed and Seed Program was honored with a national award in Detroit for its partnership and collaboration with local Key Bank, the assistant US attorney, the Cincinnati Police Department, and the Department of Justice for its neighborhood restoration project. Kathy Garrison and Lois Day deserve credit for their outstanding achievement on behalf of the Madisonville community.

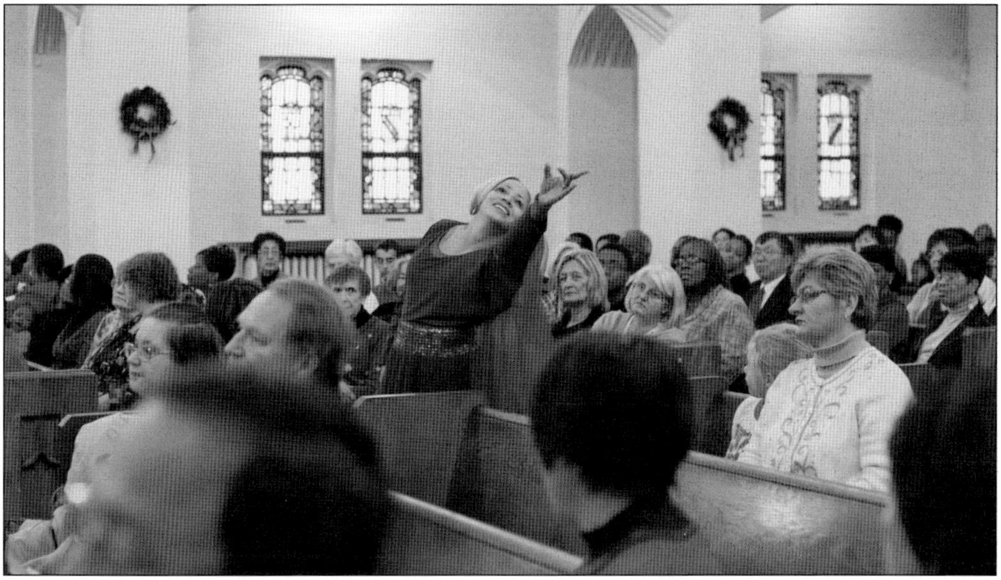

This is a view of the interior of the sanctuary of the Korean-Madisonville United Methodist Church on Madison Road on the evening of the annual Holiday Song Fest. The Methodist church is one of the oldest churches in Madisonville, being founded early in the town's history, and it is a very appropriate choice for host of the festivities. The festival began with the Madisonville bicentennial, held in December 2009, and has continued since, valuing Madisonville's multiracial community. The committee chairs of this event were Nancy Hanseman (organist), Eunshin Khang, Zachery Riggins, and Prencis Wilson. In this photograph, one of the spiritual dancers from Gaines United Methodist Church is performing.

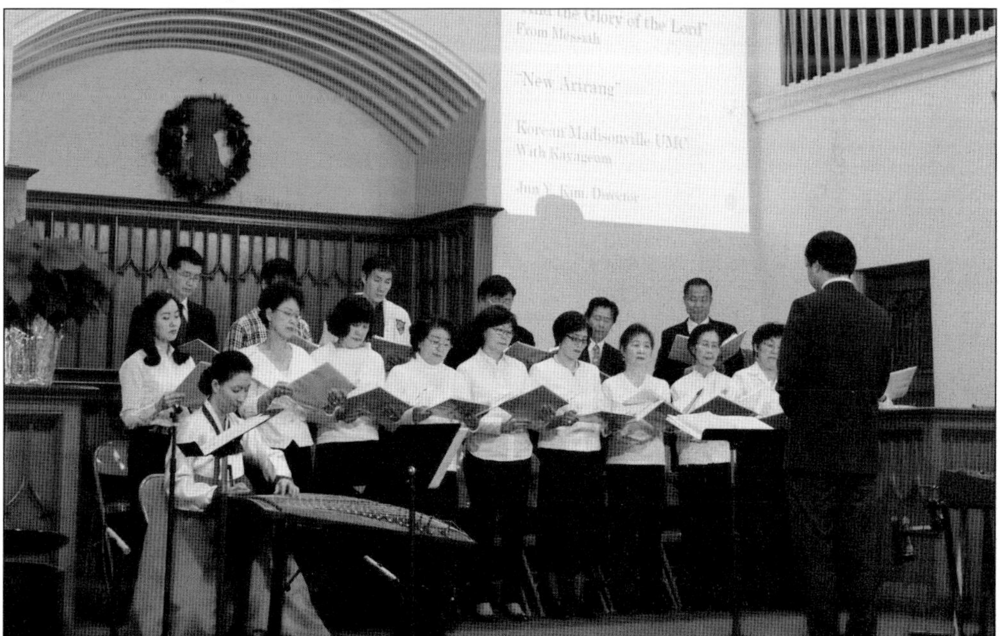

The Korean-Madisonville United Methodist Church choir, directed by Jun Y. Kim, sings "New Arirang."

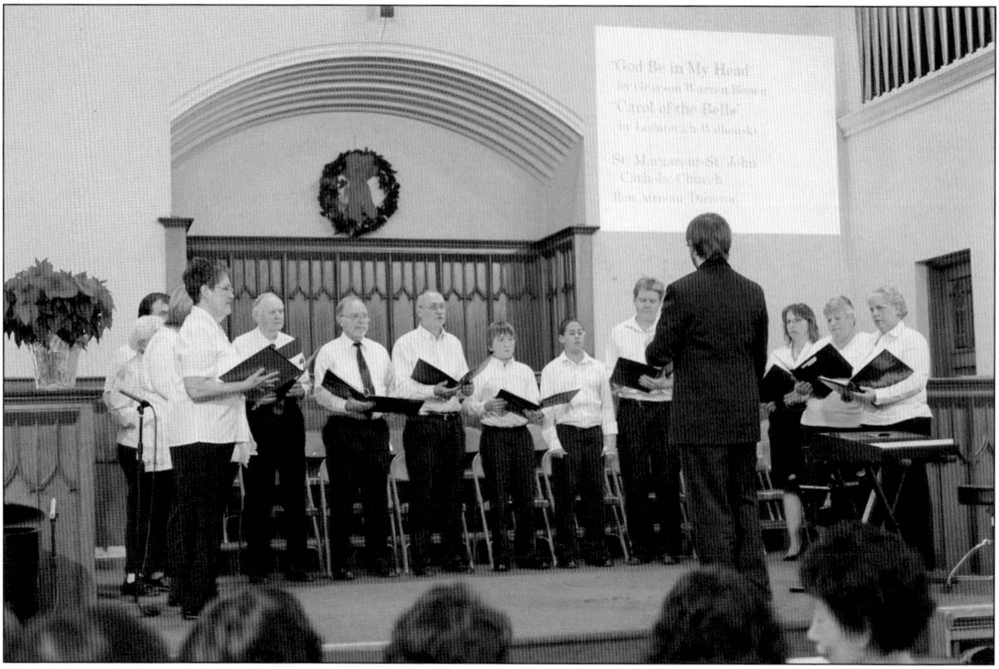

Another participant in Madisonville's ecumenical Holiday Song Fest is St. Margaret–St. John Catholic Church Choir. Ron Attreau is the director of the combined choir. It shares lovely traditional anthems for the church-filling audience.

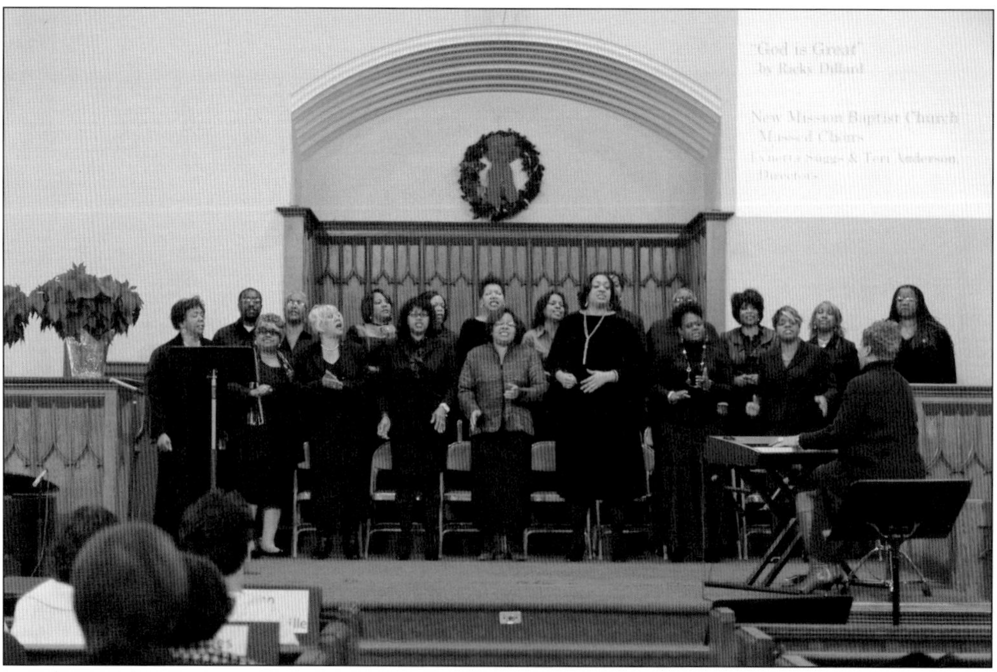

Members of the New Mission Missionary Baptist Church Choir led a very enthusiastic set of anthems that received a lively response from the audience and participants alike. The codirectors of music are Lynetta Suggs and Teri Anderson. This church celebrated its 100th anniversary in 2009 along with Madisonville's bicentennial celebration. That was a special year in Madisonville.

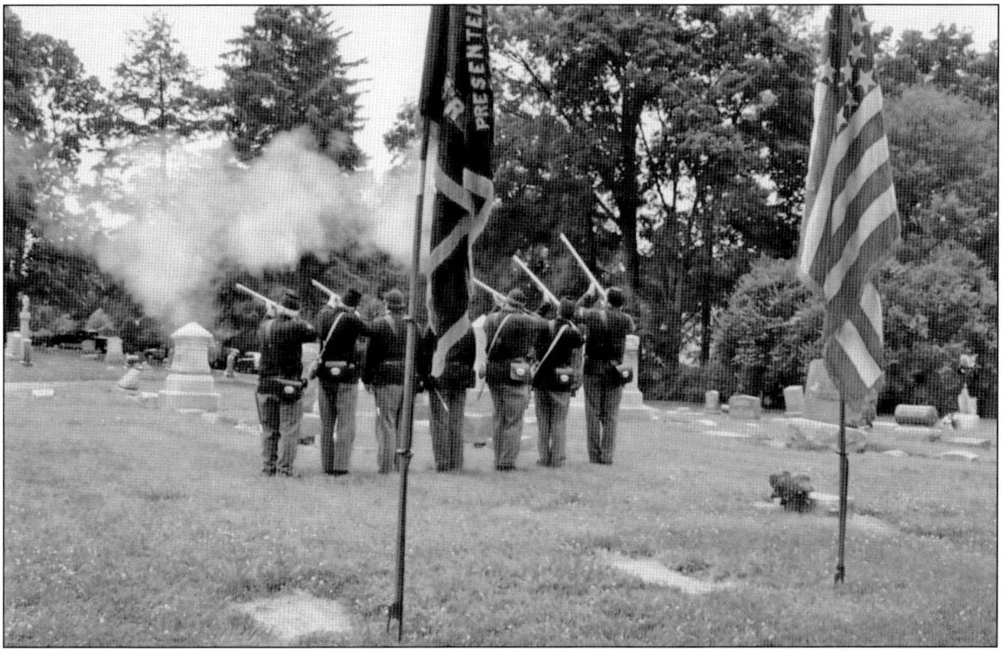

These Civil War reenactors came to Laurel Cemetery for the May 2009 dedication of the grave marker for Calvin N. Deem, a Madisonville Civil War veteran who died in 1936. No marker was ever placed on his grave until this ceremony. A distant cousin was in attendance.

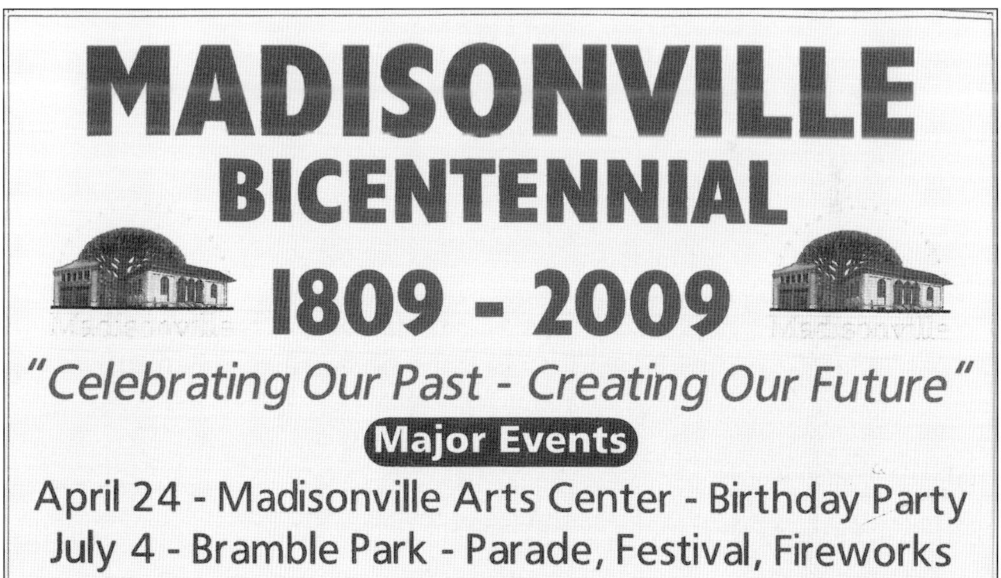

This banner and advertisement sign for the Madisonville bicentennial hung from the two-track railroad overpass for the bicentennial year of 2009. The celebration began in April with a gala at the Madisonville Art Center on Whetsel Avenue and climaxed with the Fourth of July picnic, festival, and fireworks at Bramble Park. Celebrations continued through the year until the Christmas Songfest and Community Council Christmas Party.

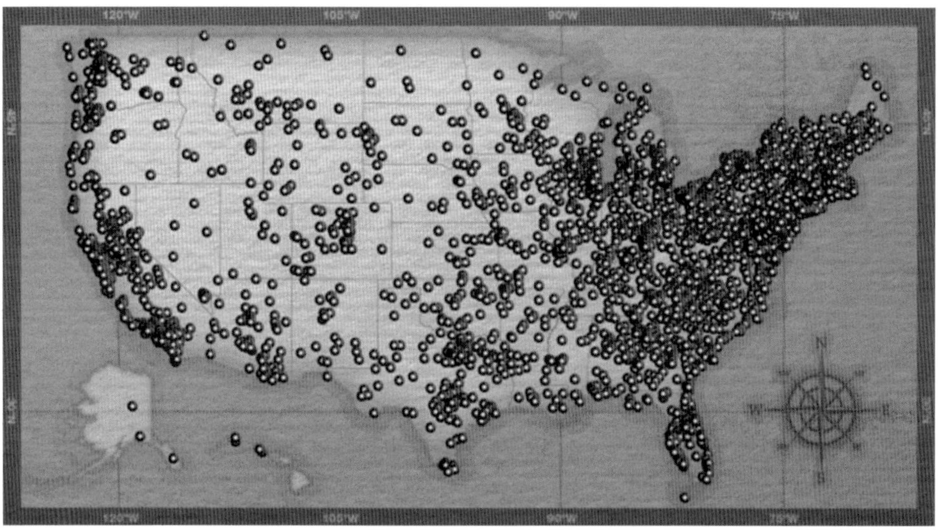

Consistent with our mission to preserve history on a local level, this book was printed in South Carolina on American-made paper and manufactured entirely in the United States. Products carrying the accredited Forest Stewardship Council (FSC) label are printed on 100 percent FSC-certified paper.

MADE IN THE USA